BACKSEAT RIDER

LAURA MASSEY-PUGH

BACKSEAT RIDER

A RECORD-BREAKING TANDEM RIDE
AROUND THE WORLD IN 180 DAYS

First published in Great Britain in 2023 by
Bannister Publications Ltd
Office 2A, Market Hall, Chesterfield, Derbyshire, S40 1AR

Copyright © Laura Massey-Pugh

ISBN: 978-1-916823-03-7

Typeset in Athelas
Printed and bound in Great Britain by CMP (UK) Ltd, Poole, Dorset

Cover design by Benjamin Fletcher-Bates

This book was self-published by Bannister Publications.
For more information on self-publishing visit:
www.bannisterpublications.com

contents

"It's not because we know we can, it's because we think we can…"

Steven Massey 2021

prologue

IT IS NOT every day a couple decide to cycle around the World on a tandem bicycle in 180 days. This is my story, from the "backseat" of the tandem bicycle, also known as the "stokers" seat or, in some cases, "rear-admiral". On the front half of the bicycle is my husband Stevie, also known as the "captain".

We met in 2015, married in 2018 and decided to spend six months riding around the World on the same bicycle to set a Guinness World Record in 2023. We are both accomplished long/ultra-distance cyclists, so this idea was not completely unfounded. Stevie is an ex-train builder, now house husband, and was responsible for handling, driving and maintaining a 50kg+ machine. I am a Veterinary surgeon cum project manager and responsible for everything else. Hopefully through my story, the importance of our set roles to our success will become clear.

And: No, we don't switch places.

part one: europe

Day 1, Berlin, 5th June 2022

IT IS quiet in the large grey expanse of Pariser Platz early on a Sunday morning. A small group of us shuffle around like the pigeons in the square, flapping over the last-minute details of getting witness statements prepared and social media accounts ready to stream live. I don't feel excited, just focused. This has been our goal for over 18 months; to get to this start line, to prove our intention, to make a start. We have everything in place, the tandem carefully packed with individually selected equipment, the route loaded and ready to go and the checklist of what I need to happen before and at 7 am.

The contingent of our "ground crew" are ready to wave us off: my parents, Stevie's brother Michael and his partner Ela, our niece Katie, and friends Matt, Megan, and Stephan. Aside from Wolfgang, one of our independent witnesses, the Platz is empty apart from the pigeons and a couple of security guards at the edge of the square. We have approached them to try and get another witness signature because our second witness is delayed, but they have declined, stating they cannot be distracted from their duties of watching the empty Platz.

The clock ticks closer to the hour and Eric, our second witness, appears bustling around the corner just in time, full of apologies for his tardiness. Days later we find out he had spent most of the night in Accident and Emergency with a broken collarbone but had still made the effort to help us. This was only the beginning of the exceptional lengths people would go to help us succeed in our mission.

All too soon it is a minute to 7 am. We get the tandem ready, she's clean and shining in the low dawn light with her bright yellow Erro panniers, front and back creating a purposeful image. Stevie and I are attired in our matching Huub Thunderbirds kit which looks and feels fresh and prepared, a sensation which will not last for long. We mount the tandem for the first of thousands of times to come, over the following days, weeks and months; both clicking into the right pedals in unison.

"Ready Laura?" Stevie asks followed by "Up", a familiar command to lift the pedal, and then everyone is counting down. I scramble to get the GoPro camera running and set the trip computer on the Garmin and before I can think about what is happening, we are off. My parents unfurl a giant banner (from where I have no idea) and cheers break the silence as we roll off the start line.

In a moment that seems too sudden, we are riding away from the towering Brandenburg Gate with its four-horse chariot atop, the stony creatures rearing with anticipation to run as we are filled with anticipation to ride. The distance between us and friends and family grows and their cheers diminish as we ring our bells in a farewell. Will we really be returning here in six months? Will the same people be here to meet us? How will we and the world around us have changed in that time? And can we possibly ride a fully laden tandem around the world in 180 days, or is this our most stupid idea yet?

It is 21st August 2020, in that brief reprieve between lockdowns where you could meet up to 30 people in an outside space at your own property. The evening is balmy after a hot summer's day and we have made the most of the relaxing of the restrictions to hold one of our summer pizza parties in the garden, carefully calculating how many people we invite. Earlier the garden was full of friends, a wonderful buzz of the too-long suppressed need to connect and socialise. Stevie and I worked in unison to keep a string of stone-baked pizzas flying out of our pizza oven for our guests.

As the evening draws in, we are relaxing with those that remain, around a large outdoor table littered with pizza crusts and empty glasses. The punch has gone down particularly well, and I am finding the remnants very refreshing after the hot work near the oven. The conversation turns to our most recent adventure, Land's End to John O'Groats on a tandem in 10 days. The trip from the Southernmost point to the most Northerly of the UK is famous in cycling circles and seizing our chance between lockdown restrictions we had completed the 1,000 miles trip at a very fast pace for a hilly route on a laden tandem. Many of our friends cycle themselves and are impressed, those that don't cycle themselves are arguably even more impressed, unable to contemplate sitting on a saddle all day and then camping at night. We regale our audience with tales of adventure and mishap from the trip, only to be confronted with the inevitable question: What's next?

Before I know it, the punch is talking, and I have confessed my plan. I have had the idea for months now, ever since I heard of the amazing female team Tandem Wow setting a new record for circumnavigation in 263 days just before the first lockdown. Their effort was tremendous, but it had got me thinking, calculating, and then starting to plan. Our Land's End to John O'Groats trip had only developed the idea I had started to conceive as we had proven 100 miles a day on a laden tandem was possible. I had been tentatively mentioning the idea to Stevie for a few months now and somehow, he hadn't explicitly said no. The possibility was there: how far could we go? Was the 100 miles a day sustainable for much longer?

And just like that we are telling our friends we are going to ride around the world on a tandem in 180 days and set a new Guinness World Record.

The city is still. Sunday morning in Derby, where we live, would have still had a small number of people rattling about the silent streets but Berlin seems practically empty. Germany has strict rules about Sunday opening, so I assume there is little to get up for and it means we can make fast progress out of the heart of the city on empty roads. About a mile or two down the road I cry out in panic: I've forgotten to start my GPS watch! My thoughts quickly become anxious; how can I forget something so important on day one and what hope do I then have of remembering to do it around the world? How can I have planned everything so carefully and then forgotten one key thing? What else have I forgotten to do or overlooked? How could I be so incompetent and who on earth am I to think I can pull off a trip like this?

Stevie however, is stoic and unphased, and quickly reminds me that the GPS watch is a backup, the Garmin GPS on the bike is the most accurate ride recording and the one which will be submitted to Guinness, whilst the watch is mainly an easy way to keep track of progress throughout the day and upload to Strava. I settle down and concede that I can do a bit of mental calculation to figure out our distance and focus on the route and riding the bike.

A lot of people starting out on an epic adventure like this cite feelings of relief and excitement to finally be setting out. A trip of this magnitude requires extensive planning and I was massively proud just to make it to the start line itself because many underestimate the work and determination required to make an idea into a reality. But the relief did not come, it just felt comfortingly familiar, we have done this so many times before; the rhythm of turning pedals, the routine of stopping for traffic lights and junctions and the usual misdemeanours of trying to give directions when you can't see where you are going. As the suburbs dissolved into the countryside, the morning was warming up and the weather was very pleasant. We were soon peckish, having felt too nervous to have had much of any early breakfast and we stopped and broke into the front pannier to retrieve crusty bread rolls filled with cheese and ham. Eating standing up on the side of the pavement was already the norm for us and enabled a speedy snack before making more progress.

Feeling more relaxed we rode past fields of cornflowers and poppies, with Kites and Buzzards wheeling overhead, interspersed with small neat sleepy villages. I was starting to settle into the ride, the day was warm, and it felt strange to be enjoying ourselves so early on when we had so much ahead.

The heat quickly rose beyond pleasant, after a cold Spring in the UK we felt like we were barely accustomed to temperatures above 10°C, never mind the high 20°Cs forecast for the day. At about 60 miles we needed to top up our water supplies and refuel in general, but with it being a Bank Holiday weekend, provisions were hard to come by and we ended up making our first detour off route to Dahme. Still, in the holiday vibe, we ordered massive iced coffee floats and relaxed outside a café while Stevie adjusted our shoe plates, tweaking the place where they attach to the pedals. Although most of our kit had been tested the SPD sandals ,which clip to our pedals, were new and sometimes it's hard to get things right until you've ridden a few miles. Feeling refreshed we headed South towards a campsite I had picked out in Radeburg. Throughout the afternoon the heat just kept climbing and became increasingly oppressive, exposed as we were on the bicycle. Not accustomed to the temperatures we began to struggle. A shady picnic area provided some respite, but then another petrol station stop was necessary for cold drinks. I was feeling frustrated that we weren't staying on top of things and Stevie was flustered had not managed to eat or drink enough which seemed like a novice error to make on our first day. We were in different frames of mind: me keen to push on, make a solid start and a successful first day, while Stevie wanted to go steadier and find our legs on the road. He wasn't impressed to be doing over 120 miles on the first day as this was too close to being "audax[1]" distance and making the trip more of an endurance challenge and less of an adventure.

By the end of the day, our good mood had been frazzled away by the heat and we were both pretty grumpy. Stevie was probably suffering from mild heat stroke, and it was hardly the triumphant end to the first day I had imagined and hoped for. To make matters worse on arriving in Radeburg I discovered it was the wrong one.

There are two places called Radeburg, just north of Dresden, about 25 km apart and there was no way Stevie was going to ride to the second one where I had pre-booked the campsite. We prioritised food, as we had found a Turkish kebab house that was still open, and I ordered enough kebab and pizza for dinner and breakfast. I set to googling nearby campsites whilst Stevie flaked out with a cold drink. My luck was in, and I found another site a mile out of town, so strapping our dinner to the pannier rack I convinced Stevie to remount the bicycle for another mile or so rather than give up and check in at the hotel across the square.

We managed to get a pitch in the busy campsite, but Stevie still wasn't feeling great, and it took a while before he was fit to eat anything. We had camped next to a young family cycle-touring and having not had a chance to come up with an alternate story had had to confess to them what we were doing. We felt like complete frauds, claiming we were going to cycle around the world in 180 days when we were encountering issues on day one. They were friendly and signed our witness book anyway, excited that they were the first entry.

By the time we had negotiated the shower complex and eaten what we could of the takeaway, we were happy for an early night and got tucked up in the tent, only to hear the disco starting up, complete with loud music and flashing lights. We certainly did not have the most peaceful night's sleep. Plenty of challenges already and this was only day one, the whole trip ahead of us was incomprehensible and the feeling that we were imposters was strong in our minds.

Day 2–4, Radeburg, Germany to Melk, Austria

At least the campsite was quiet the next morning, with the sense of everyone else sleeping off hangovers from the night before. We packed up in a familiar fashion, brewing tea and getting everything loaded on the bicycle. We are experienced at cycle touring or bike packing as it is now more fashionably known, and it felt good to settle into a familiar routine. After eating cold pizza for breakfast, we set out on the road again, losing our five-euro deposit on the campsite shower key when no one answered the bell at the office. These are the kind of sacrifices you have to make when breaking world records.

It was still relatively quiet by the time we got to Dresden, and we were lured into a second breakfast of bockwurst (Germans always have the best sausage-based snacks) at a petrol station on the way out of the city. Entering the countryside again we started to climb... and climb... and climb. Still finding our feet with the routine we had neglected to look at the elevation profile for the day and as we ground our way up to Altenberg, signs of a ski resort gave us a hint that we had certainly gained some height. It turned out we had made it to over 3,000ft, similar to the height of Snowdon (or Yr Wyddfa as it is now known), which explained our slower rate of progress. The weather was still extremely hot, but we were more focused on keeping our fluids up today although the baking sunshine left us feeling wobblier. The weight of front panniers meant Stevie cut it a bit too close to the curb and the front tyre bumped into the ditch. I grabbed the bars with my left arm and screamed in pain, feeling like a dagger had been stuck in my elbow.

An innocuous mistake, if for the fact had I not fractured my radial head two weeks before the trip so was riding with a broken arm, carefully concealed from concerned family and friends!

It promised to be a glorious May morning, my alarm going off early despite it being my last free day before we left, and I quickly threw on a cycling jersey and shorts before grabbing my sportier bicycle and heading out of the door. As I clipped in, I was resolute. Today I would hit 18 mph average speed on my favourite 25-mile route. The sun was out already but not yet too hot, the breeze was light, and I was feeling good after a Spring of training. I rolled out, keen to get going properly on the country lanes, and was happy to ride straight out onto an empty large roundabout, keeping my average speed up from the off. The light dappled around me, but I assumed I would be fairly visible in a range of coloured kit and a bright blue bike. I noticed a large SUV approaching from the left leaving it until the last minute to put on the brakes.

But it didn't stop and pulled straight out into the lane I was in. In horror I swerved to try and avoid the inevitable impact, but couldn't, and although narrowly avoiding being across the bonnet I was still off balance from being by being hit and ended up down, with my bike scuttling across the road. For a minute I thought the driver was just going to keep going, but he did pull over.

"Oh, my God! Are you hurt?" he asked,

"Just get me out of the road," I replied, still too shocked to have got to my feet and out of the middle of the roundabout.

Once in relative safety on the curb, it turned out he just hadn't seen me (which given the conditions implies he probably didn't look properly) and as a cyclist himself was mortified. We exchanged details and I quickly hobbled home feeling bruised and battered with a ripped saddle and bent shifters on the bike. The rest of the day was a write-off, and we soon decided it probably wouldn't put our families in the best frame of mind to hear I had been hit less than a mile from our front door when we had the whole world to get around. A few days later, as the bruising spread up and down my arm, I admitted defeat and accepted a visit to Accident and Emergency might be wise. Waiting for the results of an x-ray I had my range of motion checked and it was deemed very unlikely I had broken anything, and I confessed my upcoming plans to the radiography technician. The digital image appeared on the screen and I craned to try and get a peak, as given my Veterinary background I may have been able to self-diagnose. Then came the words I did not want to hear.

"Oh, that's a surprise! You've broken it!"

My whole world fell apart in that instant, 18 months of planning, massive expense on flights, insurance, kit; a job I had given up, not to mention the friends, family, sponsors, and charities I would be letting down if I couldn't get to the start line. Luckily, the practitioner picked up on my impending meltdown and hastily followed it up with the reassurance that it was an un-displaced fracture of my radial head, supported by my ulnar: a hairline fracture that didn't need a cast and given my past few days of denial I had kept a good range of motion and required very little physio. It still hurt like hell though and I was struggling to weight bear through it on my solo bike. We continued to play it down until we left, concealing the extensive bruising under a cardigan at our leaving do and hoping it would remain un-displaced for the six weeks it would take to heal.

This jolt was a frank reminder that it could still cause me issues and that I needed to be careful, but also a bitter consideration that riding a bicycle on roads comes with inherent risks and for 180 days we would be at the mercy of anyone who "just didn't see us" in their metalled boxes on four wheels...

I sucked it up and rode one-handed up the rest of the climb, luckily not too tricky a feat from the stoker seat on the back, but still in a lot of discomfort. Cresting the top, we stopped at a café for lunch, and ice creams for a bit of a refresher.

A big motivator after lunch was country number two: Czechia. Crossing a border felt somehow very purposeful and as we flew down a glorious descent on the other side it quickly became apparent, we were in a different country and culture.

The terrain was still rolling though and my routing had us following tracks more suitable for a holiday tour than a record-breaking attempt. After a small sense of humour failure from Stevie, when we ended up on the second dirt track, I rerouted to the main road.

Having not factored the elevation into my overly ambitious

goal for the day, we were looking like we would fall short of my intended night stop. I made an effort to accept this as part of the ride and not get het up about being a few miles down on day two. Researching the likely villages that would take us to our 100 miles target for the day it looked like the best options would be to find some dinner and then a campsite. It was never going to be that simple though: the wonderful-looking pizza place was shut; the next pub along didn't serve food and there was no shop to be seen. A hotel was non-existent, and I quickly started to feel out of my depth in an unfamiliar country with a foreign language. A last-ditch attempt saw us ride to the nearest petrol station, which proved to be our salvation, as a bemused attendant watched us buy out the hot counter of sausage rolls and a pile of sandwiches from the fridge for the morning.

In the car park, as we scoffed down the hot food, things suddenly seemed a lot more positive. I decided the best bet was to make our way to a campsite that appeared shut on google maps, on the basis that if it was shut, there would likely still be somewhere to put the tent up. We soon turned off the road and down a forested track and it was quickly apparent there was no official camping option no longer there. Trying to behave like the intrepid adventurers we were (and because the light was fading) we opted to pitch up in the forest on the side of the road. After another long day in the saddle and the stress of making the bed and breakfast arrangements, we failed to amicably agree on a camping spot and both went to bed feeling aggrieved and grumpy.

Waking up to rain pattering on the tent promised a cooler, damper day and it's always a frustration to pack up a sodden tent. Yesterday's sandwiches got us on the road, but the rain had set in with a damp mist rising from the woodlands around us like a tropical forest. It was not the kind of weather for roadside picnics, and we pushed on too long on busy wet roads to get to

Příbram. We must have made a sorry sight because one man in a van even slowed down to offer us a lift, but we, of course, had to decline without really being able to explain why succinctly. It was completely miserable. Saved by a pizzeria in Příbram, our moods improved, and the waitresses politely mopping up the puddles we left on the floor.

Emerging from the restaurant into glorious sunshine it could have been a completely different day to the deluge before lunch. I relented again over pushing the mileage further today and our destination for the night was set to the city of České Budějovice, which took me several goes to learn to pronounce. With beautiful architecture and a modern feel, I had located a basic but friendly hotel, overlooking a canal in the centre and we were pleased to have a night under a roof to finish drying out. Rushing through showers we were quickly on the hunt for food and again battling with the feeling of trying not to be on holiday we found an Indian restaurant close to closing, which resulted in the fastest-served meal I've ever experienced. It wasn't very late, but the craft beer hall on the way back was on last orders too, which was just as well as it would have been far too easy to get caught up in the mood of the cosmopolitan city. Before the trip, a lot of people had asked about what we would do if we came across somewhere we wanted to stay longer, and the answer had to be: come back another day. A few hours of relaxation in the evening felt like a just reward for the first three days of hard riding but we knew we couldn't risk anymore, and I made a note that České Budějovice was somewhere to return.

A glorious sunrise over the canal and a church bell tolling the morning saw us attack the buffet breakfast with relish. Trying to subtly sneak out with pockets bulging with snacks for later in the day we were certainly well supplied and ready to continue heading south and to country number three: Austria. Another up and over, as all European country borders seemed to be up mountain passes and we were whizzing down to the Danube, with wonderful cliffs and cascading rivers. Hitting the banks of the Danube felt like we were getting places and we were picking up the pace for the first time along the flat cycle track that was EuroVelo Six. The river was already broad, moving in a ponderous way, while large containers and shiny cruise ships chugged up and down. Another ice cream stop saw us treated to the kindness of strangers when an Austrian gentleman paid for our bill when we didn't have cash at the ready. Despite not feeling we warranted such kind support; we were very grateful for the refreshment. That evening's campsite on the banks of the Danube was lovely and we met some cycle-touring Chihuahua's making me miss my daily interaction with pets I had through my job. It was hard not to get carried away by the holiday spirit as we dined on schnitzel and beers in the restaurant next door. I had spent time in Bavaria in Southern Germany before and everything felt familiar and comfortable.

Day 5–6 Melk, Austria to Budapest, Hungary

The next morning, we breakfasted on the prettiest sandwich I'd ever eaten, torn between our need for speed and watching with fascination as the petrol station attendant roll thin slices of cheese and ham before dressing the roll artfully with green leaves; we were delighted when it tasted as good as it looked. The route was as convoluted as the sandwich though, as we dodged on and off cycle tracks, caught between grumpy drivers and lanes not quite designed for tandems. We opted to divert from our plan and head inland, picking up a bit of speed with tailwinds, but were then caught out again by the cycle route on the map we had been following leading to a gravel, which then led to a path, which then ended back at the Danube with green grass on either side. Backtracking to tarmac some signs, obviously designed to lure in hungry cyclists to a café, worked a treat and we had a rather substantial lunch, hoping the rain showers that were blowing over would stop.

Picking up the riverside track along the Danube again we started to feel like we were onto something as we approached Vienna or Wien as it is now commonly known. The well-marked cycleways took us right through the city and onto the island of Donauinsel in the middle of the Danube. A moment's lack of attention though and we were taken down one-way tracks ending abruptly at the edge of the river. We were becoming frustrated with backtracking, especially when we could see the intended path on the other side of the water. Not such a swift route as we'd initially hoped.

We both heaved a huge sigh of relief when we ended up on an old empty rail trail (a cyclist's dream) and were able to put our foot down all the way to country number four: Slovakia. Having made good progress for the last few hours I decided it would be best to try and get a good distance in today and push through Bratislava for a smooth start the following day on the far side of the city.

With no accommodation booked we risked the few options on the outskirts of the city. However, it was to be our first experience of 'no room at the inn' as the first, then second and third hotels turned us down claiming to be full. We will never know if it was just a particularly busy time or our slightly 'rough from the road' appearance which put people off, but a bed for the night was not forthcoming. With the only realistic option to backtrack, we headed back to the city centre confident of finding somewhere. Having circled 15 miles around the city's hotels at night we finally managed to find somewhere to take us and the bike. With the best part of 145 miles done that day and it having gone at 9pm at night we were shattered. The only saving grace was that the petrol station next door served microwave pizzas, which made a great accompaniment to a couple of instant noodles and a glass of wine. Stevie was raging though because I hadn't got him a beer! Given the late hour and the cool evening, a glass of red had seemed the perfect thing, but I should have known his relaxant of choice is made from grains, not grapes.

A bit of a giveaway of our mutual love of beer is that we didn't meet on a bicycle but at a beer festival. I was serving it, and Stevie was drinking it! CAMRA (the Campaign for Real Ale) held a National Winter beer festival at the impressive Roundhouse of the old carriage works in Derby every year. In 2015, for reasons I cannot quite recall, apart from it was something new and different and I was at a loose end, I had decided to volunteer behind the extensive bar. I think it would be safe to say I wasn't typical of the demographic of CAMRA members at this event, most of them having a decade or two on me and being men, so I was probably fairly distinctive. However, amongst the throng of eager imbibers, it took me a few half pints to notice that a tall, bearded gentleman seemed particularly keen on the pints from breweries "H–G" where I was working. A brief chat was all we managed before my attention was called to more thirsty punters. By the time my break came, he was still loitering in the area and noticed me wolfing down some chips. Wandering over to chat he came out with a completely unbelievable story of how he had cycled from Derby to Lands' End to John O'Groats and back to Derby in 9.5 days. Having researched the route myself previously, I knew 9.5 days was a fast time for a one-way trip, never mind back again. I was quickly becoming sceptical, but there was an earnestness to his account and a depth to his confidence that it got me wondering. At the end of the night, he left me his number on a "what is your favourite beer form" with the word "beer" scribbled out and replaced with "person" and I left him with a peck on the cheek, a gesture that was so out of character for me that it left me thinking who was this hirsute man of lofty stature and tall cycling tales to have enamoured me so quickly?

A groggy start after the late night in Bratislava had us make fast tracks out of the city, stopping at a Lidl on the outskirts to pick up breakfast and paint brushes. The brushes were a special request from Stevie as after our off-road section yesterday mud was accumulating on the bike and although we didn't expect it to stay spotless all the way around the world, the more we could prevent mud and grit from getting into the chain and components the better. However, it did make for a strange sight to watch a man paint-brushing his tandem bicycle in the supermarket car park and the Slovakian man we donated the excess brushes to looked even more bemused. Tailwinds were in our favour today and a picnic lunch on a bench (after a ridiculous amount of time trying to spot one) we were making good progress. I decided to stay on the EuroVelo 6 route, thinking it would be smooth, scenic riding. It was certainly scenic...

We soon hit an off-road section and I clung on as the puddles appearing underneath me got deeper and deeper. I voiced my reservations as to whether it was wise to ride such a rough track, unable to peer far enough around Stevie's back.

"Just keep pedalling and we should make it through," Stevie said confidently.

Before I had time to query him on the "should" aspect of this we ground to a halt in the puddle and unceremoniously toppled sideways. I emerged from a puddle looking like the creature from the deep, with mud all up one side, a bloodied knee, and a phone charging socket full of mud. Safe to say I wasn't impressed, and we continued on foot, pushing the bike, until we could find safer ground. Thoroughly frustrated by what would have been fantastic routes for your normal cycle tourist but we needed to make progress as we had a dinner arrangement to keep!

Dr Hedberg (Mark as he is less formally known) is an old colleague of mine from 'back in the day' at a small Veterinary practice in Dover. It had been my second job out of university and a steep learning curve, but Dr Hedberg had always brightened the day with his quirky sense of humour. Mark's family are Hungarian, and he now lives near Budapest with his wife and daughters, and with the city being on route, it was our first opportunity to see a familiar face. We had a stiff push to the outskirts of Budapest as the wind turned to crosswinds and the traffic built up: it was Friday evening and wherever you are in the world everyone is always in more of a rush on Friday evening!

Mark had sensibly recommended staying this side of the city centre and we had found a farmhouse which had a bed and breakfast room. Riding up a peaceful drive and into an oasis of calm after the busy roads, we were greeted by David our host. Google Translate was ready, but we were relieved to find that he was an 'ex-pat Brit'. It was easy to explain what we were doing and why we were in a rush to go for dinner. After we had a quick shower, Mark arrived bang on time to wine and dine us with true Hungarian hospitality; it was great to catch up, but also to briefly break out of the bubble we had been in since leaving Berlin.

Day 7–9 Budapest, Hungary to Drobeta-Turnu Severin, Romania

Our wonderful guesthouse hosts had left breakfast out for us to allow us an early start. Their advice to tackle the centre of

Budapest on a Saturday morning rather than a Friday night was certainly worth it. It was enough of a challenge to navigate via the various cycle paths and tracks and difficult to be in the right place to stay on route, but the main roads proved too busy to risk. Even out of the city, the cycle tracks were tricky as they would be smooth one moment then unrideable ruts and potholes the next. The wind behind us helped make up for lost time navigating on and off them.

We picked up supplies late in the day and headed to a nearby campsite which appeared just off the route. A mile down a dusty rutted track and Stevie was less than impressed with my definition of 'just off route', but we arrived at a beautifully peaceful campsite called Oasis Tanya. The peace was only broken by a small herd of Dachshunds who alerted the whole neighbourhood to our arrival, but they were quickly rounded up. We got pitched and I managed a brief dip in the saltwater pool before rustling up super noodle surprise on the stove. The location was idyllic, and the campsite had a laid-back feel, certainly somewhere I could happily have lost myself for a few weeks soaking up the Hungarian sunshine.

Of course, it was not to be this time, and we were soon packed up the following morning to risk the rutted track back to the tarmac. Smoother roads and some more impressive cycle tracks had us flying through the city of Szeged. Reaching the Romanian border our passports were checked and stamped for the first time since entering the EU on the way to Berlin, but the Romanians seemed friendly people, many waving from the queue of lorries at border control. There were lots of bicycles about too and it was clearly part of the culture to travel by bike and transport things this way – including an actual kitchen sink.

Our good progress was foiled by the first puncture of the trip and a rather tricky inner tube change left us hot and bothered. Pushing to get through Timişoara, the front tyre went flat again, and we found shade in an abandoned roadside fruit stall to get the second inner tube in. I'd hoped to get a lot more miles in but checking the time it was already gone 6 pm and for the first, but not the last time, we were caught out by a changing time zone of our trip having lost an hour.

Negotiating the city took longer than expected, but we were able to get out the other side before searching for a hotel. We fell on our feet and found a bed in the small town of Izvin. Hotel Roco was not quite what we expected from traditional setting, more suited to weddings and large functions and was empty on a quiet Sunday evening. Having booked online we couldn't find a way in and eventually managed to track down a young waitress at the outside trendy bar where everything was bright white, and dance music blared from a speaker. Google Translate came to the rescue and we eventually got let into a deserted reception area. With a sense of times gone by, the hotel had a big red marble staircase and a large chandelier in the lobby, our footsteps echoed eerily around the empty atrium as we unpacked the tandem and ferried everything up the stairs. Our room was Japanese-themed complete with a low-style bed and kimonos, which only added to the surrealism of the experience. We nosed around the closed reception and empty function rooms and cocktail bar before heading back to the hip-hop beats in the trendier bar, complete with multicoloured disco lights. Thankfully Romanians eat late, and we managed most of a three-course meal alone before a large family came to join the party atmosphere as the tunes still pumped away in the background.

The hotel was still deserted the following morning, although the reason for the image on the logo became clear as several peacocks came to investigate us packing up and strutted around the car park noisily calling out. There was some instant coffee provided and with leftover pizza, this was sustenance enough to get us back on the road. Navigation was easier today, essentially following the same road west to Lugoj and then heading south towards the hills. Little villages lined the road with pretty geometrical designs. Romania had a traditional feel to it, with horses and carts still on the roads and wizened old men deftly handling the reins.

Riding through farmland, I was watching the trip distance avidly as we were approaching our first big milestone: 1,000 miles! Less than an 18th of the total distance we would be riding, but still an achievement as it is the distance we had ridden from Land's End to John O'Groats when this trip was conceived (or at least we started to believe we could do the 100 miles/day). But the achievement was overwhelmed with a sense of how far we still had to go and what challenges we might encounter – the obligatory photos and social media posts were generated, and we were hastily on our way.

It got hotter as we started to climb, and the humidity rose as we summited the climb on a true mountain pass with a serious set of hairpin bends. The drivers were courteous, and we tried not to cause too much of a bottleneck on the corners. The lush green fields in the mountains had row upon row of haystacks and the feel of an alpine meadow, but we were certainly feeling the elevation gain: fully loaded tandems do not like going uphill! Finally, a beautiful winding descent along a river took us down to Orşova and back towards the Danube, now even broader. A smattering of rain hit us, and we decided it was as good a time as any for a refreshment break at a petrol station. Just in time as the clouds burst and rain poured down, fountaining from gutters, and cascading over the forecourt roof. We were more than happy to wait for the thunder and lightning to subside and the downpour to ease before riding the last flat stretch to Drobeta-Turnu Severin where we found another gem of a hotel, but this one more populated. After a brief discussion about whether the bike could come in, we agreed to lock it up outside under their security cameras and checked into a river-view room just in time to catch the sunset over the Danube. Another rare moment of relaxation to savour.

The proximity of the restaurant downstairs convinced us not to venture any further and splash out on a sit-down meal. A charming waiter called Bobbi served us and was delighted to practise his English. We found he had lived briefly in the UK, but only been able to find work at a chicken processing factory. It hadn't given him the best impression of our country, especially as the difference in the cost of living had left him unable to do anything except work and sleep in his time there. He was charming though and talked us into a surprise dessert proclaiming, "If you don't like it, you don't pay, but if it is the best dessert you've eaten you pay double!" It was very good, but we weren't charged double, and we ensured he got a rather good tip for his entrepreneurial efforts.

Settling down with a glass of wine after dinner to celebrate our first big milestone we suddenly heard another English voice call out, "There you are!"

Slightly confounded we turned to see a lean, middle-aged man approaching.

"You two stick out like a sore thumb!" he stated, pulling up a chair. We soon figured out this was not a long-lost friend but the owner of the fully loaded touring bicycle which had been parked next to the tandem. His familiarity was based on the kinship of being fellow cycle tourists and he was also on his own adventure, albeit at a slightly slower pace. He had already been on the road for 40 days though and had an air of competence. He had just been out to get a cheap meal to save cash and we felt slightly awkward pushing aside the empty dessert plate from our relatively expensive three-course meal and even more naive when confessing it was only our ninth day on the road. He was polite enough not to scoff at what must have seemed a rather ambitious plan given the relatively short distance we had come, and we enjoyed swapping route ideas and experiences with him. We couldn't help but envy his steadier pace and the opportunities he had to stop and experience life at the speed of a bicycle on his travels.

The speed we rode Land's End to John O'Groats had not just been born from our love of a challenge (although we cannot pretend that was not an aspect) but also from the fact my rota, on night shifts at the time, was seven days on fourteen days off; which I had calculated was just enough time to get to and from both ends of the country and ride in between. With military precision, Stevie had collected the hire van in the morning and loaded our kit. Just off a night shift, I napped on the front seats on the way down to Cornwall. A short ride to the most southerly point and we camped up ready to set off the next day. But Cornwall was tough with its relentless short sharp climbs, useless descents, where no speed was gained and towering hedges obscuring any view. A blown-out tyre set us back physically and mentally. A good friend came to our rescue the first night providing a bed, wonderful food, and a morale boost but the second night I was cooking dinner in the rain at 9 pm while Stevie was already passed out in the tent. Had we bitten off more than we could chew?

Smoother riding up through Cheddar Gorge and Bristol we met another good friend in Tintern for a pub lunch which spurred us on into Wales and a lovely campsite in the borders. The tandem was full camping weight, and we were carrying plenty if not too much kit. More tremendous hosting near Preston saw us pushing onto country number three. In Glasgow cycle paths sped us through the city, but we were barely halfway there and Scotland proved a long hard ride, through cities, countryside, ports, and industry seeing the whole breadth of the UK at the speed of the bicycle. Finally reaching the Highlands, it was beautiful, when you could see past the midges! On the approach to John O'Groats the road signs counted down the miles... less than 50... less than 25... less than 10 and suddenly we're rolling down to the seafront and the famous signpost! Having doubted our ability to make it in 10 days and wisdom at setting such a fast pace, we were immensely proud and knew we had overcome a lot of challenges to make this happen. But we had worked as a team and done what we had said we would. All we needed to do now was to get ourselves and the tandem back down to Derby and me back to work!

Day 10–14, Drobeta-Turnu Severin, Romania to Gebze, Turkey

The hotel buffet breakfast had us leaving with full bellies (and pockets) again and we left a card for our cycling touring friend as we unlocked our bike. Making the most of friendly Romania I got plenty of waves from the backseat and was delighted to stock up on the seasonal cherries in my nose bag on my handlebars. Whizzing past the queue of lorries at the border we were soon into Bulgaria, our seventh country in 10 days. It was another small culture shock though, as unlike Romania, card payments weren't readily accepted and we had not planned on acquiring too many Bulgarian Lev for the short time we planned to be there. At the first shop we made do with a bottle of water bought with leftover holiday money. It took a good, few miles down the road until we found somewhere to top up our supplies. The roads had changed too, and it was all too easy to end up on cobbled and rough sections, reducing our speed and giving the tandem and us a rough ride. Regretting my route choices somewhat, I at least, got a beautiful view of the Danube on the descent, but Stevie was left dodging potholes, cracks, and crevices. I feared another repeat of Bratislava when the first hotel I had aimed for in Kozloduy claimed to be full. Given the expanse of rooms towering above we suspected this might not be the case, but whether they were only partially open, or we didn't look like the sort of guests they wanted, we will never know! Trying to better our chances I booked the other hotel in the town online before arriving and we backtracked three miles to get there.

On arrival, a bored but tough-looking Bulgarian lady resided behind a chipped reception desk, and we started to doubt our chances again. Using a combination of Google translate and mime we tried to explain that we had a room booked. She looked doubtful and reluctantly started up an aged computer which made grinding noises as it flickered into life. Having convinced herself that we were entitled to stay, the next issue quickly arose. Cash only. Having planned to rectify the lack of currency situation after we had checked in somewhere we were in a bit of a predicament and had to negotiate to leave our bags in the room and our passports at the desk while we went out in search of a cash point. Seemingly convinced we weren't going to do a runner the lady gruffly agreed, and we jumped on the unloaded tandem, enjoying feeling like we had wings riding back to town without weight. We took the opportunity not just to get cash but also dinner and found a lively local restaurant and again were embarrassed by our complete lack of Bulgarian language. Google Translate helped a lot, but when the waiting staff figured we didn't have a clue what they were saying, they roped in a young student, who worked there part-time but was on her night off, to come and help. Between her and the smartphone we were able to order a veritable feast and were soon flying back to the hotel to settle our dues and bed down for the night.

The following morning it was quickly apparent that the

online advertised breakfast was not going to be forthcoming, so we rapidly packed up and rode back to the town for the third time and joined the queue for the bakery. Ordering items solely based on appearance we hit the jackpot and had fresh pizza and warm hot dog pastries washed down with peach juice. Baked goods are the way forward in Bulgaria. Soon we realised we had made a massive error though: no caffeine. Whilst we are not coffee aficionados or energy drink fiends, I am particularly fond of a proper cup of tea and previous experience has taught me going cold turkey has serious consequences. An emergency stop for caffeine was required and after an iced tea, my mood dramatically improved.

We couldn't resist a café lunch in Pleven and Bulgarians not only have a strong baked goods scene but also create amazing salads, a nice treat to keep the vitamins up.

A few stiff climbs after lunch saw us reaching Sevlievo that evening for a pre-booked and paid hotel to go through the nightly ritual of showering, washing clothes and charging everything up before heading out for another taverna and dinner.

The next morning saw us stocking up the calories with a slice of pizza as long as my arm; I knew it was going to be a good day when it started with pizza for breakfast! But we were soon to burn it off as we approached the Shipka pass, any road that has the title of "pass" is inevitably going to involve a lot of ascent and we were set for 30 miles of climbing to reach the top. Tandems, being notoriously hard to ride uphill, there was relatively little we could do except settle in. I counted the switchbacks on the GPS screen, watching our progress inch slowly up and played games with myself as to how long I could last without checking the screen.

By the time we got to the top, it was most definitely lunchtime, and we had a slightly surreal experience of admiring the view with the tourists and sampling some Bulgarian cuisine in a school dinner-type canteen with large trays of Bulgarian favourites lined up, apparently awaiting an influx of tourists that didn't arrive while we were there.

A tremendous swooping descent down and we got to test the disc brakes on the tandem to the max, me clutching the bars for dear life with one hand whilst trying to film with the go-pro in the other and not put Stevie off. Despite the time lost on the climb, we were still pushing for big miles that day and the last 22 of the 122 miles dragged awfully. The centre of Bulgaria had seemed more modern, with fewer horses and carts and more posh petrol stations and English speakers, but as we were heading south the landscape had changed to more arid. The people again seemed more traditional, but the culture was subtly different as we neared the edge of Europe. We certainly felt like foreigners as we attempted to check into a small local hotel for the night. The hotelier was friendly enough, but it was clear we were complicating things by not having a word of Bulgarian. However, once we got across, we needed somewhere to put our special bicycle she quickly rallied some younger relatives to open a large set of white wooden gates and had the bike safely installed in a courtyard. She then proceeded to manage to explain where the nearest restaurant was and what time it closed without a word of English. Once settled into a comfortable but quirky room with three single beds, mismatched scratchy towels and everything else seemingly pink, we rushed to get to the restaurant on time and enjoyed a wonderful meal of kebabs on our last night in Bulgaria.

The border checkpoint loomed large before us with "Turkiye", and the crescent star displayed in large letters above the lanes. An indication of the proud nation we were entering where flags are flown from most buildings and the national emblem is displayed everywhere. Making it through without issue I was excited to see the Turkish countryside with its friendly faces herding tough-looking sheep over dry scrublands. We were quickly thrown into Edirne and had to find our feet with Turkish food. We established soup was on the menu and despite the heat outside decided this was a good safe bet especially as it came with a bottomless breadbasket and çay tea. I knew from my research before the trip that the çay was likely to become a staple for our time here and was delighted to be getting an authentic cultural experience from the little bulbous glasses filled with the hot sweet tea.

The road had started out rolling and became even more so, but without the chance to make the most of short descents, we were losing time, and it was getting tough. The afternoon call to prayer rang out from a nearby town and we were pushing hard to get to our destination on the edge of Istanbul that evening.

I had made arrangements to stay with a Warmshowers host. Warmshowers is an organisation for cyclists to enable them to stay with a host free of charge, either camping or inside and have a warm shower. Many provide food, entertainment and local tips and knowledge too and with us being so recently arrived in the country I had high hopes for what sounded like a tremendous host for some insight into Turkish customs and some advice on what to expect whilst we were there. As we battled the rollercoaster though, it became apparent that we would not be arriving any time near late afternoon as I had hoped. Stevie was apprehensive, as even though we had used Warmshowers on our test ride around Wales, I think he felt that it was a bigger risk in a new country, especially when we were tired and feeling rather anti-social after a long day. I urged him on though, assuring him the host sounded very accommodating and friendly and would surely understand the nature of our challenge and how shattered we must be after several long days of riding.

To make matters worse, the road was getting busier and as it was the main highway towards Istanbul, the building up of traffic and many slip roads on and off was making riding extremely hazardous. Stevie later stated it the most dangerous road he has ever ridden, but there was little other choice leading into the confluence that is Istanbul. At each slip off I was obliged to twist in my seat, try and establish if any vehicles were peeling off and then we would make a break for it and cross the lane if all was clear. The opposite had to be done on the slip roads on too and with speeds picking up it was not always easy to judge where the gaps were. I had already warned our host we were running late and received a brief but seemingly affirmative reply, but by the time we reached our turn it was 8 pm and we entered a gated complex where the security guard eyed us suspiciously. With no further directions I tried calling the contact number at first to no answer, but then when I finally did get through, the directions were not easy to understand and seemed mostly to consist of "find the orange buggy". Starting to wonder if I had overestimated our host's fluency in English, we wandered around beautifully manicured gardens with tiny streams and little bridges trying to find some form of orange buggy. Eventually, we gave up and called again and this time the host said he would come and find us. I apologised for the inconvenience but was massively relieved to finally be able to relax after such a long day.

The host finally spotted us, wandering out from his house with his long-legged pretty girlfriend in tow on his arm. The orange buggy turned out to be a garish orange dune buggy out the front and around the back was an idyllic swimming pool. It was too late to be thinking of a dip though as we were guided in, the host seemed strangely preoccupied and quiet, and his girlfriend ran off unexpectedly, chasing some frogs. On entering a large, modern open plan house we were introduced to another man but exactly who he was wasn't clear until we needed somewhere to put the tandem.

"He was here first" declared our host "so he gets his bicycle in the room."

We realised that this was another Warmshowers guest who had arrived earlier that day. As events started to unfold, it turned out that they had been barbequing and drinking all afternoon and despite being very clear we intended to come today in my messages the host had assumed it was too late and we would not arrive until the following day. It seemed the novelty of having guests had worn off somewhat and we were shown to a room with a small sofa bed, which did have a warm shower as stipulated but no light bulb, loo roll or bedding. Not quite what we had expected from the glowing reviews of his hospitality, I somehow convinced tired and grumpy Stevie that we should be grateful for what we had and that at least it was somewhere to sleep. The next issue was food. We were ravenously hungry, and the host had promised to cook up vegan culinary delights for his guests, but this is not an obligation of hosting, so having found his girlfriend, I tentatively asked if there was somewhere we could get any food or order a takeaway.

"Chicken! We have chicken," she exclaimed and showed me to the fridge and also said I was welcome to have barbeque leftovers. Again, not quite what I had expected, but thankfully we don't have many dietary restrictions so I started to see if I could rustle up a meal while the host and his girlfriend canoodled in the other room. The original guest came to join me, and seemingly less tipsy, we had an interesting chat about our experiences on the road and I felt obliged to come clean about the extent of our trip, if only to justify our late and unusual arrival.

Stevie joined me as we sat down to eat a basic, but much-welcome dinner and I could sense his eyes lingering on the bottles of beer being drunk, but it seemed impolite to ask when the pair seemed to be having their own private party.

We had finished eating and feeling exhausted were ready for bed, when the host came over, eventually developing an interest in us. He then not only offered us a beer but a rather nice local craft beer which I knew would go down a treat with Stevie and we were obliged to stay up and enter into conversation. The local advice and feel for the culture I had hoped for was not to be though and talk quickly turned to politics, or at least our host's view of the world and politics.

"Paris is full of rats!" he announced, "They do not have enough cats, so it is full of rats! Everywhere! Dozens in every trash can, crawling everywhere, it is a filthy place."

We were not sure which part of Paris he had visited, but this certainly had not been our experience, but we opted to stay quiet on this front. He seemed determined to start some discord though.

"Your Queen is a bitch!" he stated between puffs on a joint, "You should get rid of your royal family." As much as we aren't devoted royalists, we weren't quite sure how to take this statement and rapidly tried to change the topic of conversation and then excuse ourselves to bed as it was already too late at night. It was a brash statement from someone who had the inevitable portrait of Atatürk on his wall; the "Father of the Turks", as near to royalty as modern Turkiye has!

We left early the next morning, silently retreating from the graveyard of beer bottles and full ashtrays and we slunk onto a quiet street. Having had too short a time to sleep, restless and squashed on the tiny sofa bed, I felt drained and deflated at an experience completely the opposite of what I had expected. I knew I had let Stevie down; his recovery was vital after such long testing days, he needed to keep his focus on steering the bike and I felt guilty I had compromised this. Thankfully, it was a spurious experience and other hosts we have had before and after have been amazing. We had arrived at the wrong time and in too contrasting a situation to make the most of the previous night's offer; maybe in a different time and place we would have swum in the pool, eaten barbeque, drunk many beers and defended our monarch's honour more successfully.

Breakfast had not been forthcoming, so we took the opportunity to try the first Turkish bakery we spotted and we were not disappointed! Fresh from the oven wondrously flaky boreks (cheese pastries), a loaf of sweet soft bread and the gloriously sticky baklava cheered us up immensely; the sugar high got us to the coast of the Marmara Sea and thankfully out of the increasing chaos of every sort of vehicle trying to get everywhere in all directions as fast as possible. Unexpectedly serene cycle paths along the shoreline lulled us into a false sense of security and we stopped for an early lunch and ice cream with the waves lapping across the road from us. Briefly into the fray again to get to the ferry port and a scramble to get a ticket – we needed coins, and all our denominations were too large; I dashed to buy a couple of drinks and split a note. It was only when I got back to the queue to board, I realised I had been horrendously shortchanged, but with not enough time to try and find the culprit. A very helpful ferry steward helped us get tickets and board before the ferry sailed, mellowing my irate mood.

And then we were leaving Europe across the Bosphorus Strait. The sense we had made significant progress was overwhelming and I was so proud of what we had already achieved. The water was sparkling around the boat, and in another bit of karma we met a wonderful local guide and teacher called Nur (or at least that was the only version of his name our ignorant tongues could pronounce) who proceeded to give us a rundown of all the landmarks we could see from the ferry and all the culture and history we were missing by flying through one of the most historic cities in the world. We were truly grateful for such insight, and it only made our transition to Asia all the more poignant and memorable.

We disembarked and I attempted to navigate us to the outskirts of the city as quickly as possible, which turned out not to be very quick at all, because we were soon embroiled in industry and factory works. Desperate to get out of the fumes and pollution it was a tough and busy ride out towards the suburbs. I soon plumped for the closest hotel I could find, trying not to let my irrational brain be frustrated with our first day under 100 miles. I knew the crossing of Istanbul would be challenging and time-consuming, but as ever I had been overly optimistic and assumed we'd be able to keep up the 115–120-mile days we had been averaging.

It was a relief to stop though, especially as it was an uphill finish. Happy to get into a hotel that evening I rushed to try and get sorted and find food so we could get the rest we both needed. Now very much in a different part of the world, I tracked down a kebab shop but instead of skewers of meat, these were durum kebabs, made from a kind of wheat or bean paste. It was obviously a local café, and they were rather phased when I walked in and tried to confidently order, dubious that I knew what I was ordering (which I didn't) and Google translate came out again. I ordered four wraps between us for good measure and, on recommendation, a couple of Ayran salted yoghurt drinks. A quick skirt of the nearby convenience stores led me to believe that beers would not be easy to come by now we were in a Muslim dominant area, so I accepted food versus beer was more important and headed home to our room. Sitting on the balcony I watched the sun go down over the huge city, listened to the call to prayer echo between various mosques, ate the spicy wrap and drank the salty creamy Ayran; not a bad way to spend a bit of time before bed.

Day 15 – 21: Gebze, Turkey to Arhavi, Turkey

Good intentions for an early start the next day were quickly foiled with a soft rear tyre. Stevie had suspected a slow puncture the previous evening but this morning we were definitely losing air so, to the bemusement of the hotel staff, the back wheel came out and a new tube went in.

We were feeling relieved to have made it through Istanbul, but the incessant schedule was starting to wear on us, and fatigue was sinking in, feeling like we were continually on the back foot and a late start was the last thing we needed. A wonderful descent out of Gebze served to lift our spirits somewhat as we flew back down to the coast and the aquamarine waters of the Marmara Sea.

And then a suddenly audible "pssst!" and a not-so-slow puncture had Stevie making an emergency stop on the hard shoulder as the front tyre deflated this time. The culprit was easily identifiable as a shard of metal from the debris that littered the side of the road where we had been riding.

Feeling the pressure to push on along the flat before hitting the climb up to Bolu, the next disappointment was a "twang". It was certainly not our day for mechanicals as we identified a broken spoke. Pulling over into a petrol station forecourt it was everything off, tube and tyre, rim tape, cassette and disc brakes as the spoke had snapped in an awkward way at the nipple end. Stevie could only justify this as a spurious flaw in the material. He opted to slacken all the remaining spokes slightly, regardless because we were feeling rather paranoid after a run of misfortunes. Our ambitions to push further now curtailed, we settled for a stay on the high plateau in the small town of Düzce.

We found a basic hotel on the outskirts and just got in before a group of Slovakian motorcyclists turned up, which initially seemed like it was going to descend into a fight over the last rooms, but then turned into a discussion about the bicycle and our trip, as the hotel staff managed to squeeze everybody in. We had to venture out for dinner and initially enjoying a chance to walk and relax, it soon became clear that we stuck out like a sore thumb with people staring and looking bemused by our presence. Muslim seemed to be the main influence here and I felt a bit self-conscious of having my hair exposed, until I saw another woman without a headscarf. Alcohol was not readily available and there was again a sense that the culture had shifted with the change of continent. Definitely not a tourist hotspot, one local even asked us what on earth we were doing there as: "no one comes here!" and seemed relieved when we said we were just passing through. No one was unwelcoming, just bemused by our presence.

I stayed up too late that night, trying to negotiate with the patchy hotel Wi-Fi to get photos uploaded and publish the weekly blog. An amalgamation of the posts that went on social media, with extras and photos added, it should have been a straightforward job but even half an hour was a lot of time to lose from sleeping. We planned to be up and away early the next morning as we were conscious of the race to get to the Caspian Sea and were aware that our timings there could make or break the whole record attempt.

. . .

PART ONE: Europe

The Caspian Sea Ferry is a bit of a legend amongst the worldwide cycle-touring community. It runs from Azerbaijan to Kazakhstan or Turkmenistan across the Caspian Sea, the biggest body of inland water in the world. And when I say "it", there isn't a single boat but several different cargo vessels which take passengers, and "ferry" is probably giving an exaggerated, luxurious idea of the crossing. There are no bars or restaurants on this ferry, no luxury cabins, entertainment, or shops. There are shared bunk bed-type cabins, shared toilet, shower facilities and a mess room that serves basic food three times daily; nothing else is available to purchase. Being such a large body of water, crossings are unpredictable with the shortest crossing from Azerbaijan to Kazakhstan taking a day but with waiting to board, customs and weather issues some crossings have taken over a week. And there is no timetable.

All these factors make a crossing irresistible to adventurers and travellers, there to have the experience of a lifetime. But for a pair of world record hopefuls, the uncertainties surrounding the ferry were a great source of stress. I had banked on five days to wait for a ferry to turn up and get across the sea but knew this might not be enough. Even so, this had put us on a particularly tight schedule for the first leg of our trip, with the added pressure of knowing that the earlier we got there the more flexibility we would have if we did encounter delays.

It may sound foolish to have chosen such a route to begin with, but we had been determined to try and sustain the integrity of our trip, not just by Guinness standards but also by our own, creating as complete a circumnavigation as possible and not "skipping" places we considered could be more challenging such as the Middle East. I had researched extensively before the trip, reading stacks of books and reams of online blogs and reports, and established we had few options. Being UK nationals there was no way we would get visas for Iran, and Pakistan would have been problematic politically. Another option would have been to follow the wheels of Mark Beaumont and

Jenny Graham, the two male and female solo bicycle record holders and to take a more northerly path through Europe to cross Ukraine and Russia. Jenny's account of the main roads, dangerous trucks and fear for her own life put us off and by the time we left on our trip, travel in this area would have been impossible with the political unrest.

Left with very few options, and having initially ruled out the sea ferry as being too unreliable and problematic, it seemed the only one left and all we could do was research the scant information available on obtaining tickets, finding when boats were running (either involving tracking the movements of the vessels online or contacting a local fixer who could help) and get there as soon as possible.

So, an early start it was and having finished short the day before we had inadvertently saved all the climbing for today heading up and over and through the mountainous area across the centre of Turkey. The heat was incessant, and even though we had somewhat acclimatised over the past two weeks we suffered with the long climbs, baking in the heat. With the sense of needing to make up miles today we were pushing hard, but going slowly with the rising elevation and it was difficult not to be frustrated instead of proud of our progress in tough conditions. A swooping descent to Gebze improved Stevie's mood as he got to let the tandem stretch her legs, topping 50 mph as I tried not to lose my nerve as we plummeted down the valley. With the road ahead not visible to me and with no control of speed or direction, I had to place implicit faith in his handling skills.

Grabbing food quickly I found a savoury wrap inedible, which is usual for me. My guts started rolling. Thinking it was the heat and exertion I focused on topping up my fluids, but by late afternoon I felt distinctly queasy.

We were starting to make better progress and my guts settled a bit through the afternoon. With most of the climbing done, we enjoyed a few more stretches of descent with mountains surrounding us and we rode through some of the most spectacular landscapes of the trip so far. The queasy feeling was at bay and feeling more confident we pushed for our stretch distance of nearly 120 miles, and I booked the hotel online from the backseat to make sure we wouldn't get turned away once we got there. Rolling up to a luxurious spa hotel it was already gone 8 pm and heartbreakingly we had to decline the use of the spa facilities on checking in, prioritising dinner and bed. Feeling accomplished after a long day, we felt we deserved a nice restaurant dinner, so we were rather put out when we got to the restaurant just before 8:30 pm to be told it was closed. Disappointed this hadn't been mentioned when we checked in, a grumpy waiter went to see if the kitchen could do anything for us. We thought we'd make the most of the wait by grabbing a drink from the bar only to find out it was the only bar we've ever come across not to serve alcohol. A few soft drinks and some leftovers from the kitchen later we felt we had had rather poor compensation for our epic efforts that day but were just relieved to be fed before pushing onwards again in the morning.

Being the first to the buffet breakfast was worth getting up for and once we had consumed as much as we dared with copious cups of çay we were soon packed up. Much to the horror of the staff it was pouring with rain and thunder was rumbling across the mountains. We struggled to explain our urgency to leave in such weather and tried to look as cheerful as possible rolling out, but my guts started rolling again too and it was apparent that something was still not right with my digestive system.

The rest of the morning was horrendous.

I hunkered down on the back in the pouring rain which quickly had me shivering. Stevie tried his best to negotiate a vicious rumble strip of a sometimes-non-existent hard shoulder which did nothing to settle my stomach and by the time we pulled over in 25 miles, I was a sodden, shaking, and miserable mess, heading straight for the bathrooms.

As if by magic, the clouds parted as we ordered multiple cups of the sweet çay and a wonderful family sitting next to us were obviously concerned for our safety (or sanity) and gave us cheese pastries, vine leaves and cake from their service station picnic. The sweet tea went some way to revive me, but I couldn't face the food; an unusual situation for me indeed.

I needed regular stops and still couldn't face food for the rest of the ride, surviving on multiple cups of çay and electrolytes. In total, I consumed 10 cups of çay and Stevie managed 13! With the "rear-wheel driver" feeling sorry for herself we were happy for some descents at the back end of the day, and the arid terrain changed to paddy fields with long-legged white storks striding through defiantly. In my ignorance of global agriculture, I had not realised there was such a large area of rice farming in Turkey, and they were very proud of their local produce, selling it in every shop and service station.

The descent into Osmancik was a great end to the day, with us able to see the town and river winding through from miles away and swooping down into it. It was bustling and we struggled to find the hotel before a man stopped to help. Initially we were suspicious of his intentions because he seemed to be taking us in the wrong direction. It turned out he knew better than Google Maps and not only got us there, but helped us get checked in and negotiate a rate.

Another brief interlude from the relentless pushing of the pedals we had an evening stroll to the charming riverfront where a trendy café bar served us alcohol-free cocktails and burgers, and the waitresses all posed for selfies with us. I managed a bland meal of chicken burger and chips and hoped that I would be back to fitness the next day.

A solid night's sleep did me the world of good and I felt much more prepared to tackle more climbing the following day, especially after chips for breakfast. The climbs were steady but felt more achievable, until I felt a bouncing on the back when nearing the top. The back tyre had punctured again, and despite Stevie checking the tyre, no culprit could be found. The clouds overhead were accumulating, and I can read the weather well enough to know the tailwinds meant that a storm was heading our way. Rushing Stevie to get the tube in, we saddled up and pedalled hard down the hill trying to beat the storm behind. The dark clouds soon engulfed us, and we had to admit defeat to the weather by donning waterproofs at the side of the road. Thunder and lightning soon followed and the interval between claps and flashes was disturbingly close. Suddenly there was a massive clap overhead and I saw the bright white fork hit the hillside to the left. I was concerned we could be next, but thankfully the storm veered away.

The continued rain made the last few climbs and then the fabled long descent into Samsun, technical and anticlimactic. I had read so many accounts of this road down to the city on the shores of the Black Sea, but the weather only let up as we reached the city and skirted around the centre to try and avoid the congestion. Just making it through at sunset, we were optimistic about getting a good few more miles before calling it a day when the back tyre went flat again; another check and another change and we decided to rule it out as being from debris on the roads.

A flat ride should have had us in good time to get to the next town at sundown, but the third flat couldn't be called a coincidence. In a rather surreal situation on a grassy central reservation, Stevie struggled, with not enough light, to see what he was doing while I tried to explain the situation in my basic German to a local who had come over to see what the issue was. It seemed German tourism was popular in this area and English holiday-makers non-existent. Regretting our choice to push past Samsun, we got a cheap hotel run by a beady-eyed proprietor and a gang of teenage boys. Suspicious that the price had already been inflated (it was a big jump in price here from in the mountains), we almost lost our sense of humour entirely when his card machine wouldn't work. We didn't have enough Lira in cash and he wouldn't accept Euros. Finally, coming to a truce and paying from our emergency dollars, we secured a room and Stevie got to work fixing inner tubes while I hunted down some kofte kebabs from the takeaway over the road.

At least the morning's breakfast was substantial enough to compensate for a very expensive, but basic room. With flaking walls and a dodgy aircon, it left a lot to be desired and I was trying to beat a hasty retreat in the morning whilst attempting to get the Wi-Fi to load. I had been finalising our master plan to get to the sea ferry in time and was doing some last-minute checks on the Georgia-Azerbaijan border. It had seemed the borders, including land borders, had opened just before we had left but now, I was struggling to find this information online. With plentiful warnings of no-go areas and the risk of conflict with Armenia, it wasn't sounding dreamy, and I eventually stumbled across the sentence I had been dreading, hidden deep within the paragraphs of warnings and cautions: the land borders were closed.

The next bit of bad news probably wasn't the biggest surprise; the rear tyre was flat again. Being in no position to elucidate the cause in the dark last night we were determined that following morning to find the culprit and took turns examining the tyre under the bright daylight; in between me researching what other options we could have to get to/across the Caspian Sea. A tiny flake of metal was removed and although still feeling unconvinced that we had found the culprit, we had little option but to push on. We were now in urgent need of a bike shop to stock up on inner tubes, this being the fourth puncture in 24-hours.

The nearest bike shop proved to not quite be what we needed with shelves piled high with all sorts of paraphernalia and bicycles of every size and shape, except anything sportier, and no inner tubes with the Presta valve we needed. More googling showed us the next realistic option would likely be in Ordo; the best part of a day's ride. Having done an epic 132 miles yesterday and with it looking increasingly unlikely that we would be rushing to catch the ferry, we decided it was best to head there and call it a day, giving me the chance to do some research and book a more upmarket hotel so we could have some rest and recovery after what felt like a very tough start to the ride: we would have covered close to 2,200 miles in 19 days by this point.

Making this decision felt like a weight off our shoulders so, when the next inevitable puncture happened, we were pragmatic and approached it systematically, using the cooking pot to find the hole in the tube, marking it up with a permanent marker and then marking the corresponding place on the tyre, or so we thought. Still nothing visible no matter how hard we checked. Eventually we called defeat in a urine-smelling bus stop, where we had found some shade, and reinflated to continue.

We could have predicted the next puncture in about 20 miles, and it seemed unsettlingly consistent. This time we pulled into a garden centre in the hope of a cold drink, but even better they provided a bowl of water and an air pump! My basic

German again went a small way in explaining our predicament and frustration, but the owner was wonderfully kind and tremendously excited to hear about our trip calling her daughter up to translate. She couldn't do enough to help us; except find the culprit of our puncture issues. Near defeat, I examined the tyre in the suspect area for what felt like the millionth time when a tiny hole glinted in the sun.

"Quick Ste! Get the pen knife!" I shouted and the German lady looked confounded by the sudden excitement. Enlarging the pinprick hole with the knife the shiny speck was eventually visible and by gently prising, we were able to dig out a tiny shard of wire – just long enough to embed thoroughly in the tyre well enough to have avoided detection but just the right length to cause an intermittent puncture. We were ecstatic, having started to feel like we were completely incompetent to have lost so much time with such basic issues. The German lady soon twigged what had happened and joined in celebrating with us too. With a rapid pump up from the electric pump (Stevie's foot-pumping muscles were aching a bit), we sped along the shores of the Black Sea with a massive feeling of relief...until it happened again.

Seriously questioning our sanity at this point we were straight into the routine of locating the hole this time, with me clambering down to the lapping seashore to get the water for the cooking pot. Fearing a repeat issue, we checked for bubbles and didn't quite know whether to be happy or frustrated when they came from the rim tape side of the inner. Like the first puncture of the trip, we suspected a combination of the material of the inner tubes we had been using and the exposed rim tape. This solidified our need to get traditional rubber inner tubes. So having fixed the seventh puncture in 24-hours we eventually reached Ordu much later than expected. The bicycle shop we had located was great and, despite the language barrier, soon not only equipped us with the tubes we needed but also a pair of free neck tubes and took photos for social media, proud to help us in our record attempt.

The upmarket hotel seemed impressive at first and it was a relief to speak English instead of using Google Translate; the Wi-Fi was abysmal though and we soon went in hunt of dinner and internet. The town had a much more touristic vibe and with licensed bars and restaurants and even a pub. We got talked into the local spirit, which was not dissimilar to French pastis but far too aniseed-based for my taste. It finally felt like we could relax a bit; I had felt quite self-conscious in the more rural places with my head uncovered and suspected that customs and culture regarding women might be quite different. I had had no negative experiences but did not want to inadvertently cause offence.

After finishing eating, we headed to the pub to use Wi-Fi, but this made me a rather poor conversationalist and Stevie, who was feeling the two strong drinks was left to his own devices, as I tried to figure out flights, costs and options. Eventually he was flaking, and we had to head back to the hotel, the day having run away with us and all intentions of an early night left somewhere on the road with all the punctures.

We awoke to a dull start and to find the flights I had booked to Kazakhstan the night before had been cancelled. Time to call a friend and I messaged Nigel who was our contact at the agents that had booked all the original flights. It was a sombre day's ride waiting for callbacks and feeling deflated, maybe due to the uncertainty of our plans, maybe after all the excitement of the past few days or maybe just because it felt like the race was off and we had wasted energy trying to go so far and fast.

To compound our flat mood, we then encountered the first hotel that refused somewhere safe to put the bicycle and lost time searching for another option. More research into routes and options, and Stevie was increasingly concerned about news that dust clouds from the dried-up Aral Sea in Uzbekistan posed a real risk. I had felt more blasé about such things planning from the comfort of our own home, but now on the road this issue seemed more tangible. Friends and family were increasingly concerned for our safety in the Middle East and despite the numerous reports I had read, it was beginning to sway us. There was an alternative option: if we missed that leg entirely, we could make up most of the distance in India and rely on the fact you always accumulate more miles than planned, to account for the rest of the 18,000 we must accomplish to meet Guinness World Record requirements. I nervously calculated distances. It was possible, but was this what we really wanted? I had been excited about the ferry and the more exotic places we might visit, but could I justify this against our commitment to the record?

Guinness World Records are essentially the Governing Body for world record circumnavigations. They set the rules and they can change the rules. They also verify the evidence and ratify the record within these parameters. The main rules for a tandem bicycle circumnavigation are as follows:

- *You must start and finish in the same place.*
- *You must move in the same direction: east-west or west-east and any significant deviation in longitude may be discounted. (It is up to Guinness what they decide is a significant deviation).*
- *You must pass through two antipodal points on opposite points on the globe: ours being Wellington in New Zealand and Madrid in Spain.*

- *You must travel a minimum distance of 18,000 miles by tandem bicycle and 24,000 miles in total.*
- *You must use the same bicycle (but parts can be exchanged) and the same two people.*
- *You must use public transport, not chartered or private transport.*

There is more detail to the rules than this, but as the basics, this is what must be adhered to. Many people ask us how we plan to cross oceans if we are cycling around the world or why miss out whole continents like Africa, but these are the rules we must adhere to and by following them closely we were giving ourselves the best chance of success at a new hard to beat world record.

Not without its sacrifices in terms of holiday versus record attempt, that was the decision we made.

An early night and a late start, lying in until 7am, had us feeling a bit better the next day and we used more time to swap the chain. Borrowing a chain tool from a local bike shop as ours had got lost in a late-night puncture fixing session. It was all we could do to convince the mechanic that Stevie knew what he was doing and just needed the tool, not assistance. We offered to pay but he declined, just determined to be helpful. Meanwhile, my phone rang, and Nigel had limited options for me, flights to Kazakhstan were possible but it would be a long wait and we would likely miss our flights at the other end in Kyrgyzstan and have to put those back too, or we could have a shorter wait and fly to India direct, albeit the significantly more expensive option. Not in a position to make a snap decision we put the new chain to the test and made good progress along the coastline.

We needed all the concentration we could muster to deal

with the Turkish tunnels, something I had been aware of and mapped out before the trip, but still, as each one approached, I would strain to see around Stevie to assess the distance. Some were short and over in a matter of seconds, but the longer ones were terrifying, no choice but to put the foot down, ignore the roar as vehicles approached from behind, and hope our lighting and Hi Vis was enough. Given the rugged cliffs lining the coast there was rarely an option to bail onto backroads but riding the tunnels was far from ideal. It had taken quite a while to realise that the honking of horns didn't mean motorists were angry, just impatient and we had encountered some lovely gestures on the road from being handed fresh pears from a passing lorry to being bought dessert when we stopped for a break. Less could be said for the dogs though and we had taken to carrying "dog bread" in Stevie's back jersey pocket to put off attacks. Some were fine, but out of the blue, you would hear the yelps and barks and know that you were in for a chase. The scariest had been in the hills where I had sighted three huge herding dogs from half a mile away, galloping over the fields towards us. Knowing we would stand little chance if they weren't confined, I had screamed at Stevie to keep pedalling and came out in a cold sweat as they gained on us. Luckily, we reached a summit, and they reached a fence at the same time, but still an unnerving experience. Working as a Veterinary Surgeon I am quite used to nervous and fearful dogs, but these were something else. My skills had come in useful with less intimidating hounds where a short sharp shout would often stun them into thinking twice before pursuing their attack.

The last challenge of the day was an incredibly steep incline up to a rather wonderful restaurant with a couple of attic rooms overlooking the Black Sea. I watched the sunset and grabbed a brief pause to reassess our situation, before finding a glow worm and chasing it around the bedroom to show Stevie. I also spoke to my parents briefly about our options with the flights and they agreed to give me some birthday money towards the flight changes if we went for the more expensive option straight to India, making it quite clear which option they preferred. Over a beautiful dinner in the restaurant, we made up our minds: to India it was.

It seemed simpler and more likely to keep our 180-day target in our grasp, eliminating a lot of the unknowns in the Middle East and after all, curry is Stevie's cuisine of choice.

Day 22–23: Arhavi, Turkey to Khashuri, Georgia

With the pressure of the race to the ferry lifted we enjoyed a leisurely breakfast overlooking the shimmering Black Sea before returning to the route and heading to the border: today we were to enter Georgia!

I was apprehensive about the border crossing as it was our first major border out of Europe and tales of thorough searches, delays and bureaucracy weighed heavy on my mind. We whisked past queues of lorries from all different Middle Eastern countries, the drivers seemed relaxed in the face of miles of queues, standing next to their vehicles chatting, smoking, and occasionally making tea from small stoves.

On arrival at the border, there seemed to be some confusion as to where we were meant to be, we were stamped out of Turkey and then directed to the vehicle lanes for entry into Georgia and had passports checked again. Just when it seemed to be going smoothly, we were directed back around to join the pedestrian control gates and had to queue again to get rechecked. This wasn't too much of an issue as everything seemed to be moving quite efficiently until we realised that we couldn't get the tandem through the dogleg in the security gates. The border officer at first seemed unable to get their head around the fact that the bike wouldn't fit and just kept beckoning us through until a more senior guard came to our rescue and rearranged the whole gate structure.

And then we were out and away! With the excitement that comes from a new country and culture we initially lapped up the different landscape with its lush plants, rolling hills and lots of bamboo. Quickly we hit Batumi and it felt like a massive shock to the system with busy chaotic roads, with some awful paving work. Stopping for something to eat we yet again had a dilemma with trying to find cash and communicate, now not only unable to recognise the words but also the characters used because Georgia uses the Mkhedruli alphabet made up of a beautiful swirling script. We somehow managed to negotiate some wholesome soup and what was to be my Georgian highlight, "Eggy boats" or Khachapuri as they are officially called. Now, these wonders are essentially boat-shaped pieces of dough, similar in texture to a stone-baked pizza, but formed into an open calzone-type shape. This is then filled with a wonderful cheesy mixture and topped with more cheese and an egg which must poach in the filling as they cook. I had never seen the like and was instantly a huge fan (I'm a huge fan of anything pizza based!).

It took a bit of effort to get going again but we had a much more pleasant ride up the coast once out of the city and the roads became more rural. All sorts of domestic animals roamed the quiet village streets, dogs, cows, chickens, pigs and even horses.

Having been unable to predict the speed of crossing the border, it made it hard to guess where we might end up that evening and riding past one rather rough and basic-looking roadside motel we decided to push onto the next small town where there appeared to be two hotels visible on Google Maps. Arriving at the town and matching the photos online to what we had in front of us, it became clear that one was now a supermarket and attempts to locate the other had us heading down a dusty track on the outskirts with no accommodation in sight. We tried asking the locals via Google Translate but they just looked confused by the concept of a hotel in this small provincial town. I was frustrated by the technological failure and losing my nerve a bit with what seemed to be another accommodation disaster, but Stevie remained calmer and set out our options: ride back to the first motel and look for wild camping spots along the way or ride on into the unknown and hope we came across something sooner rather than later. With no obvious accommodation up the road for at least 20 miles we decided to retrace our steps, and with Stevie keeping our spirits up, we were quickly back at the motel.

It felt very much like a place used by truckers and locals, and I felt quite nervous, but there was a lady behind the counter who soon went to get a stern-looking older man and we managed to communicate that we needed a room. There was indeed one available and although basic with a shared shower, it suited our needs and was dirt cheap. Freshened up, we ventured back downstairs and into the bar cum restaurant cum shop and the owner helped us get the tandem securely stored under cover and then served us a hearty stew and bread with a delicious bottle of Georgian wine, even though we suspected the kitchen had already closed for the night. We were delighted with the turnaround of events and looked forward to seeing more of Georgia the following day.

It was still quiet when we got up and packed the bike, with the shop just opening to serve coffee to motorists and truckers. We felt it was best to get on the road and hunt down breakfast there, so waved our goodbyes to the family who had been so welcoming despite our preconceptions and rode back to the town where we had attempted to stay the previous night. We did a good job stocking up at the supermarket, but our attempts to buy coffee fell a bit flat when we found what we had thought was a coffee shop only sold coffee beans!

We snacked on the side of the street and soon were surrounded by a pack of pleading eyes from the local dog population. A particularly scabby puppy managed to twist Stevie's arm for a scrap of bread, but I warned him to be careful, as we weren't sure how the locals would respond to these innocent beggars. They seemed in worse health than the street dogs we had seen so far, ribby and with telltale signs of external parasites. When Stevie spotted one laid out in the middle of the road, motionless, I cringed. Not just at the horrible sight of a canine casualty but also because I knew Stevie would take this badly. The dark-furred form must have been recently hit as we hadn't seen it when we pulled up. On the verge of dragging Stevie away from the scene, another dog yapped in triumph at finding an unexpected scrap and miraculously the casualty jumped up and lolloped over to investigate. I let out a massive sigh of relief that this was not a hideous hit and run, but a dog so laid back he had just had a little nap in the middle of the street!

The free-ranging animals continued. When we had to pull over to check a squeak (which turned out to be the belt drive running too tight) Stevie got a shock as he stood up to find a pig staring back at him.

At the next stop, we picked up more baked goods and the bakers were proud to show me their massive clay oven, essentially a large wood-fired pit that worked like a giant tandoor, expertly using a paddle to slap large rounds of bread onto the sides to bake in a matter of minutes.

We made an executive decision to stick to the main roads and not risk running into dirt tracks, but this proved to be a rather gruelling ride through the makings of a new super-highway across the country.

The air was thick with dust from the construction and the trucks and cars were all crammed onto the narrow original road and were not overly pleased to be held up by a tandem. The road climbed fairly steeply as well, and the construction and pollution just went on and on. Reaching the summit, we were confronted with a surprise tunnel and weighed up our options to go over or through? With the light fading we decided to power through and hope it wasn't as terrifying as some of the tunnels in Turkey had been. Taking a deep breath, we lunged in, and with lighting and two lanes it wasn't that bad, but I was glad to reach the other side and descent down to Khasuri.

We were running behind schedule, and I was stressed because we were late for the guesthouse I had booked online, worried I had gambled wrong, and we should have stopped before the pass. The town seemed dark and the guesthouse was up a dirt track with deep puddles and children playing in the dark. Arriving at some big wooden gates we waited to be let in and the local kids were delighted to practice their English and were fascinated by the tandem. The doors cracked open and a small middle-aged lady showed us into a beautifully ornate house, with a high ceiling and pristine decoration: not quite what we had expected at all!

We managed to track down somewhere to eat and did a hasty turnaround to potter up the road, still avoiding potholes and puddles with Stevie struggling to keep up with his flip-flops. I wanted to rush to get there to ensure we got fed and watered but had to wait for his less-than-ideal footwear, but we got in and got seated. The restaurant was traditionally Georgian, and we will never know if it was a special event such as a birthday or if the locals were just very lively people, but the raging disco music, interspersed with deafening karaoke wasn't quite the peaceful dinner we needed. After some delicious starters, a main course of local specialty chicken dish seemed to be more bones than meat and the pungent garlic would surely be emanating from our pores for days! Not the worst meal we had had, but not the best either, and after such an eventful day we were happy to pass out for some well-deserved sleep.

Day 24 – 28: Khashuri, Georgia to Tbilisi, Georgia

We flew down the biggest road we'd seen for a long time heading into the heart of Tbilisi, having had a steady back roads ride to the city. The traffic and congestion seemed to come up quickly and I juggled trying to check directions with holding onto the bars and signalling from the back. Navigating down a side street we found the hotel, for once not the cheapest we could find, as we desperately needed rest and recovery and had a few celebrations coming up.

Starting the usual negotiations about the bicycle the hotel staff were helpful enough, but didn't exactly feel friendly. We found that Georgians aren't the smiliest of people and quite matter of fact: if they can help you, they will, if they can't then that's that!

These cultural differences were to prove a challenge for the next few days when we would need all the help that we could get, not only getting the bicycle ready for the flight, but also rerouting approximately 2,000 miles.

As with many airports Tbilisi airport was situated outside the city centre, about 14 miles away from where we were staying, and the obvious answer would have been to pack the bike at our leisure in the hotel and taxi it there, but I had put my foot in it with Guinness World Records several months earlier.

. . .

PART ONE: Europe

Determined to get everything right I asked for clarification regarding the rule around the use of private transport including taxis. According to Guinness, this is forbidden, and only public transport may be used, presumably to prevent someone with more money than sense from chartering private jets to speed up their journey. The clock never stops so travelling time counts and I can see how this would cause an unfair advantage. However, the rules specifically mention taxis and I couldn't get my head around how on earth we were meant to get two massive bike boxes filled with tandem to the airport on public transport? I assumed the taxi rule only applied until the end of a leg of the trip i.e., if you got to a rubbish bit of road you couldn't jump in a taxi. So, with full intentions of staying above board, I asked the question and was rather shocked to hear not only that taxis were absolutely forbidden, but also that Guinness expected us to cycle to the end of each leg, right to the airport. This seemed different from what others had done, but Guinness makes the rules and can also change them at any point (most famously changing the solo record rules halfway through Mike Hall's circumnavigation attempt negating his record) so now I had it in writing I had no chance but to abide.

Stevie was livid.

In an attempt to make up for the complications I had caused, I had already been in contact with a bicycle shop in Tbilisi to ask them to keep hold of a couple of boxes from the new bicycles. The tandem has two "couplings" integrated into the frame just in front of Stevie's seat-post and allow us to split the tandem into two half. It is not quite as straightforward as that, as the rear brake needs disconnecting too and to try and ensure the safety of all the components; wheel, saddles, pedals, stoker bars and disc brake rotors, all need to be disassembled and carefully packaged before the front bars are turned and everything fitted into two boxes. So not only did we need boxes, but we also needed packaging material and strong tape.

After an early night and a much-needed lie-in, mission number one was to track down the boxes. After about a two-mile walk we located the bike shop and in typical Georgian fashion, they were helpful to a point. They did have boxes, but what they hadn't mentioned was they were at the back of a dank garage and not exactly in perfect condition. After following the mechanic to the back corner by the light of our phones and ignoring any rustling noises that might have indicated we weren't the only ones down there, we did the best we could to recover two boxes in the best condition and some packaging. Mission number two was then to walk the mile back to the hotel in flip flops carrying the two boxes between us, an exercise that felt very foreign after so long on the bicycle.

Arriving back at the hotel the manager David had come to see what the fuss was with two guests that now wanted to store empty cardboard boxes as well as a tandem bicycle in his garage.

We had tried our best to impress David with our record attempt and epic tales from our trip so far, but we weren't convinced it was working and he remained quite sombre and practical. A welcome drink of white Georgian wine (which turned out to be orange) was offered but the hotel "bar" appeared to serve only this from unmarked bottles and no other varieties of wine or beers were available. Alcohol and food were also forbidden in our room, except the glasses of wine were delivered there, which was slightly confusing and Stevie was bitterly disappointed not to kick back with a beer.

We pushed our luck by asking David for help sourcing strong tape and made some headway in that he could tell us which shop on the other side of the city would stock it. We had hoped he'd pop up with some from the garage or know a friend who could have dropped some off for us, but the information was better than nothing, but this was a job for another day; we also had a route to replan.

All my routing prior to the trip was done on computers and as much as I can navigate and make minor changes on my phone, I was not prepared to do 2,000 miles of rerouting on its tiny screen, so mission number three was to try and locate an internet café or use of a laptop. When I had travelled decades earlier internet cafés had been plentiful and a blessing for those on the road. In the modern age of smartphones, they appear to have become redundant and the only ones I could find seemed to be aimed at hardcore gamers and not somewhere I fancied spending several hours of my life. Plan B was to try and rent a laptop from a computer shop, but in typical Georgian fashion, this was an unusual request so met with flat refusal from the half dozen shops we visited. A friend of a friend of a friend very kindly found one we could borrow but it was too far outside the city. On the point of desperately considering buying a new, but cheap, laptop I had a brainwave: a pawn shop!

Making a deal with a man behind a wire barrier we purchased a second-hand laptop on the agreement we would return it the next day and sell it back to him for a reduced price.

Getting back to the hotel I started furiously rerouting while Stevie caught up on some more sleep. Routing the trip hadn't been as simple as just picking roads from A to B and involved checking road surfaces and missing bridges on Google satellite (I'd spotted one on our original route that would have resulted in a 50-mile detour) and looking at heatmaps and other functions to see which roads were going to be tandem-friendly. Working into the evening I eventually gave up for the day and we went out for a feast of a Georgian meat platter and a couple of wind-down beers.

Up early the next morning the race was on to get the route finished, uploaded to Garmin and the laptop back to the shop. It took me well into the afternoon and then a trip to the other side of town to hunt down the tape we needed and by the evening I started to feel like we had gained some control over the situation. Having a three-day layover whilst waiting for the flight to India wasn't ideal in some ways, but at least had given us time to find our feet with a new route and catch our breath. I'm sure we would have made mistakes and had more complications if we had rushed to fly out the day after arriving. Now things were in order I started to feel like I could relax and on an evening trip up to "Turtle Lake", we dined lakeside on "eggy boats" before Stevie dared risk the longest zipline in Europe! I took the cable car back down and found him looking ever so slightly shaken at the bottom.

The following day was special for two reasons, my birthday and our wedding anniversary. I had thought it a good idea to combine the two four years ago, giving Stevie no chance to forget, but in fact this just means he gatecrashes my birthday every year claiming it's his anniversary too! Regardless of this, we had our first day of complete relaxation: massages, a long jacuzzi bath, acting like tourists and seeing the sights of the city and indulging in a few restaurant meals. Little did we suspect at this point, that this would be the last time on the whole trip, we would experience anything we could consider approaching a holiday.

A wild night on the town had been curtailed by an early start to get to the airport in plenty of time and with one final hair-raising dog chase in the final 14 miles in Georgia. David had come through though by arranging a car to meet us at the airport with the boxes and then all we had to do was package the tandem.

Three hours later it was done.

We still had hours until check-in opened but the staff gave us the runaround having to pay extra for the boxes, go back to the ticket desk twice, obtain a receipt, return to check in and then to oversized baggage to scan the boxes. Finally navigating security and border controls it was a long tedious wait to eventually board the first flight and the end of the first leg.

---

1. Audax is a club for long-distance cyclists, with origins in France their rides are measured in km, with the quintessential brevet randonneur starting at 200 km or 125 miles.

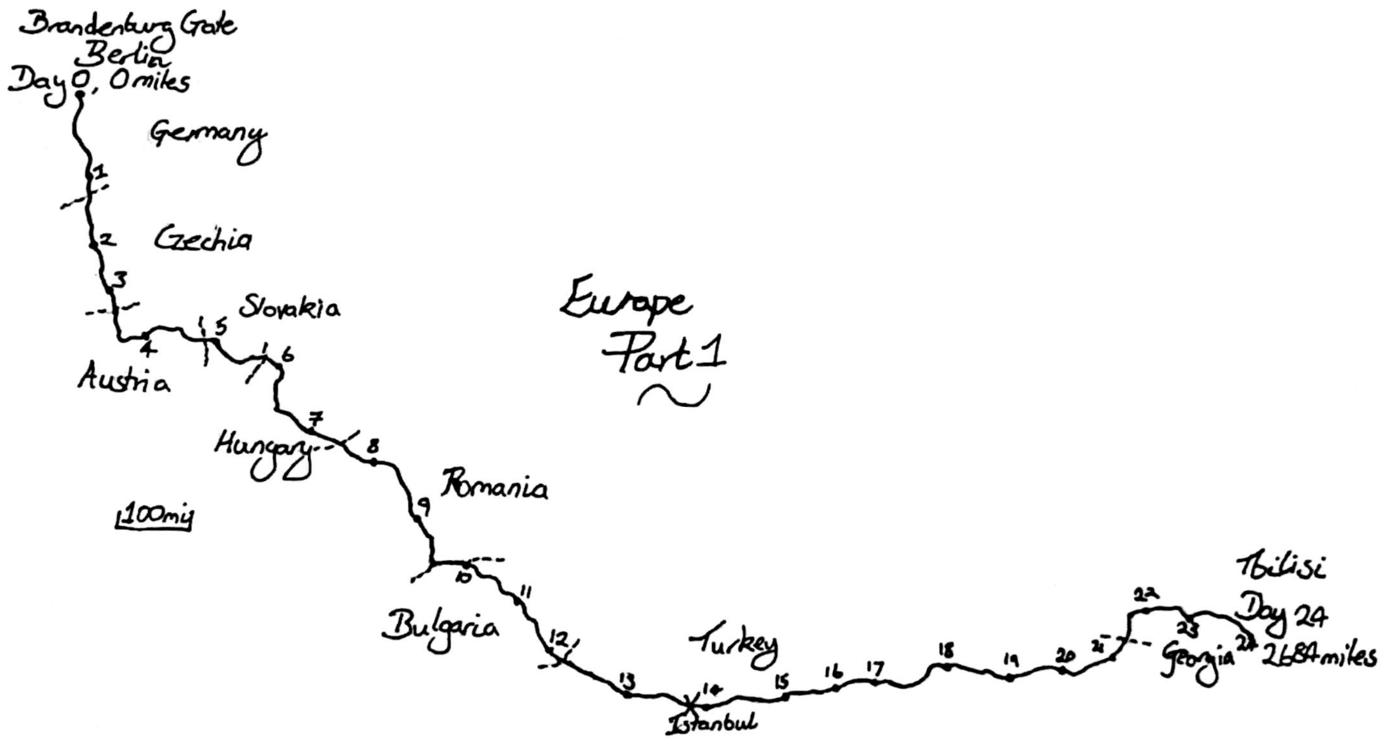

Europe
Part 1

Brandenburg Gate
Berlin
Day 0, 0 miles

Germany

Czechia

Slovakia

Austria

Hungary

Romania

Bulgaria

Turkey

Istanbul

Georgia

Tbilisi
Day 24
2684 miles

100mi

Boxes packed Tbilisi

Everything including the...

Into Asia

First border into Czechia

Georgia

Departure

Farm animals roam free in Georgia

Late night puncture, number 3
in 'puncturegate2022'

Muddy crash
on Eurovelo6

part two: india

Day 29 –36: Ahmedabad, India to Kankavli, India

I HAD ALWAYS VIEWED flying days as some kind of wonderful hiatus from frantically chasing the distances on the tandem. This wasn't quite the case. The first flight to Abu Dhabi was not too bad, but too short to get settled in enough to get any rest and we landed for our connecting flight late in the evening. With hours of layover we briefly toyed with getting a hotel, but eventually settled for jumping into some more comfortable seats when they became free. This airport was a hub of flight connections and filled full of excited families and people from all different time zones which made it noisy and chaotic right into the early hours of the morning. It was a relief to board the second flight, but this one was packed, and we were the only Caucasian passengers with large families having come from the USA or Europe. As we went to disembark the air hostess asked us if we were travelling for a wedding or funeral and was amazed to learn that we were travelling by a bicycle in the hold.

It was early morning in Ahmedabad when we landed, and we quickly fell afoul of looking like tourists when it took a bribe to get the bike boxes out of customs and out of arrivals. It was a close call as to whether we would be stung for a hefty customs fee on the bike too when they found out how much it cost, but we convinced them it was for riding not resale.

And then India hit. People were everywhere, swarming to get in and out of the airport on mopeds and in cars with horns honking. We were stuck with two boxes on a trolley and needed to build the bike, to get out of there. Making our way to the back of the car park just in time for dawn we found a grassy area that would have to do for the job. Stevie set about reassembling as fast as he could. I watched as a man cycled up, a few hundred metres away, dismount, stand on his head for what must have been a good 10 minutes, get back on the bike and ride off again. I had no explanation for this, but it gave me a sense of the inexplicable nature of India to come.

It was a stressful enough experience rebuilding whilst so sleep-deprived but was only made worse when a group of men came to watch. Stevie did not appreciate their questions and prying hands, so I acted as crowd control while they seemed happy to stand and stare.

They finally got bored and dissipated as we finished rebuilding the tandem up and then had to navigate out of the airport and into the new country. I was partly excited but partly overwhelmed by the contrast with what now seemed a much more familiar culture in Georgia, and we struggled with basics like getting cash and finding something to eat; cashpoints didn't always have money in and the petrol stations and supermarkets we had come to depend on for food were non-existent.

Feeling unsure, we eventually settled for a local restaurant and enjoyed our first real Indian curry. We had been given a lot of advice on how best to try and avoid getting stomach upsets so were now sticking to vegetables, religiously washing our hands, and not eating any uncooked vegetables or salads. The curry came with freshly chopped onion, which we agonised over and then left, but thoroughly enjoyed the rest of the meal.

Delicious as it was, the heat of the curry did nothing to cool us down and the temperature was soaring. I was struggling to adapt, and it was tough going on the baking hot highway. A miscellany of vehicles passed us; small trucks adorned with tassels and hand painted signs, tuk-tuks bouncing along with an assortment of cargo and motorcycles with ladies in saris glamorously riding side-saddle but, less glamorously, on mobile phones, presumably on social media!

We were gradually adjusting to the bustle and even though busy, the pace of traffic felt slow; it seemed everyone expected any sort of vehicle to come from any given direction at any time (even on the wrong side of the road) so at least it felt drivers were aware of us. Stevie's kind nature was quickly tested as we were soon asked for a "selfie" by a passing moped rider; from accounts I had read about in my research I knew that this was likely to be a frequent occurrence and if we stopped every time we were asked, we'd take twice as long to get around the world. Firmly saying no seemed to work initially, but we soon found that they would then just ride ahead and take a selfie whilst driving, which was even more disconcerting. We did start chatting to one couple on a moped though, and it turned out they spoke brilliant English and were on their way to an anniversary night away having got married last year. We were pleased to have a selfie with them and enjoyed telling them about our trip.

Having made good progress along the National Highway, I took us on some more minor roads to shortcut to the hotel I had booked. This turned out to be a mistake and we were quickly faced with mud, massive potholes and puddles, to the point that we had to get off and walk around one. Stevie was not impressed, and I quickly learnt the lesson that not all roads in India are rideable. We located a rather luxurious spa hotel feeling completely exhausted from the loss of a night's sleep on the flight and the excitement of India. The sudden exposure to heat had taken it out of us and my leg had broken out in red swollen patches of heat rash, a problem I occasionally suffer with, being both sore and itchy and requiring antihistamines and cold towels to try and stop them acting like small radiators.

As we settled in the hotel restaurant for our second curry in India it seemed a crispy cold beer would be just the treat to celebrate a whole new country. What we had not realised was that we were in an alcohol-free state of Gujarat, and it was illegal to sell or drink alcohol here! Now, in my research for the trip, I'd checked a lot for details, from what side of the road to ride on to what plug socket we needed for each country, but it had never occurred to me to check where we could get a beer! Settling for soft drinks to go with the delicious curry it didn't matter too much as we were soon passed out for an early night, without enough energy to join those frolicking in the spa pool below our balcony window.

The next morning, we felt 100 times better after 10 hours of sleep. It was curry again for breakfast, or at least a South Indian style with masala dosa and sambar (a large rice pancake with a spiced potato filling and a lentil sauce).

Back onto the National Highway was a relief after my detour down the back roads last night and we made good progress with slightly cooler weather. Feeling like we were getting the hang of India we weren't even put out by what we thought was a monsoon-level rainstorm at the end of the day.

We opted for a basic, but pleasant enough place to stay called "Hotel Fun City" just off the highway.

The following morning, we cracked and had our first non-curry-based meal since arriving, opting for cheese toasties for breakfast. Our culinary ignorance only got worse when Stevie spied the famous golden arches of McDonalds coming into the town of Vapi and we dined on spicier-than-normal veggie burgers while the manager insisted on selfies to post on social media. With so many options for accommodation I had become more relaxed again and was willing to play things by ear depending on how far we made it, but that evening it fell through. I confidently walked up to the first large hotel and an old, bearded man took one look at me and told me in a very direct tone that they were full. I had no doubt they weren't, and it may have just been that they consider the hotel for locals, not tourists, but I couldn't help but wonder if Stevie would have had a different response if he had asked.

We hadn't experienced issues with different cultural approaches to gender so far, but this did make me think that I shouldn't take it for granted that I would be treated the same here as in the UK and there may be some situations where Stevie was best to be the spokesperson.

I know I am extremely privileged; I have never felt truly discriminated against for my gender. During my childhood, I spent summers running feral around my grandparents' farm and my Nan would call me a tomboy as I'd come back for dinner with muddy knees and hay in my hair. An all-girls secondary school did little to feminise me, and I refused to wear skirts other than the mandatory school uniform for many years after. I still abhor the colour pink. My balance came, when through my younger brother's Cubs' group, I was introduced to

Sea Scouts and when given the option to join their troop instead of Girl Guides, there was no decision! This led to summers messing about in boats on the river Thames and winters in a sports hall giving as good as I got in games like British Bulldog (a full contact game, I suspect now banned). I was determined that anything the boys could do I could do too and luckily no one told me otherwise, it was only when puberty hit and they quickly surpassed me in strength I had to concede that I would have to adapt to keep up. So that is what I did, and to this day I will use technique and adaptability over pure brute strength, never asking for allowances or concession for my gender.

My academic environment helped as well, and being surrounded by other girls with high aspirations meant there were no careers or job options viewed as "for the boys," even though I had had my heart set on being a Veterinary Surgeon from a very young age I never experienced any sort of stigma when it came to what I could achieve academically.

My university days followed a similar path with weekdays studying with a mostly female compatriot of high-performing classmates and weekends piling into a minibus full of lads to the whitewater kayaking rivers of Scotland, and as long as I mucked in and kept up, I was never made to feel out of place.

My cycling career only really took off through Stevie and I skipped the traditional path of joining a club and going on ladies' group rides, turning up at my first Audax event to a room full of middle-aged men with the only other female pouring the tea. With my upbringing, I wasn't fazed at all though and it immediately felt like an inclusive atmosphere, even if there was a bit of curiosity at the young lady Stevie had brought to stoke his tandem. Being unsupported, audax rides were perfect for me, as everyone is treated the same; there are no prizes or concessions for being female and you are expected to look after yourself as much as anyone else. I have seen an increase in the number of women at Audax events (historically some of their most accomplished riders are women so it has never been an exclusive club) and this means that I don't always get the smug feeling of walking past the long queue for the men's loos at control, to stride straight into the ladies. I have mixed feelings about the way inclusivity for women in sports is treated, initiatives like all-female rides and a quota of places for women at events can surely be no bad thing, but I find it unsettling to think I should be treated any differently from anyone else. I want to ride on a level playing field and if that means adapting myself instead of adaptations being made for me that's fine by me. But I am aware of the massive privilege I have had that my life so far has given me an outlook to not see the barriers, only the opportunities and to not worry what others may think, only to want to push and challenge myself on my own terms.

The next hotel was a no-go as well and I was starting to get edgy that we were running out of options. To make things more urgent, it had also started to drizzle and then rain and then pour. Reaching Vasai-Virar, I spotted a more expensive hotel online, at over £40 for the night; double what we had paid before. The Golden Chariot Hotel was a huge opulent building with marble floors and a gated entrance where we had to persuade the security guard to let us in. Trying not to look too bedraggled from the rain we checked in, but soon sensed it had had its heyday and the room was the least comfortable yet and the food not quite the amazing explosion of flavours we had come to expect. At least, now in the state of Maharashtra, we could get a beer even if the prices were eye watering.

That night both of us tossed and turned and the following morning it wasn't clear if we were suffering from the spice of the curry or something worse. Trying to keep the food bland at breakfast was a challenge but we needed to fuel up before riding off into the rain again. With the humid heat, it was hard to know whether to have waterproofs off or on, sweating or soaking occurring in equal measure.

I had planned to give Mumbai a wide berth as I suspected getting sucked into the city would be an unwise move. Then the rain and the traffic just got heavier and heavier, the heavens had truly opened, and it was relentless. I desperately tried to reroute from the back without getting my phone soaked and shouting directions to Stevie above the horns and traffic. We frequently ground to a halt amidst a pile-up of rickshaws, mopeds and tuk-tuks all trying to go in different directions, cutting in front and across us. Mind-bogglingly some of the major junctions just seemed to be controlled by a traffic officer with a whistle which just added to the cacophony of noise. It felt like a tap had been turned on overhead and we couldn't risk the puddles due to the treacherous potholes. We rode past tall buildings and slums packed full of an incomprehensible amount of people living basic lives, that must be so different from our own and we felt very much the aliens passing through. After moving about 15 miles in two hours we called defeat at a Biryani restaurant. We ate our food seated on newspapers with puddles forming around our feet. The young waiter was delighted to practice his English and take selfies, so we fuelled up on mountains of rice whilst getting ready to brave the downpour again.

We'd finally reached the city limits and had some beautiful, challenging roads with misty verdant hillsides, waterfalls and resident monkeys perched on the barriers, but horrendous potholes and road surfaces. We decided to call it a day at this point, after a mere 81 miles, and checked in at an empty holiday resort which was very much out of season. The evening was spent desperately trying to get everything dry, especially our precious Brooks leather saddles which had been doused by the monsoon rain and were at risk of severe hammocking. Stevie balanced and wedged everything near the air conditioning, and we braved the rain again to run over for dinner at the roadside restaurant.

That night was horrendous, I sweated and shivered, tossed and turned, and made frequent trips to the basic toilet. We had learnt at this point to carry our own toilet paper as it isn't supplied in India (the locals preferring to splash down with a scoop and bucket) but after that night we were running seriously low. Thankfully Stevie had done a fantastic job salvaging the saddles and we triple-bagged them the next day as without our comfortable seats, moulded to the inverse of our sit bones we were in for a world of pain. Unbelievably the rain hadn't stopped and had only gained intensity, pouring off the rooftops like a hose had been left on. A couple of stray dogs watched us load up the tandem- they are much calmer here, wary but wagging and not like the chasers in Europe.

We set off as quickly as we could, but the mixture of rain and road surface hammered our speed, along with the fact I had eaten nothing and Stevie only biscuits. Eventually finding an open restaurant I braved an omelette and sweet masala chai tea to try and keep my strength up but I still needed to stop frequently. The saddles were now triple wrapped, but the rain seemed to get everywhere else, and we needed to upend the panniers to get what must have been at least a pint of water from the external pockets. A bit of elevation on the road felt more challenging than it should, and we were haemorrhaging time so ended up calling it a day early at the first hotel we found, very basic and for the first time in India the owners spoke very little English but did their best to make us feel comfortable. I felt guilty for sticking to the blandest food on the menu and hoped they didn't take offence, just thought we were weird foreigners, but I was still up and down in the night and as much as I could still ride, there would be only so long I could go on when eating so little.

The next day didn't get any easier, we were riding National Highway 66 which was in the process of being resurfaced, but this was not a straightforward job. We would later find out that the works had been going on for years and no one knew when it was expected to end with large sections of the road dug up on alternate sides forcing us to cross a muddy potholed gravelly central section each time the sides switched (which seemed to be every few hundred metres). Sometimes the whole road was blocked by construction, with mopeds skidding around the mud at the edges. The combination of this and the effects of the stomach bug made progress incredibly frustrating again and in desperation, I briefly tried to divert from the national highway to cut off the corner, but we soon ended up on pure gravel and had to backtrack, wasting more time. We just couldn't afford to be losing this much time, but with frequent loo breaks and not risking the integrity of the tandem over the road surface and speed bumps, we had no choice. Back on the route and going the long way around we realised we would have to cut our losses and find a hotel before it got dark as the area had become more remote and we didn't want to risk a night in the monsoon. Paddy fields filled the countryside so there was no option of a dry wild camp spot.

Just when it seemed things couldn't get worse, we punctured.

Pulling over to a dilapidated building it ironically turned out to be an old hotel and we set about trying to fix the puncture as soon as possible without getting everything drenched. An Indian man on a moped pulled up and stood beside us and I desperately hoped he wouldn't ask for a selfie or the standard questions of where we were from and where we were going as I feared Stevie's patience was out.

PART TWO: India

Thankfully, he remained silent and eventually drove off, but it reinforced the impression that privacy is a very different concept in India and if we were forced to wild camp we would probably wake up to a crowd of people outside the tent. Puncture fixed in record time by Stevie's skills, we now had a night ride to the hotel in the town I'd spotted and were both trying to stay positive, despite the challenging situation: unwell, soaked through, nowhere to stay, nothing to eat and severely under-distance again...

I often think one of our major strengths as a team is how we react to situations like this when everything seems to have gone against us. Without a doubt, we both get stressed, upset, and angry and sometimes at each other, but when it really comes to "the crunch" we seem to always sort it out between ourselves. It is the mutual "get it sorted approach" that has gotten us out of many a tricky situation and there is always a solution if you stay calm and logical.

Once we found ourselves sitting outside a closed McDonald's at 6 am, both of us basically in tears, watching a young hooligan doing doughnuts in his car in the car park. We were exhausted, having ridden all night, hungry with no real food and resigned to the fact we were going to miss our coach back to the UK which was leaving from Dijon a few hundred miles away later that afternoon. We'd given it everything we had, and it wasn't enough. We were done.

The whole situation had arisen due to confusion in booking coach travel. There had been a mix-up between the coach timetables and the assumption that it left from the same place every time. This wasn't the case and we had realised, with about 40 hours before it left, that we had 600 km to ride to make it. This is a distance we could have ridden fresh and without luggage in that time, but after a holiday of col-bashing in the Alps and with full touring weight, our chances were slim to begin with. A desperate attempt to ride there had proven excessively hilly, resulting in us being stopped by the police at 2 am wondering what on earth we were doing and then grabbing one hour of sleep behind a crash barrier on the main road when we couldn't stay awake anymore. And now it was clear we wouldn't make it.

I'll never forget sitting on that grassy bank, feeling like it was all over because we couldn't get a cup of tea and a McMuffin but somehow, we pulled ourselves together, we thought things through and then somehow, we came up with a better plan: ride the tandem back to the UK. If we couldn't get the bus and couldn't easily get the tandem on a train or plane that was our only option. With me having contacts in Dover, if we could make it to Calais and get the ferry, we would have enough time to leave the bike with them and get a train to collect it at a later date.

A few hours later we had breakfast and a new plan; we spent the next days enjoying touring quickly to the north coast of France before an early hour's race to the ferry and homeward bound.

In this case, the lights went on and we prioritised finding somewhere to stay as the most pressing issue. Mileage and the record could wait, we needed to stay safe and recover first and foremost. After a few false alarms due to "hotel" not necessarily meaning accommodation, just a restaurant in a lot of cases we finally narrowed it down to spotting "ac/non-ac" signs as a giveaway for somewhere that had a bed. Pulling over in an eerily dark town, except for the lights from vehicles accompanied with incessant beeping of horns, we were pretty frustrated when somewhere that was obviously a hotel seemed to draw blank looks from the people there. It was unclear who worked there or not, but we became insistent, desperate to get somewhere to rest and unclear what the problem was? We had been soaked for hours and my feet had become itchy and then sore and now felt like they were on fire; I dared not look until we had somewhere to stay sorted out.

After several phone calls and being asked to wait for something, but not clear what it was, we were on the verge of leaving when a young man, with perfect English, turned up and he was to be our saviour this evening.

It turned out he was the principal of the high school, a role of some esteem, but was staying in the hotel. He informed us the hotel, and in fact, the whole town had no mains electricity and suddenly the strange lack of lights from shops and houses made sense. He encouraged us to stay at the next hotel along which he assured us would be more upmarket and likely have electricity, and made the calls to book us a room. He then helped us order food from the hotel we were stood outside, speaking rapidly to the staff and things suddenly seemed to happen very quickly. Under his breath he offered to get us a couple of beers but warned us they must be hidden as alcohol was legal but frowned upon. We were absolutely taken aback by his kindness and he couldn't do enough to help us, we almost felt he would ask for a fee or at least to spend the evening with us, but once he helped us get through the rigamarole of getting passports checked and settling in, he left us to it ,humbly accepting our profuse thanks saying that it would please his God that he had helped strangers and he needed no thanks (we suspect he was Hindi, but are awfully ignorant of the religions of this region).

Finally getting into the room, I dashed to the loo again before peeling my feet out of sodden sandals; every step I had taken since stopping had felt like walking on hot coals and, as I suspected, my feet were spotted and pitted with foot rot, likely a fungal infection from the damp. I washed, dried and slathered them in Sudocrem and hoped they would recover. The room was very basic again and left us wondering what the hotel the gentleman was staying at was like if this was the more upmarket one. As tired as we were we still needed to shower, wash our clothes, eat, and charge everything up before bed. We couldn't even finish the beers he had so kindly brought and with no air-conditioning for the first time, we hung clothes from the ceiling fan in the vain hope they would dry before getting soaked again tomorrow.

The following morning was another struggle. Stevie had gone down with a gastrointestinal upset as well, leaving both of us taking it in turns to be up and down in the night. The rain continued to pour, and we were on the same National Highway 66 now until Goa and the local information was that it wasn't going to get any better in terms of the road surface. We were riding ourselves into the ground in terms of health, nutrition and recovery, and something had to give soon. It was still 120 miles to Goa and, given the struggles to make 80 miles for the past few days, there was no chance we would make it in a day in our condition. Stevie managed to get some biscuits down but not much else and I made the decision to get to Kankavli 50 miles down the road and reassess there.

Those 50 miles were the toughest so far of the trip, both of us were drained and unwell, my feet still blistered and sore, and the incessant rain, road humps, and potholes were too much for us to take. We felt pathetic and soon pulled over for a hot chai at a basic dhaba, feeling like the hygiene precautions we had taken to avoid such places were in vain and the warmth and comfort of the hot sweet tea outweighed the risk of the cup not being washed.

A shiny new car pulled over and a young man got out to buy chai too and it soon transpired he was more interested in us than refreshments; a cyclist himself. Instead of the normal blunt questions: Where are you from? Where are you going? He actually showed an interest in us and the bike. It was refreshing to have a proper conversation. We hadn't realised how oppressive the endless questions had become with mopeds/cars/trucks pulling over multiple times a day to ask us the same thing, with no follow-up or further interest in our trip, and then wanting the inevitable "selfie" whilst precariously driving and angling their smartphone. We found it confounding that the "selfie" seemed to be the main goal and wondered what they did with these photos, except post them on social media with a caption of "look at these weird foreigners I saw" with no further knowledge of our epic adventure. And the questions were asked with so little regard for the answers that we had taken to giving the simplest answers, usually picking the next main place along our route to satisfy them; trying to explain that we were cycling along the majority of the coast of India just caused confusion, whether due to disbelief we were attempting this or, in some cases, lack of geographical knowledge outside of their locality it wasn't always clear.

This young man was like a breath of fresh air though, and a civilised conversation about cycling and the roads going forward wasn't just a relief but also very informative; it was only when we came to leave after him, we found he had paid for our chai as well as his.

Day 37–42: Kankavli, India to Bengaluru, India

I stared out at the drizzle dripping down on the grey overpass, with the horns and engines already creating a din, as we prepared to finally leave the hotel in Kankavli. We had ended up taking two whole days off the bike and three nights there recovering, reassessing, and replanning. Arriving after the awful 50-mile day we were done in but massively relieved to find a decent hotel and even more relieved that there was a pizza takeaway just below it so we could try and get some bland food. I caved and put out a call for help to some doctors we had contact with and got advice on the right medication to get us sorted out; and in another blessing, the best-stocked pharmacy in India was just around the corner, not only stocking all the medications we needed (including anti-fungal foot cream and anti-diarrhoeal) but also Mars Bars, granola and Dairy Milk!

This was more important than it may sound, as except for the pizza takeaway, we had been struggling to find anything we could stomach to eat. On the first morning we had gone for breakfast in the hotel and ordered boiled eggs...

"Fried." said the waiter.

"No, boiled eggs please," we replied.

"Fried eggs?" he reiterated, with a blank expression on his face as if he'd never heard of boiling an egg.

"Not fried; boiled eggs?" we asked more hesitantly despite these options being on the menu. We couldn't imagine they had run out.

"Boiled eggs, fried." he responded and at this point, we gave up and agreed. True to his word some minutes later a plate of fried, boiled eggs arrived. Not quite what we had in mind.

We realised that taking the route directly south from Mumbai had been a mistake, partly due to my rushed planning in the Tbilisi hotel room and we should have headed inland to Pune for better roads and resources. I had made contact with Audax India and offers of help and suggestions were coming in thick and fast, but in particular, I had been put in contact with another tandem rider called Meera who was keen to help replan a route. We had found out that the roads south were in even worse condition and busy with trucks and traffic; given the amount of time/distance we had lost over the past days we knew we were going to have to cut India short to have any chance of making our flight. She suggested cutting across through Bengaluru where she lived and helped me replan a route.

Taking the medications I reacted badly with vomiting and spent the whole day in bed waiting for them to work. I felt pathetic and an idiot for attempting the whole trip. It seemed we were falling behind with no chance to catch up and all my plans had been far too ambitious and based on an idyllic idea of riding around the world. I felt like a fraud and a failure.

But somehow, we pushed on and after two days of rest were eager to get back on the bike again. Stevie still wasn't brave enough to put his bib shorts on properly leaving the straps lose around his waist, but we were a damn sight better than we had been two days ago. Finally, we were on the road to Goa!

The rain was less dramatic than the past few days, and we had found out that a large proportion of Mumbai and the surrounding areas were on red alert due to the severity of the monsoon and flooding, so we had caught the brunt of it. Managing to track down omelettes and toasted sandwiches buoyed our spirits more and I was enjoying the ride, watching little kingfishers perched on telegraph wires, intently watching for snacks from the paddy fields. I spotted a tree full of big black birds making a ruckus. They somehow looked odd though and it took me a minute to realise that they were hanging by their feet and not birds, but bats! They were massive, as large as seagulls and due to their size, could only be fruit bats. There were hundreds of them across two or three large trees. I managed to convince Stevie to stop (he needed to check something on the bike anyway) and hopped over to the central reservation to get a proper look. It was a rare moment of feeling like I was somewhere exotic and special but after a few minutes we needed to press on. Our next goal was somewhere less exotic. On approaching Goa I had spied mainstream fast-food options and still not being brave enough to go back to curry we had our eye on at least a McDonald's and my stomach was rumbling at the prospect of a solid feed. The roads got busier as we approached and I spotted the golden arches on the side of a shopping centre, only to have Stevie ride on past.

"What are you doing?" I exclaimed distraught, "You've missed it!"

"We don't want to be getting caught up in there," he replied nonchalantly, "It'll take ages, we'll go to the next one."

He was under the impression the streets would be lined with golden arches throughout Goa, but I was less convinced. My fears came true when we swept onto a large flyover around the edge of the city with barely a peel off in sight. We'd missed our chance and I was fuming.

We bickered about whose fault it was, Stevie was adamant I hadn't made it clear that was our only chance and I was adamant that I wasn't to know that. Given it was only the second western takeaway we'd seen in India, how could he think there would be more down the road? I was just on the verge of a complete meltdown when, as if by magic, we came across a Domino's Pizza, and all was right with the world again.

The fact was, not only were we desperate for familiar food, but also to get the calories in to fuel our ride without fearing the consequences of a spicier curry on our delicate gut; it was much more than just a craving for junk.

Feeling well sustained with pizza we had a decision to make; there was a stretch of the route through what appeared to be a forested area and we needed to decide whether to stop before or after this stretch, either a 90-mile or 110-mile day. Given it was our first day back on the bike we were reluctant to push ourselves too hard, but at the same time keen to hit that magic "100 miles" figure which would give us the confidence we were back on track. We were moving well, so opted for the latter and rode past the last town at 90 miles to push on to the next.

BANG!

Stevie brought the bike to an emergency stop and I had a sinking feeling. I knew what had happened, having heard a noise like this before – the rear tyre had blown out.

We were just on the way out of town, and it had started to rain. We dodged between the chaotic traffic to try and rolling the bike to try find somewhere to assess the damage. The tyre's side wall had given way and, in hindsight, we suspected that the multiple punctures and times it was levered on and off in Turkey had weakened it. We were, of course, carrying a spare so Stevie quickly got to work swapping it out, but more time was lost and the opportunity to ride in before dark was lost.

The forest road was tougher than expected and Stevie, in particular, was frustrated with the odds being stacked against us again, preventing an early daylight finish. It didn't get any better when we struggled to find the hotel and then spent more time convincing the security guard we couldn't just lean the tandem up against a pile of rusting bikes, outside and uncovered. Then the hotel's card machine didn't work and running low on cash none of the cashpoints in the area worked either. Standing in the corridor which was the only place I could access the hotel's patchy Wi-Fi I tried to find a restaurant in what had appeared to be quite a touristy village near the beach on the outskirts of Goa. When we ventured out it became apparent, through Covid lockdown or other factors, it was run down and most places were closed up. The only open restaurant had a private function and the only open shop was a liquor store, with the first drunk person we had seen in India outside it picking fights. We hurried back to the hotel and spent all our cash on the room and bottled water, before eating leftover cold pizza for dinner.

The following morning, we were relieved to find an open restaurant serving omelettes early on, but then resorted to crisp sandwiches for the rest of the day, still too nervous to go back to full-blown curries with our guts only just settled. We got a brief glimpse of the Arabian Sea for the first time before turning east and climbing up through the jungle to cut off the tip of India and the roads we had been warned about. The jungle was dense on the sides of the road and we saw monkeys, but more alarmingly, several road signs for tigers!

Midafternoon we cracked, and with no other options for hot sustenance, we had daal and rotis and hoped for the best. It fuelled us for the 10-mile slog uphill to come and we overtook a few underpowered lorries chugging up the gradual climb. The small town of Yellapur had limited accommodation options and after last night's poor stay, we tried to go for the most upmarket. We should have trusted our instincts though, as it quickly seemed that the staff weren't the most accommodating. The first issue was the bike and after the usual argument that the bike doesn't have a stand and cannot stay upright of its own accord (this happened throughout India as all Indian heavy steel bikes have stands and they cannot accept that ours doesn't) we then had another issue because they would not let the bike go anywhere undercover. They are very particular about removing shoes when inside, presumably for hygiene as well as cultural reasons which is no bad idea, given the number of men we saw defecating on the side of the road. This extends to bicycles too and we were never allowed to bring the bicycle indoors in India. We eventually compromised on a spot directly outside the hotel where it was at least sheltered from the rain and could lean up, but was visible from the street and very exposed. The hotel staff reassured us there was 24-hour security and cameras, so we reluctantly accepted and went to check the room. Just as well, as we had to negotiate clean sheets and a towel each before settling the moderate amount (for India) for the room. The staff seemed unabashed to have offered a room with dirty sheets, just keen to get our money. It was only after we settled in, I noticed the muddy footprints on the walls which they hadn't got around to cleaning. The staff here struck us as lazy, a contrast from the cheapest and most basic places we had previously stayed in India. We went to get dinner at the restaurant attached and were accosted for selfies whilst trying to eat a disgusting tasting bowl of greasy noodles (it was a "multi-cultural" restaurant so served Chinese dishes as well as the usual curries). Suddenly, we spotted a crowd forming around the bike outside. The hotel staff who had offered "24-hour security" were clustering around it and seemed to have invited all their friends along too. They inched closer and closer to it, and I sensed Stevie about to crack as they started to touch the components. He abandoned his dinner and went outside where he was bombarded with questions from the crowd. Meanwhile I tried to fend off more selfie-takers in the restaurant. All we wanted was to eat in peace!

Stevie eventually got the crowd to disperse and we gave up on the rest of dinner, but were now seriously worried about the bike being tampered with overnight, not through maliciousness just curiosity. We had come to learn that culturally they would quite happily pull, ping and test any moving components without any understanding of if they were causing damage. Our fears were only compounded by the one man who had been insistent about knowing how much the tandem cost. The true figure would seem like a small fortune given the difference in cost of living here so we settled for saying it was sponsored by an American company and there would be big trouble from them if it was damaged! We came up with a plan to try and further ensure its safety and with Stevie making a show of storming up to bed I demanded to speak with the hotel manager.

"We were told our special bicycle would have 24-hour security," I said in my most assertive voice, "and now it has been tampered with and my husband is very angry! We have been harassed in your restaurant and we do not think you will keep our bicycle safe!"

The manager offered his apologies, but didn't look particularly upset by my complaints, so I persisted until I thought he had got the point; if anything happened to the bicycle, we would be expecting him to pay and I would inflict the wrath of my husband on him. We could do little else but take the risk overnight and leave early.

We left the quiet hotel at 7 am, leaving the 24-hour security snoring on the reception sofa and beating a hasty retreat from the worst accommodation yet. Breakfast on the road was bananas, biscuits and Snickers bars. Now in more remote areas, we struggled with food options. We found a café that only served one option, idli (a kind of ground rice patty with lentil sambar and chutney) which was tasty enough, but the rest of the day was fuelled by more junk food. The jungle had opened now first to paddy fields and then to open skies over cotton and corn fields in the flatter terrain. That evening usual dilemma of getting the tandem safely stored saw us stage a walkout to get the tandem locked in the garage and in a new accommodation quirk that we hadn't thought to check before paying, there was no Wi-Fi. Not just useful for updating social media we had also become reliant on internet access to check the weather, the route and upcoming accommodation. I was on the hunt for a new spare tyre too and it was not proving easy to source what we needed. Having tried a few bicycle/mechanic shops it was clear we would need something specially shipped in. Bailing out of the grungy hotel to find dinner we dodged puddles and mopeds down muddy streets and managed to locate a pizza restaurant, which was more of a small café, filled with teenage boys from the local boarding school who were very engaging and interested in our trip and followed our trip through social media from that point. They also got us a tuk-tuk to save the half-hour walk back to the hotel although I'm not sure if the little vehicles are more terrifying from the inside or outside!

We slept in our sleeping bag liners that night, not convinced by the cleanliness of the sheets, and the following morning had to leave via the fire escape, as yet another 24 hour security guard snored on the couch. Getting harassed by beggars as we tried to depart, we were relieved to leave another bad night's stay behind us as were finding the cultural challenges wearing. A roadside café served freshly made stuffed parathas which made for an amazing brunch, and we watched a pair of kittens using the tandem as a gymnastics frame and daring each other to scale the heights of the tin roof of the restaurant.

That night we decided to head for a reasonably large town called Sira as there were a range of hotels and we also needed to top up on cash. We rode into the town past the first few accommodation options only to find the cash machine empty. This being a familiar situation now we opted to try our luck at a hotel instead, but they were cash only, so we rode further into town picking out ATMs on google maps. After the third try, still failing to give us cash we were becoming frustrated as we had finished early to give us the time to rest and recover, not ride in circles around town. The usual selfie-taking and question-asking were occurring and one young man on a moped seemed keen to help when we explained our predicament and offered to lead us to a cash point. We retraced the roads we'd come down and followed him in and out of the traffic and up a hill. When we turned towards the National Highway I started to panic as there was no way there was a cashpoint up there and he seemed to be leading us to a more isolated location. Stevie, obviously thinking the same, tried to turn around, but the youth used his moped to obstruct us. It was looking like we'd put ourselves in a bad situation.

Eventually, Stevie gave up trying to turn and stopped the bike before we got any further. The moped driver stopped as well and approached us, I was ready to pedal like hell if he showed any signs of wanting to mug us or worse, but he then waved his phone at us and cheerfully called out the familiar "Selfie! Selfie!" request.

We were livid.

Not only had he wasted our time and energy to get another stupid selfie, but he'd also given us quite a scare and we couldn't fathom what had possessed him to lead us all the way out here. If he had shown us to an ATM, we would have been happy to have as many blooming selfies as he wanted, but now we were livid.

Six foot three of furious Stevie is quite a sight and the driver soon panicked and got back on his bike when he realised that we were not having any of it.

"You are a dishonest man and a disgrace to India," I shouted after him, in the hope he would realise how stupid his actions were.

We both simmered quietly on the way back to town and retraced the way we had come to a relatively expensive modern hotel we had seen on the way in, convinced this would take card payments. Yet again, India was never straightforward, and the hotel was so new they had no card readers, no Wi-Fi, and no restaurant. This was the last straw for me, with the daily stress of logistics, every night a different challenge, a string of crap hotels and a scare with the moped driver on top of the exhaustion of riding the bike I was in tears trying to get online payment apps to work. Stevie did his best, but the staff were just not helpful, insisting on cash but not able to help us find a working cash point and given the hotel was barely finished, insisting on the full rate for which we were about two pounds short with the cash we had. Stevie showed them the contents of our wallet and tried offering dollars or euros at a higher rate, but they would not budge.

The hotel had a safe space for the bike though and they accepted a deposit for the room, I sat on the bed and cried as the "staff" found reasons to come in and out with towels and toothbrushes, blatantly angling for a tip, quite how they thought we would manage that when we couldn't pay for the room I don't know!

We now had no option, we had to find cash and, reluctant to get back on the bike, we walked the mile back up to Sira and started a hunt for an ATM that worked. A long time later and on the eighth ATM I had all but given up but then by some miracle we finally managed to get 2,000 rupees out! This was the equivalent of about £20 so we tried a few more times until we had enough to cover a couple of nights' accommodation and food. Mission accomplished, we headed back to the hotel via a restaurant and finally got to bed rather late. We'd managed to turn things around, but at the cost of an evening of rest and recovery, which we sorely needed.

The following morning, we still felt drained from the night before and the routine of getting on the bike, trying to find food, and trying to push the miles was becoming exhausting. However, today we had the offer of some assistance in the form of Meera who I had been in contact with previously. She had insisted that Audax India would host us in Bengaluru and was trying to arrange to meet up. We had no idea what to expect and Stevie was a bit reluctant to commit to plans when we had such a tight schedule. She sent me a list of directions for when we approached Bengaluru which seemed to make little sense and after Mumbai, we weren't best pleased to be cycling through another city but with the road layout, we had little choice.

As the traffic built getting closer, we saw something we hadn't seen since reaching India: other cyclists! Not just people riding bikes for transport, but a couple of lads dressed in Lycra out for sport. They chatted, helped us with directions and took some great photos as well as the usual selfies before zipping off through the traffic as the rain set in.

I was sure we would miss our rendezvous with weather and traffic, but Meera's messages were insistent, and it was clear she was determined to track us down. Finally identifying the correct overpass, we pulled over and a short lady came bustling across the road through traffic. Meera was enigmatic and efficient and quickly shepherded us towards a hotel to meet another Audax India member, Deepak, who also was the organiser for India's biggest ultra-distance cycling event. We had been a bit reluctant to stop this early as it was only mid-afternoon and we had only covered 85 miles, but between them they convinced us it wasn't worth the battle with the traffic and Deepak would chaperone us out early the following morning and that they would "host" us here at this hotel. We were a bit taken aback but agreed and then everything happened very quickly.

Meera had the whole thing under control barking orders at the porters to make sure the bicycle was safely stored in an underground secure parking, then whisking us inside to an air-conditioned paradise of a hotel and speaking rapidly to the check-in staff. She had made arrangements in minutes and then we were seated, handed cooled drinks, and had a traditional Hindu welcoming ceremony with a small spot of red paint placed upon our foreheads.

We could hardly refuse a short video interview with them

and were being treated like some sort of celebrities and it was clear they were very excited about our record attempt. We had a short chat and I learnt that Meera was in awe of our custom-built co-motion tandem, the one she rode being off the peg, and given her diminutive stature, not the best fit, but she was obviously a tenacious rider and had to overcome the obstacles of having a riding partner who wasn't her husband and the prejudice around her riding solo. We take it for granted that in the UK we can source any parts we need, but in India, they were much more restricted in the components they could get hold of. We were just getting into the conversation, but Deepak and Meera were adamant we should make the most of the opportunity to rest and bundled us off to our room. The hotel was the most luxurious we'd been in since arriving in India and not only was the room paid for by our hosts as soon as we got in, but we also had a call to say that dinner had been included too!

We couldn't believe it and felt like we had been transported to a different world from the trials and tribulations of the past tough days on the road. That night we slept very soundly with clean sheets and full bellies.

Day 43–57: Bengaluru, India to Chiang Mai, Thailand

There was no lie-in the following day though, we were up and "at 'em" at 5 am and in the quickest I have seen Stevie get ready we were on the bike and set to follow Deepak and his daughter out of the city on their motorcycle. We had been given jerseys from the Tour of Nilgiris that Deepak organised, and I was enjoying the change of scenery, staring at a different design on Stevie's lower back. The streets were calm, but not dead and Deepak very patiently rode ahead to each junction, not so close to be considered drafting but not so fast that we lost him in the early morning traffic. It would have taken a lot of concentration to take the most direct route without his help and yet again we felt rather overwhelmed by the assistance we had had from these wonderful people. Finally reaching the outskirts he waved goodbye, and we were off into the countryside again.

It was still early morning, but with the wind behind us and a gentle downhill to the day we were making tremendous progress and it felt so good to let the tandem stretch her legs (or wheels). Unbelievably we hit 100 miles by 2:30 pm and a pizza lunch buoyed our spirits more!

We made the most of the easy miles and pushed on to Tiruvannamalai making it a 130-mile plus day. A sacred temple there made it a spiritual hub and therefore the area was set up for travellers and tourists and we had a very pleasant hotel to stay at (albeit not as fancy as the night before). We were just settling down to dinner when we spotted another hotel guest, and it took us a minute to realise what felt so unusual, they were Caucasian! We were unable to detect their language, but we suspected the couple were Eastern European travellers. They were the first white people we had seen since landing in India almost two weeks ago. It certainly gave us the impression, due to the legacy of covid or not, we were pretty unique in our journey across the country.

The following morning, we frequently passed orange-robed pilgrims visiting the temple and they looked as road weary as we felt, giving the impression they had travelled a great distance to get to this special place. It was a travesty due to the nature of our trip that we couldn't detour to see the temple, but needed to push on down the road and head for the second coastline of the Bay of Bengal on the East.

Sugar cane and banana plantations lined the sides of the road and we passed alarmingly motor-powered belt-driven machines, clanking and whirring away as they pressed the cane into a liquid we were never quite brave enough to try. Our culinary adventurousness was tested to its limits at lunch when our idli and dosas were served on a large banana leaf. Stevie's face was priceless as the no-nonsense waitress flopped one down in front of him and started to ladle out daal and coconut chutney; he doesn't like messy food at the best of times!

Still, in high spirits from the relatively smooth progress of the past few days, I was optimistic when I found a nice resort hotel with a pool online. My positivity was short-lived when we found the place locked up. The next hotel too much of a stretch to ride to that day and we pleaded with a local to help us out and make a call and the owner eventually arrived in a tuk-tuk. He didn't look best pleased to have his evening disturbed by needing to accommodate guests and after showing us the green algae-filled swimming pool we declined the first offer of a room which had rat droppings on the table. The second one appeared cleaner, and he wrote a modest sum on his hand, with little choice we agreed and hoped we were the only occupants. He tried to push us to have dinner there too, but with no evidence of a kitchen, we smelt a rat and decided to try the takeaway joint down the road. The heavens opened just at the wrong moment on the way back and we darted home to avoid the warm rain. Thankfully our sleep was undisturbed by rodents.

The following morning we packed up to leave only to find the gate firmly shut and the hotel owner blocking our path. He spoke rapidly at us in Tamil, and we became frustrated trying to figure out what he wanted. Finally, he wrote the word cleaning on his hand and another figure. Feeling fairly outraged that we were being held hostage until we paid more money for a room which he obviously hadn't bothered to clean before we stayed, and we very much doubted he would after, we grumpily handed over the amount. I got the impression he rubbed his hands with glee at getting one over on stupid tourists like us. The pleasant bubble of the nicer side of India we had been in for the past few days had now burst.

We often had the sense that people were hearing only what they expected, or wanted, to hear from us. It may have been a language barrier but despite using fingers and repeating ourselves we had to order brunch twice over to get the portions we wanted at a roadside café. The views over the massive estuaries were pleasant though and we appreciated the change in scenery. It was a hot day again and approaching Chennai I was determined not to get sucked into the melee as we had in Mumbai. There was one issue though, our wonderful Audax India friends had managed to contact the most experienced tandem mechanic in India there and he had managed to source us the spare tyre we needed and had it delivered to his shop which was slap bang in the middle of Chennai. I dreaded entering the heart of the city. Then, in another amazing altruistic gesture, he offered to bring the tyre to us and using the tracker managed to locate us on the ring road around the city and turned up not only with the tyre but also ice-cold drinks and cake. He had brought a contingent of his staff with him and we sat and enjoyed a pleasant break from the heat. It must have been the middle of a working day for him, and we couldn't quite believe all these people had gone to such efforts to help us.

Faith in humanity was restored and with Chennai successfully navigated we were pleased with an air-conditioned hotel room after a scorcher of a day.

The temperature still soared for the next few days and we struggled to stay hydrated and cool, stumbling into a roadside service station cum restaurant we were less than impressed when one lady wouldn't even give us the chance to sit down before shoving her children in front of us to take photos then walking off without asking us any more about our trip. The selfie culture was certainly becoming more and more infuriating and seeing two mopeds collide with each other as one driver tried to take a selfie and steer, we had no doubt it was very dangerous too. Luckily it was low speed so neither party appeared seriously hurt, but it just seemed such a stupid thing to do, risking injury for the sake of a photo! The heat didn't help with the noise either, horns sound continually in India for what seems to be no apparent reason most of the time and with the hot dusty roads the cacophony only added to the discomfort. Stevie had taken to wearing earplugs on the bike to muffle out the continuous din.

Over the next few days, we had a couple of even more disturbing experiences. Riding into a town one evening the muddy walkways on the edge of the road were busy as ever. Watching the throng of people pass by from the side view I got from the back of the bicycle I suddenly saw a heap of rags next to the road. It took me a moment to compute that it was a human form lying motionless while other people stepped over him.

"I think that was a dead person," Stevie said in horror, and although I tried to deny it, deep down I was not convinced; we had seen open coffins here and knew there was a different attitude to life and death.

The next day we had just managed to pick up the pace on a descent, and with Stevie concentrating on avoiding the swerving mopeds and tuk-tuks, yet again we didn't realise what we had seen until we were past the scene. A motorcycle had skidded off the road and a man lay sprawled on the floor with a couple of people standing next to the incident. It was only as we passed, I realised he had a puddle of blood around his head and was at least unconscious. We rode for a few moments in shock and silence.

"We should go back!" I then exclaimed, "We might be able to help!"

The bystanders hadn't seemed to be proactive and we had just had an ambulance pass us without stopping so it didn't seem help was on its way. From what I had seen I was fairly sure the injuries were fatal, but I still had the belief that even if that chance was minimal, everything should be done to preserve human life. Stevie was more cautious. We had no idea what we would be getting ourselves into if we turned back; we knew how to get urgent medical assistance for ourselves but not for a resident and had no idea what the implications of two foreigners trying to help would be or how it would be interpreted. By this time miles had passed, and we continued to ride on. I was overwhelmed with guilt and disgust, feeling incapacitated to help.

I watch the abdomen move up and down in a horrid slopping fluid movement. I know that is a bad sign. I know deep down that our efforts are futile, or at least they would be if this was one of my animal patients. But this is a human; so, I keep the rhythm and continue CPR as paramedics swarm around me placing IV lines, pushing fluids, and reading ECGs. A car has hit a pedestrian and with my basic CPR skills from my veterinary training, I am assisting. All I can see is the wreckage the vehicle has made of the body. I desperately hope these human medics, with skills far superior to my own, can work some sort of miracle, but I know a broken body when I see one. It is bad enough seeing the aftermath of a road traffic accident on a cat or dog, but to see the damage done to a human is indescribably horrendous.

It was no surprise when the call was made well over an hour later, but the scenes stayed in my head for a long time after, the contrasting feelings of wanting to have done more and knowing it had all been futile anyway.

One tiny lapse of concentration and a large metal box is allowed to destroy a vulnerable human form. It horrifies me.

Increasingly I find car culture confusing: how can we be so blasé about what essentially is a dangerous machine, a fatal weapon? A complex machine that we have a tiny bit of training on, usually in our teenage years, that we are then expected to competently handle for the rest of our lives. A small mistake and the damage done to a pedestrian, cyclist, or motorcyclist is easily fatal. We don't run up and down the street waving knives, taking children to school with loaded guns in our pockets, thinking it is ok to take our eye off the target to check social media. Motor vehicles are responsible for the highest number of accidental deaths in our country, and no one seems to care, mis-sold a story of wide-open roads and putting their foot to the floor...

An extreme point of view I know, but this is how I feel every time I have flashbacks to bodies lying dead on the road.

The next day, it was a street dog that was the victim.

"Don't look!" I screamed at Stevie as a horrible thud and yelp happened behind me, the gory scene only compounding my sensitivity to our vulnerability on the roads. It seemed there was less respect for animals here in general and we had even seen calves that appeared to have been hit. I was feeling very low, oppressed by the heat, and depressed by what we had seen over the past few days.

Salt encrusted our clothing, and we drank litre upon litre of tepid water, getting cold drinks in at every opportunity, so we were relieved when the storm broke in an explosion of thunder and lightning over Guntar. In a basic hotel, we had evidence that it was not just us that suffered gastro-intestinal disturbance echoing through the thin walls in the morning and this wasn't the last time we would hear vomiting in the next room; evidence that it was not just our hygiene causing a problem, but potentially endemic in the population.

Riding up the coast and crossing the massive estuaries we were relieved the temperature had dropped a bit, but even more relieved to hit a major milestone: 4,500 miles, a quarter of the way around the world!

It was day 49 now though and through the days in Tbilisi and the roadworks, monsoon, and sickness in India we had certainly lost time and miles.

This meant it was time to swap the belt on the crossover of the tandem (which links Stevie's and my pedals) and the chain, which was showing wear when checked with Stevie's lightweight chain tool. We were carrying a spare belt and the plan was to swap these over every 4,500 miles to ensure they meshed with the rings and didn't become too worn. Having lost the chain tool in #puncturegate Stevie was forced to snap the old chain so was a bit flustered when fitting the new one.

A few miles down the road he wasn't happy though as there was an odd noise from the new chain. Wise enough not to just put this down to the chain settling, he stopped to check and realised he'd made a simple mistake by threading the chain the wrong way through the jockey wheels. Now without a chain to spare and no chain tool, it was a bit tricky to fix, needing to separate the derailleur arm and remove the jockey wheels, then re-guide the chain correctly. Whilst in the middle of this a tuk-tuk driver pulled over and ignoring me approached Stevie and tried to get involved and help. I sensed this wasn't going to go down well but instead of completely losing his temper with another unsolicited interference with the bicycle (something we dealt with every time we stopped) he decided to check our assistant's credentials.

"So, are you familiar with the Shimano GRX gravel groupset?" Stevie asked him. The man looked dumbfounded.

Not so easily put off, the man still tried to get involved and it took quite a degree of determination to convince him that we knew what we were doing, it was under control, outside his area of expertise and no; we did not want to try and strap the bicycle to the tuk-tuk!

This may sound very petty and rude when someone was offering help, but these situations were so frequent we hid from plain sight whenever the bike needed tweaking as all too often people with no idea of how it worked would interfere and refuse to back off. We were tired and feeling the pressure of having our personal space and property continually invaded. It was a relief that evening to manage to order a takeaway to our room and eat in peace without selfies, "Where are you from/going?" questions or the food being served onto our plates for us by overbearing waiters.

The next morning's second breakfast stop was at a rather basic dhaba with dirt floors and staff, yet to start work, still snoring on camp beds in the corner. As we frequently found in these most basic places, they were the most honest, helpful and had the best food. It seemed those that had become more affluent were prone to lazy staff and poor hygiene, but the cheaper places had a feel of integrity and honesty. We had ordered just by saying "veg" and "roti" and were treated to a veritable feast.

The heat was building again and as water buffalo wallowed neck-deep in cool mud I almost wished I could join them. That evening's moderately priced hotel proved my theory of being underwhelming and had some of the usual problems of poor Wi-

Fi and unfriendly service but did have amazing views over Lake Chilika. I took a precious moment to stop and watch the fishing boats come into the harbour and the eagles soaring over the glassy waters that evening before returning to the nightly routine of washing myself and my clothes, and doing the daily admin.

Signs for elephants crossing added excitement to the following morning and today's cheap but wonderful Indian feast was vada – fried doughnut-shaped bread with chutney and sambar and three portions of a form of cheesecake for Stevie. The cheap and cheerful establishment proved friendly as ever, but a silent lady intently watched us eat. After we had finished, she followed us to the bicycle, never saying a word but staring fixedly. She gave no indication she understood English and did not attempt to communicate, just seemed intrigued and it was a complete contrast to the in-your-face selfie-taking culture we had seen so much of. As we left, I waved goodbye and wished I could have known more about her, but she just stared and didn't acknowledge the wave.

It was soon back to typical India though with Stevie almost losing me in a crowd of staring, selfie and video-taking men who swarmed around us as soon as we stopped in one village. We had the sense again that we were very much aliens, and this was not a tourist hotspot.

After a few false starts for a hotel that evening; the first one refused to tell Stevie the price and insisted he wore a facemask (the first indication of the covid pandemic so far in India) and the second claimed to be full without a car in the car park or evidence of any guests. I relented to stay in a pricey (over £30) boutique hotel boasting a bar and restaurant. We settled in and after issues with a lack of towels (and the shower not working), Stevie tipped the staff and we got clean. We tried to get to eat in the restaurant, but the staff were insistent we ate in the room and there was a constant stream of comings and goings bringing different courses, clearing plates, and offering drinks. It took me partway through the meal to figure out that Stevie had given a rather generous tip as we were lacking the smaller denominations of notes and the over-attentiveness of the staff became clearer, even to the point that they were still at the door after we were trying to get to bed.

It was the same the following morning and it was all I could do to stop them from taking the panniers down before we had packed them. We were then massively overcharged for the breakfast that we had initially been told would be included and I was spitting feathers by the time we left, feeling we had been taken advantage of yet again.

These swings in extreme from kindness and honesty to opportunism and laziness were becoming exhausting. When we stopped at another tiny dhaba for an all-you-could-eat lunch at a fraction of the cost of breakfast we didn't care when we noticed the plates were washed outside on the floor under a hand water pump; at least we had more faith in these people than those that just seemed to see us as marks to be ripped off.

We managed to stay on the good side of things for the rest of the day though. As Stevie went to buy snacks and I went to see what was keeping him only to find him apparently deep in conversation (in Hindi we assume) with an elderly couple that insisted on giving him 10 rupees (10p) change. Then on to a basic but spotless hotel run by a serious turbaned man and a host of earnest and polite young men and to a roadside restaurant serving beautiful curries on plastic plates. The mosquitos had descended at this point and were so large it felt like you were being stabbed when they bit; but kind restaurant owners brought out incense to ward them off.

Back on the road, it was still crazy as ever with anything and everything piled onto tuk-tuks and mopeds, from dozens of immaculately dressed school children to stacks of cages of chickens and what appeared to be a six-legged calf on the back of a truck! The road surfaces had let us down again though and although not as bad as National Highway 66 the roadworks and speed bumps were slowing our pace and affecting our morale. We were finally approaching Kolkata though, and having lost distance to the southern tip of India were planning to approach it from the north to get some extra miles in. A final night on the road in India and we were doing well with another relatively upmarket hotel with a gated entrance, buffet restaurant and even a bar – although it wasn't proving easy to get the refreshing beer we craved; everything was well over 5% abv and seemingly designed to get you drunk as quickly as possible! Not what we needed.

The following morning, we thought we had cracked it and having had a posher hotel stay without an incident that had left one or other or both of us fuming, until Stevie collected the bike from the secure parking garage that it had been locked in.

The cycle computer had been ripped from its mount and the locks bent where someone had tried to move it. Again, we suspected curiosity and a lack of respect for other people's belongings rather than malicious intent to damage or steal, but it was still infuriating, and I demanded to speak to the manager. He was very little help even though I emphasised the importance and expense of the machine and that he was lucky more damage hadn't been done by meddling with components. It very much felt like a relief to be riding towards the airport in Kolkata.

It was a tricky ride through the city trying to navigate the under and overpasses, some of which were toll roads and the first roads we had encountered where the bicycle wasn't permitted. I was flustered as we approached the airport and our pre-booked hotel. We almost got there when we confronted another slipway that two-wheelers were not allowed on and I stopped to check the map. Confoundingly the hotel then appeared to be in the opposite direction and Stevie was pretty unimpressed to have to backtrack. It was only on arriving at the second hotel I figured out there were two hotels from the same chain within very close proximity to the airport, but I had managed to book the furthest away meaning we would need a transfer to departures the following day.

We had intentionally left ourselves plenty of time to prepare for the flight and yet another amazing person came to our assistance providing the cardboard bike boxes we needed in the form of Sumanta who had been following us on Facebook. Meeting us at the hotel he immediately instructed us to come and have some refreshments with him and his friend, deftly making sure to order foods to cater to our European palates and cover the bill with a dismissive wave of his hand when we tried to offer to split it. He left us with the boxes the following morning and spoke to the hotel staff on our behalf to arrange the transfers and then we were finally able to get some downtime and an early night before boxing up the next day.

A lie-in until 8 am felt like luxury and Sumanta was initially on hand again to help, but got called away as his son was ill. Lacking our local support our plan to box up in the car park was foiled as it started to rain. Wet cardboard does not make for effective tandem protection, so we dashed for cover but were only just about able to fit under the eaves of an outbuilding for the electrics of the hotel. True to the rest of India they were adamant the bicycle would not come inside and not particularly happy with us half in the outbuilding, but we had little choice. The last monsoon in India made the whole process a nightmare and to this day I have no idea how we managed to get everything in and safely stowed when working on a one-metre ledge with water pouring from the roof above. Finally packed and taking a break in the weather we got the boxes stored in the hotel until that evening and tried to rest up. The excitement had negated any prior ideas I had had of a nap, so I settled for a swim in the rooftop swimming pool instead. A thoroughly surreal moment of floating above the chaos of the Indian city below, with pigeons perching on the pool edge drinking the water and the monsoon rains still rippling the water's surface. I heaved a sigh of relief. India had been incredible in every sense of the word and at times completely incomprehensible, I was sure I would view our time there more favourably in the future and knew I had been extremely privileged to have this experience when we had seen many people who had not travelled beyond their village or town but for now, I just had a massive sense of relief to have made it through. I soon dried off and went to pack up the remainder of my kit for the flight.

Of course, it wasn't over yet though, after a nail-biting 30-minute wait for Stevie to turn up (both boxes wouldn't fit in the same vehicle, so we had had to split up for the first time since the start of the trip), we had to fight our way into the airport, denied entry without evidence of passport, visas and onward tickets. Finally finding some paperwork the security guard would accept, it was just another hurdle to overcome. In the airport, it felt like a different world with more diversity than we had seen for a month and we were soon approached by a young couple from the UK who were touring the world on separate solo bikes. We were soon swapping stories and I had no choice but to come clean about our intentions, to explain why we had skipped some of the cultural experiences and sights they had targeted. We were both heading to Thailand but on different flights, but it still felt exciting and a relief to interact face-to-face with fellow Brits.

Our flight to Bangkok was 2 am local time so we were pretty exhausted by the time we boarded and then had a completely surreal experience waiting for the transfer to Chiang Mai seeing so many different nationalities and hearing so many different languages. There was western food and shops, and I took the opportunity to stock up on pharmacy supplies before we both had a pint of Singha lager and a full English breakfast!

With one flight left to go to Thailand, my excitement was mounting, and I was looking forward to the next new country.

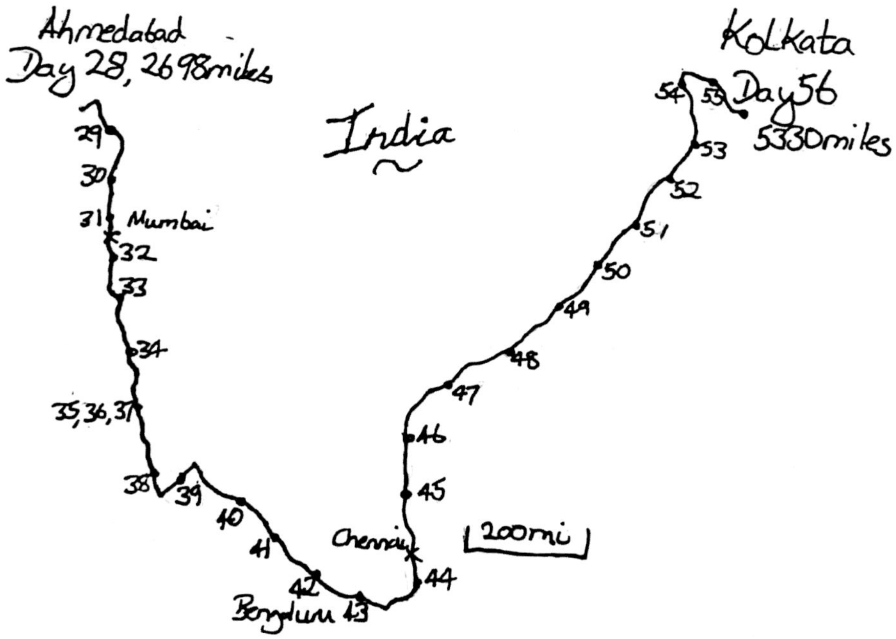
Ahmedabad
Day 28, 2698miles
India
Mumbai
29
30
31
32
33
34
35,36,37
38
39
40
41
42
Bengaluru 43
Chennai
44
45
46
47
48
49
50
51
52
53
54
55
Kolkata
Day56
5330miles
200mi

Getting
swarmed
in India

The lady who just
stared India

Wet in india

lunch in India

India

Dhaba break in India

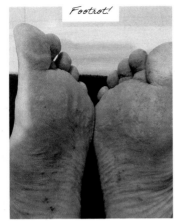

Footrot!

Monsoon rain India

part three: south
east asia

Day 58–66: Chiang Mai, Thailand to Surat Thani, Thailand

IT WAS like a breath of fresh air, literally! The air conditioning in the airport was beautiful but we were soon hit with the oppressively humid Asian heat as we stepped outside. We found a quiet spot to rebuild the bike and a couple of iced coffees helped progress no end. We had been avoiding ice in drinks in India having been warned it was often made with contaminated water, but the stylish airport coffee shop here seemed like a safe bet, especially as I saw them restock commercially bought ice into industrial freezers. It was still tough work through the heat of the day, and it was a relief to get rolling out of the airport and the city. We had a relatively short ride of 25 miles, to stretch our legs after the flight, mostly along the river Ping. I was loving it. It was relatively quiet on the road and the countryside was peaceful, it seemed lush without the intensity of the jungles in India and the river was beautiful. Thai temples and architecture lined the road and the people lived up to their reputation of being the smiliest race on earth.

Stevie, however, was grumpy and struggling, he had had a harder time of it; building the bike up and he hadn't eaten or drunk enough. So, he seemed relatively underwhelmed compared to my excitement at reaching a new country. When we got to a stunning newly opened hotel with a turquoise outdoor pool he declined to come for a dip before dinner.

Being distracted by the novelty of loo rolls in the toilet and spotless white towels folded into the shape of swans on the bed, it was close to 8 pm by the time we went down for dinner. In India, we had gotten used to eating out late, but here it was a different matter and we felt rather embarrassed when we realised the family that ran the hotel were sitting down to dinner too, probably assuming they had finished for the day. The waitress was very patient with our struggles to interpret the menu and soon plates of delicious food arrived: and it wasn't curry! The family were very welcoming and shared some of the whisky and soda they were drinking; on the house.

The next day we had slept far too well having lost a night's sleep on the flight and it was a bit of a struggle to get going, but we had a light breakfast at the hotel and started up a moderate climb into the jungle. "Elephant crossing" signs gave us hope of spotting some wildlife and I was rather disappointed to fly past an elephant sanctuary on the side of the road without so much of a glimpse of a trunk. If this had been a holiday, I would have insisted we stopped, but we still had many miles to go. The familiarity of a KFC lured us in the late morning and I was impressed when Stevie came back from the 7-Eleven next door with a replacement battery for his cycle computer, we wouldn't have known where to start looking in India! Things were certainly feeling like they were going smoother and even the monsoon rains blowing overhead seemed less intense. The rolling road meant we didn't quite make the progress I had hoped to, and we settled for stopping at an off-season resort near a large river. The accommodation was much more basic and we were quickly invaded by wood ants. With no restaurant on site, we had a mile walk to the nearest roadside kitchen which was a very basic open affair with stoves in the middle and plastic picnic tables around it. The menu was typically in Thai, but at least had pictures and having learnt a couple of keywords we did our best guess at ordering some food. The staff got straight to it, getting ingredients out of cool boxes and checking which sort of rice we wanted before cooking everything up fresh. What we had thought was going to a fish soup arrived first and I took one look at the white chunks and was horrified! My veterinary training left me in no doubt this was not fish but bovine spinal cord!

"Ste, I don't think we can eat this!" I hissed at him, embarrassed that we had made such a faux pas when the cooks had been so kind, but we were unwilling to risk it and made the most of the other dishes we had ordered. It made for rather a light dinner and on the second can of Chang lager I had a tipsy walk back. Beer in India had either been too strong or illegal so it was nice to have a drink, but I think we would have both preferred more dinner and ended up snacking on biscuits when we got in. We bribed the ants to stay away from our bed with some sweet popcorn we had picked up and hoped that would be the worst of our visitors through the night.

Stevie had slept badly, with strange dreams and rolling guts so it was a grumpy start on the bike, knowing we would need to find a decent meal asap. Thailand came through again though with first a petrol station that not only sold snacks, but also hot meals and then we discovered the joys of everything microwavable in a 7-eleven including pizza slices and burgers. I was still loving Thailand with its beautiful scenery, and we even came across a cycle lane to aid our progress, but Stevie still seemed down in the dumps and hadn't perked up since we got here. I thought my trump card of another resort hotel, this time run by an Austrian gentleman and his Thai wife would cheer him up especially as they served spaghetti Bolognese (we had been craving pasta). They did us a solid "Amerikanische" breakfast too and it was yet again a wonderfully calm surrounding where I would have loved to stay longer.

Back on the road we had 7-Elevens down pat now and knew the layout and options well enough to decide what we wanted before we got there. It was a hot day again and I was daydreaming on the back when there was a rustle in the bushes.

"A massive lizard just ran across the road," said Stevie excitedly but I didn't quite believe him, so it was a bit of a shock when, several miles later, an even bigger one ambled in front of us. These Monitor lizards were massive, probably close to two metres in length. Joining up with the river Ping again made for some pretty riding and after a couple of false starts we got a riverside hotel in Chai Nat and a room with a view.

The buffet breakfast served us well, but we were feeling groggy and it was a tough day on the road too with both of us struggling with morale. The prevailing wind in Thailand seemed to be in front of us, making the riding hard. The scenery was still lovely and paddy fields had started to become more frequent alongside large, flooded fields with little water-wheeled boats paddling across them. There was one negative compared to India though: the dogs were less amenable and became more likely to give chase as we were approaching the busier stretch on the outskirts of Bangkok. An instinctive reaction on my part jarred Stevie's knee badly through the timing chain and ruined his mood for the afternoon.

On reaching Nakhon Pathom I feared a repeat of Bratislava as the first four places were full, but finally we found a large hotel in the centre. The next challenge was finding dinner, and not being in the mood for greasy fried chicken, the other options looked challenging: one noodle restaurant would have been great except there were no chairs and diners sat on the floor with their legs neatly folded underneath them. Fearing Stevie would never get unfolded again and both of us wincing at the idea of getting up from the floor on tired legs we ventured further down the road and plumped for the first normal-looking restaurant, happy with whatever it was serving as long as it wasn't spinal cord soup!

The menu was thankfully simple; noodles with a choice of protein. What we hadn't realised was that this restaurant had a quirk where you cooked it yourself. I feared Stevie would lose his rag when the waitress came and turned on a hot plate in the middle of our table and dished out a large bowl of broth. The ingredients then came fresh and uncooked on a separate plate, and we were very grateful when the young waitress gave us a demo of how best to cook everything up. It turned out to be a delicious and healthy dinner despite having a bit more involvement than we had wanted.

We had picked up breakfast from the 7-Eleven the night before so were able to make a prompt start directly from the hotel. We were passing Bangkok today and heading for the coast, so the roads were busy and facilities were frequent but we were still battling the wind so were soon hungry again. We completely over-ordered in McDonald's and left feeling stuffed. What had looked like a coastal road was frustratingly separated from sea views by a block of buildings. Signs for seafood restaurants and beach resorts made me yet again question our wisdom in racing through this holiday destination and missing so much.

We picked a hotel inland, but it left a lot to be desired and had a distinctly damp smell. Stevie seemed exceptionally affected by this and claimed to still be full after the

McDonald's, having been feeling bloated and nauseous. We found the nearest restaurant anyway and ordered, but as soon as it was placed Stevie dashed out claiming to feel unwell and uncomfortable in the otherwise empty restaurant. I was left sitting at a table by myself waiting for a meal for two and was not impressed. I managed to communicate to the waitress that my husband was unwell, and could we take the majority of the food away? She was very obliging, and I ate one dish while the others were packed up. On returning to the hotel, Stevie was already in bed and not wanting to eat anything. I was tired too and slightly concerned, but couldn't understand what was wrong as we'd pretty much shared every meal and I was fine. We put it down to pushing too hard into the headwinds and Stevie felt he still hadn't recovered from the lost sleep on the plane and this combined with the general exhaustion of handling the bike was impacting his mood. We bickered about whether we would need to put back another set of flights and I stayed up too late doing admin which did not make for a good night's rest. Stevie continued to struggle with thirst and indigestion through the night and the following morning we were both tired and moody.

We started steadily and had agreed to cut the day as short as we needed to give us some chance of recovery. I was concerned Ste wasn't drinking enough and reminded him to take a drink every 30 minutes. I was also trying to take some of the slack on the tandem to give Stevie an easier ride. It seemed the 7-eleven fare was getting tiresome and Stevie wasn't having much to eat, and the highways were feeling like a long drag too. We were both pretty rock bottom in terms of mood and motivation, so it at least added a bit of interest when we turned off onto some rougher roads and then finally, we saw the sea! Waves crashing on picture postcard beaches cheered us up a bit and we stopped at a restaurant on the beach to get something more nutritious than junk food. It was also a great opportunity to get some social media fodder for the next big milestone: 6,000 miles.

I wrote the numbers in the sand and cajoled Stevie to pose for what would become one of the most iconic photos of our trip. Another stop to lubricate the cassette which had become noisy, and we decided to call it a day sooner rather than later; I tracked down accommodation in another out-of-season resort. I was relieved to find that, although the kitchen was closed, there was a restaurant a short walk down the beach and after the nightly washing routine, we wandered down. I thought the food was great, fresh and spicy, but Stevie was less impressed and just wanted something bland. Alarm bells started to ring when he failed to finish his beer, but I was reluctant to give up on what felt like a tiny fragment of pretending I was on holiday and splashed through the warm waves on the way back up the beach before taking the plunge in the darkness and going for a brief skinny-dipping swim in the sea. Stevie trudged back to the room, obviously not in the mood for any fun and I felt frustrated we were missing a rare opportunity to enjoy some of our trip.

I was becoming increasingly concerned that he hadn't seemed quite right since we had landed in Thailand and wasn't sure quite what to do. His symptoms seemed unspecific with a bit of bloating, nausea, and loss of appetite, but he had seemed to deteriorate over the past 24-hours. That night made my mind up for me: he was tossing, turning, and belching foul-smelling burps. I had my suspicions about what was going on but caved and asked for advice from one of the wonderful medics that had offered to help us. While waiting for a response I let Stevie lie in a bit longer to try and get more rest before we made a steady start, ignoring the necessary distance for the day and just seeing how far we could get.

With only a bit more riding along the coast, we turned inland to palm oil and rubber plantations which made for more monotonous riding, and passed stall upon stall of durian fruits. Durian is the most pungent fruit in the world and is banned in many buildings and enclosed spaces and the smell from the passing stalls and lorries wasn't doing anything for Stevie's nausea. That evening we had a response from the doctor and my suspicions were confirmed: Stevie more likely than not had contracted Giardia in India and it had incubated for a couple of weeks before he showed symptoms here. Giardia is a waterborne parasite that lives in the guts and is transferred via dirty water sources. Other mammals can contract it too. I was feeling a bit daft for not putting the dots together sooner because in hindsight Stevie's gut upsets and grumpy moods since landing now made perfect sense. We started him on the medication (which we had luckily picked up in India) and hoped it would kick in quickly. He still couldn't face much food and we ordered room service but after a few mouthfuls, he passed out asleep, completely exhausted.

The next day was similarly tough with me trying to encourage him to take on as much food and fluid as possible, and him still feeling wiped out and occasionally wobbly. The weight was flying off him too and it was only in the hotel room that night that I realised quite how skeletal he was becoming. I knew this was a serious risk as having his body in negative energy balance would not only affect his ability to ride but would have knock-on effects on recovery and immunity too. Determined to find something he could stomach I walked out from the hotel that evening to a 7-Eleven a mile and a half away, half jogging at times to try and make the trip quicker. I stocked up on noodles, cereal, milk and any other treats I thought he might try, then rushed back. The streets had been dusking on the way out and I hadn't considered the neighbourhood I was in, but started to think I should have paid more attention when I scuttled past what was at best a lap dancing club. Stevie managed to get some dinner down and I just hoped we'd be fit enough to keep pushing on tomorrow. We were toeing the line a bit in terms of the distance to cover before our flight and if we couldn't pick up the pace it was going to be another big expense to rebook the flights...

Day 67–70: Surat Thani, Thailand to Hutan Melintang, Malaysia

Thankfully Stevie seemed a bit better in the morning and managed a solid breakfast. His change in body shape had resulted in a reduction in padding on his derriere though and an act of desperation occurred outside a 7-Eleven where he hacked the pad out of one pair of bib shorts in an attempt to double up. This wasn't successful, but we knew he just needed to get to Singapore to get a new set. Pushing towards the west coast we ignored tourism signs again and stopped at a basic hotel. In the morning an elderly lady kindly offered me coffee and asked questions in basic English, and I felt bad that I couldn't communicate better, but there was a sense of a shared beverage and kinship. There was a sense of cultural change as well, moving from Buddhism to Muslim and we saw more headscarves being worn by ladies. A long procession of school children, all dressed formally for some sort of festival, walked down the road and I waved from the back.

Then we started some serious climbing; it was just as well Stevie was feeling a bit stronger. Weaving up through the jungle, the terrain almost became mountainous, and it felt like we were heading to the back of beyond, but we were steadily approaching the Malaysian border: our first land border since Georgia which felt like an age ago. Getting through swiftly was a relief and it was a flying descent down the other side of the mountain range. It immediately felt similar but different to Thailand and I felt we would have a better chance at communication with the Roman alphabet again. With the sun setting wistfully over paddy fields I was looking forward to riding through another country. An upmarket hotel that evening was very welcoming and the most touristy place we had visited for some time. It was great to be able to speak English and have a range of choices on the menu – I made sure Stevie had his fill. Raiding the buffet breakfast served to fuel us more and we enjoyed a brief respite from the heat as the mist hung low over the paddy fields before it was burnt off.

Things were starting to seem more positive, and Stevie was finally regaining strength, so we were still in with a chance of making the flights. A roadside café proved a winner for second breakfast and the good things I had heard about Malay food proved true with doorstop slices of bread topped with fried eggs, baked beans on a bit of lettuce, a large frankfurter dressed in mayo and a small jug of gravy on the side. It seems like an unusual combination but was wonderfully tasty, we even risked some fresh juice to wash it down. The roads got busier and the heat rose towards Sungai Petani. I tried a diversion to get us out of the traffic, but similarly to India, just because it looks like a road on the map doesn't mean it is paved and after taking us down a dead end which resulted with a walk down a rutted dirt track used by mopeds, we were both hot and bothered. Then out of nowhere a moped pulled up alongside us and handed me two bottles of isotonic iced cold fizzy drink. Unless he regularly picked up cold drinks on his travels, I suspected he had seen us, bought the drinks and come back to drop them off. A wonderful gesture of kindness from a stranger.

The next morning was a steady start with Stevie still recovering his strength, but I had tracked down a Domino's pizza the night before, so at least we were well fuelled for the ride. We were grateful to get on a quieter road as there was a similar volume of mopeds and motorcycles as there had been in India, but here they seemed to ride faster and be in more of a hurry from A to B. The back roads took us through dense dark palm oil plantations where the brilliant sunlight was completely blocked from the forest floor by the thick fronds. The homogeny of the plantation was quite depressing especially when we knew there were mangrove swamps just to our west on the coast and signs warned us of "tapirs crossing" but I suspect they were far too sensible to venture into the quiet lines of trees. We started to worry going off the beaten track was going to leave us in a pickle as we hadn't seen a single 7-Eleven all morning; a luxury we had started to take for granted!

We happened upon a quirky roadside café just in time for lunch. Typically, they only served one option, and this turned out to be a speciality of smoked meats with a variety of vegetable accompaniments. The set-up was unfamiliar but luckily the owner spoke good English and helped direct us to a queue where our meal was served canteen style out of large trays. It was unusual but tasty and we were just glad to have found something to eat that wasn't another microwaved burger (the novelty had worn off by this point). The staff soon managed to get our tale out of us and treated us like royalty, and then refused to let us pay. We felt quite embarrassed and the least we could do was pose for some selfies with them. Feeling well-sated we headed back to slightly more main roads and settled into the afternoon stint for a few hours. The afternoon was hot, and I was daydreaming, not really paying attention to my surroundings.

BANG.

An impact.

I was on the grassy verge. I struggled to breathe and lift my head.

Stevie! Where was Stevie?!

I struggled with the bike still on my legs and tried to see him at the front. He was already moving, starting to get out and stand up.

I tried to speak but the pain in my chest was too much initially.

"Are you ok?" he asked.

"Yes," I managed, but realised I wasn't sure if it was true.

"My ribs!" I exhaled in agony.

"Ok, stay there," he started to move the bike off me and assess the damage. A young Malaysian man was approaching, and I tried to turn to peer up the road where another man was limping. Their motorcycle was about 50 metres further up the road also on the grassy verge and the limping man had a large open wound on his knee. I wanted to get up and help but couldn't move.

Stevie was livid.

"Where is the pannier?" he shouted at them, "the other yellow bag? You have to help me find it! We need it!"

Still feeling disorientated I realised that of the two panniers bags on the left side of the bike; the front was ripped off and the back was nowhere to be seen. I vaguely recalled the sensation of the impact from behind and being thrust forward, but it was all unclear. Stevie started searching for the pannier with the men and I tried to assess my wounds, my ribs were making it hard to breathe and I was worried they were broken but judged I didn't have anything as serious as a collapsed lung... yet. I tentatively moved my arms and legs and my chest seemed to have taken the brunt of it, presumably where the motorbike rider hit me. I also had a 1p-sized chunk of flesh missing from my elbow where I could see tendons, if not bone, glistening underneath the road grit. I gradually attempted to stand and managed it but felt breathless and sore, so decided to sit again as Stevie came back with the pannier. The two young Malaysians did not speak English and it was only later we pieced together that Stevie had seen them racing another motorcycle recklessly, not uncommon behaviour in this country, and they had swerved to overtake a car and cut back in without seeing us, then collided with the right-hand side of the bike and ripped both right panniers off. It was pure luck that we all had a soft landing. The young men weren't wearing helmets or any form of protective clothing, so we all could have come off a lot worse.

By this point, we had attracted some attention and a short woman called Nasi soon took hold of the situation. We quickly declined offers to call an ambulance or the police, preferring to assess the situation ourselves and asked for help getting the damaged panniers to the nearest hotel. She was local and offered to take us in a car, an offer we quickly refused unwilling to leave the bike or squeeze it in a vehicle. We settled on following her slowly with another man who had stopped to help following us from behind on a moped. I wasn't sure I could ride but tenderly got myself in the saddle and let Stevie turn the pedals for the final mile to the next town. We had made good progress already that day so our total distance would have not looked unusual and we kept our Strava GPS running, unwilling to break the news to friends and family yet.

While Stevie made the hotel arrangements for a change, I made a call to Dr Rich from World Extreme Medicine to assess how concerned I needed to be about my injuries and whether we did need to go to a hospital. Having given me some serious warnings about signs of internal injuries to be aware of, we agreed between us that it would be sensible to monitor overnight, although he was quite impressed by my new "armpit".

Having got us into a room Nasi was still determined to help and having done some nurse training bustled off to come back with a bag of exactly what I needed to flush and dress the wound. The man that had followed us in was dispatched to locate an adjustable wrench to help straighten the derailleur hanger which had been bent. A full assessment of the bike would have to wait until the next day. As she was desperate to help more, we sent Nasi out again to get us a KFC and then finally watered, fed, wound dressed and with plenty of painkillers I tried to lie down on a pile of cushions and sleep.

Day 71–76, Hutan Melintang to Malaysia – Singapore

I squinted my eyes open to fumble for the packets of painkillers next to the bed. It was daylight and my chest was propped up on a pile of cushions, but the last dose had worn off and every breath was agony. Initially, all I could think of was the medication but, as I slowly came to, the trauma of yesterday's events put an end to my slumber. I groaned and tried to sit up and fathom what had happened and what on earth we would do next. The room was more of a bomb site than normal with empty KFC boxes, wound dressings and emptied panniers strewn about. Last night had been about getting safe and dealing with the most critical problems but now we had the rest to figure out: When could we ride again? Did we want to ride again? Was it all over?

Questions I couldn't bear to answer right now.

Stevie was soon groaning awake too, he was battered and bruised too and had some badly scuffed knuckles but had come off better than me and we started to formulate a plan in order of importance. Firstly, I needed to field social media as it would be quickly picked up by our avid followers that the tracker wasn't moving this morning and we didn't want our families to panic. I put a brief message up, playing down the severity of the crash, implying the bike was the main issue; it was just as well as, unbeknown to us, the man who had helped chaperone us in and obtained the wrench for us, had taken photos and videos of the crash and then us riding (presumably whilst he drove his moped) and it didn't look good. This made me feel very angry, we had just narrowly avoided much more serious injury from the lack of road safety and if those photos had been seen by our families before we had contacted them, they would have been distraught! We could do little apart from put it down to cultural differences (the man had blocked out my exposed legs to presumably preserve my modesty) and he had helped us, but it made me feel more uncomfortable in this foreign country.

Next up was the bicycle: Stevie had done a rough assessment last night, but we ventured down to check for further damage. Aside from the bent derailleur hanger the front pannier rack was bent and the bar tape was scuffed, but she appeared otherwise relatively unscathed. The main damage had been to the panniers, but this was a blessing, as they had essentially acted like airbags and cushioned both us and the bike from the impact. The contents had been squashed to the point where a small glass bottle of beard oil in the middle of our washbag in the middle of the pannier had been smashed; I avoided thinking about the forces involved. The two panniers themselves were worse for wear having had the mechanism where they attached to the rack ripped off and it was clear that they were irreparable, which left us with a dilemma of four panniers worth of kit and only two that could mount on the bike.

I started to look at options for replacement and then we

moved on to the next issues: breakfast and more dressings for my arm. Thankfully the pharmacy was very well stocked and using my veterinary training I was able to spot a couple of familiar brands and get what I needed for a couple of weeks' worth of dressing changes. Breakfast was a trickier matter, but we eventually settled on a nearby noodle café as I was struggling to walk far with my ribs aching. Over breakfast/brunch, we considered our options; we could pack it all in and get a taxi to the nearest airport which was Kuala Lumpur but as much as I felt like this right now, I suspect I would regret deciding to quit today. The risks of continuing weighed heavy on us though and although we had known that cycling on roads for 180 days straight statistically put us at a high risk of an accident, the behaviour of motor vehicle users in Asia certainly increased that risk. Our flights were from Singapore and in the grand scale of things this wasn't much further than Kuala Lumpur and we had a contact waiting for us there. There was no chance we would make our original flights as we had already been on a very tight schedule due to a couple of shorter days where Stevie had been unwell and even though he had speculated we might get a few miles in later that day, I very much doubted I would be prepared to sit on the bike again until at least tomorrow and the flights would have to be put back.

At his lowest Stevie is often quick to blame me for my "stupid idea" and "cracking the whip" to make our 180-day target, but his suggestion to ride sooner rather than later (when I couldn't imagine anything worse) would give me confidence in the weeks and months to come that this wasn't all down to me and he was focused on the same goal too; even if he would occasionally refuse to admit it. And to his credit, there is a lot to be said for getting back on the bike as soon as possible after this sort of accident so not too much confidence is lost, but I was just too bruised and battered to contemplate it that day. Further into the future was too much to take in and for our mental stability, we agreed the aim was to get to Singapore and reappraise. We had flights booked to Australia so we might as well go, even if we gave up on the record and spent time touring on holiday, but it was too soon to know what we would be capable of.

The next job on the list was to meet up with Nasi, who had insisted on arranging a meeting with the boy's grandfather, implying he wanted to make amends. On returning to the hotel, we were not quite so convinced that this was the case when confronted by a rather grumpy-looking old man and I had my suspicions that the goodwill had mostly come from Nasi as opposed to the boys' families. We sensed they were not affluent people but wanted them to have a sense of the damage the boys' reckless behaviour had caused. We showed them the damaged bags and they were quick to point out that they wouldn't be able to buy replacements in this country and offered to buy us a backpack, we quickly declined and said we would source some ourselves. It was very disappointing that the boys themselves had not come to apologise but even Nasi was of the opinion, "that's just the sort of thing young men do," so it felt we had little chance of changing this mentality. Realising the meeting was a waste of time we quickly curtailed it and I tried to rest up a bit while Stevie tidied up.

There was a knock at the door and Nasi had come back up to check up on us again and reiterate how much the grandfather wanted to help. Before we could express our doubts, her son appeared, having followed her up the stairs. He was sadly very overweight for his age and wheezed and puffed in the corner while Nasi rambled on.

"Oh, don't mind him, he's just a fatty!" she said, noticing our concerned glances. Eventually, it boiled down to us being given the equivalent of £40 in Malaysian Ringgit, which we were told and sincerely hoped, came from the boys' families (not Nasi). It was a strange conundrum as I am sure this felt like a significant amount of money to them, but once we had checked the price of new bags and rearranged flights (not to mention the cost of other damaged parts and dressings etc) it came to over £2,000 of extra expenditure. I later let Nasi know the full cost, staunchly stating that we did not expect this money from the families but wanted in particular the boys to know how much their actions could have cost them and that the consequences could have been a lot worse.

The day was rapidly passing and I had started the ball rolling with obtaining new panniers, we found our sponsor, Cycling Touring Life, could arrange for some prototypes from their sister company in Taiwan: Woho Bicycle Adventures, to be shipped directly to Singapore in a matter of days and free of charge! I also rearranged the flights for two days later to account for the day off the bike and give us less daily distance while we recovered. We had some dry bags already from Woho and with the traditional combination of duck tape and cable ties Stevie affixed these to the front pannier rack so that we could still carry the vast majority of our belongings. I finally got to bed early with the knowledge we would be riding again, but now it was a very different race to Singapore...

It was a sore steady start the next day, but we managed to get back in the saddle and push on. The admin continued throughout the day making arrangements for the new panniers and rearranging flights and we both felt quite sober given the events of the last few days. I managed to obtain some pizza for dinner though and we were both relieved to reach the hotel at the end of the day without incident. The following morning the roads were busy again as we were near Kuala Lumpur. We had both lost confidence and I flinched every time a motorcycle went past which was not doing my ribs any good. I was already feeling worn down and despondent when on checking my phone I found a couple of missed calls and a voicemail from my dad. He had sad news that his father, my grandfather, had passed away. Grandad had been well into his 90s and had suffered some ill-health more recently but had taken a turn for the worse over the past week and with the drama of the crash I had not known he had been so unwell until Dad left the message. It was a shock and I felt guilty for being on the other side of the world from my family at this time, but Dad was quick to point out that Grandad would have wanted us to continue to try and complete our challenge.

I felt broken.

My ribs hurt with every breath, the challenge seeming too dangerous, too frivolous, too much for us to overcome and now I just wanted to go home and mourn the loss of my last living Grandparent. I cried silently on the back until Stevie pulled us over and tried to console me, but there was little he could say and I just wanted to quit and go home.

I once quit an Audax; a 400 km event called Moors and Wolds starting from Alfreton in Derbyshire and heading north to Scarborough before looping back down over the Humber Bridge. It was a local event and roads I knew, and I had set off full of energy and optimism knowing this distance should be comfortably within my capabilities. With it being a qualifying ride for the infamous Paris-Brest-Paris Audax ride later in the year I was determined to finish well. Things went great to begin with but as I pedalled on, I struggled to keep my pace up and a well-earnt fish and chips at halfway should have boosted my morale but left me slumped. Crossing the Humber Bridge in the dark I picked up a bit and turned the pedals a bit quicker but come dawn I was feeling drained again, lethargy overcoming me, and I knew I was just going too slowly. Stevie knew this too and having been patiently riding his solo bike around the course with me, pressed me to keep the pace up but it was no use. My legs were jelly, my bum and undercarriage sore and my neck and hands seized from too much time on the bars. I had failed, I couldn't go faster, I was a rubbish cyclist and my place at Paris-Brest-Paris was not meant to be. It was all too much. I was pathetic.

So, I cried like the pathetic person I was, with the dawn breaking and still at least 50 miles to go. I quit. I gave up.

But, I rode to the finish and completed the ride within the time limit and succeeded in getting my place at Paris-Brest-Paris.

As, even though I had given up, the easiest way home was to pedal back to the start and although my speed was not spectacular, somehow managing to keep going through the exhaustion and pain I still managed to succeed. It was an interesting lesson that day in what success and failure actually are and what I was really capable of. The mentality of riding long/ultra-distance is arguably more important than physical prowess and if I had kept my head that day, I would have ridden a lot better, but equally, the will that says go on was still there and got me to the finish line. I think I experienced something similar to that, that sad day in Thailand, where I cared nothing for the challenge and the record attempt, but somehow kept pedalling and waited for brighter times to come.

Another empty resort hotel that night did little to lift the mood though. There were signs warning that couples would have to produce a marriage certificate to be allowed to share a room and we were glad that rule seemed not to apply to us, as it was the one thing I hadn't thought to bring a copy of, and I was not in the mood to argue. I managed to speak to my dad which was some consolation, but a noisy room and an insufficient dinner did little to improve matters before our final full day of riding in Asia.

Asia wasn't done with us yet though and the heat just built and built the following day with the humidity we thought we had become accustomed to, but apparently not. We were tantalisingly close to the coast again but saw little of it except signs for hotels and beach resorts, stuck in the hot traffic on the main roads. Pushing on to get the ride over and done with, we snacked on junk food and skipped a proper midday meal to get to the seaside town of Pontian, where I had booked the nicest hotel that I could find, to make up for a couple of nights of less-than-ideal accommodation. This worked out well as not only were the staff lovely and happily rearranged their whole reception area to fit the tandem in, they also gave us ice-cold pineapple juice and we had a room with a sea view. Having freshened up we ventured out in search of western food for dinner, regrettably having lost interest in developing our culinary taste buds with more traditional fayre and found a restaurant a short walk up the coastline. I had underestimated my recovery though and a short mile walk there and back left my chest aching and me struggling to keep any pace up. Seeing the sunset over the ocean though was one of the brief moments where we could briefly pretend that we were on holiday and not racing around the world.

Breakfast on the terrace the next morning was equally pleasant and my mood towards Malaysia was starting to mellow somewhat, but I was still keen to beat a hasty retreat to Singapore. The weather broke and a final monsoon shower was welcomed to cool us down a bit, but I was toe-tapping and impatient when Stevie stopped early for a McDonald's, desperate to reach the end of this leg as soon as possible.

Navigating onto the island of Singapore was tricky as it wasn't signposted as "Singapore" and we had to aim for the correct bridge and then it wasn't clear which lane we should be in. We opted to join the other two-wheelers with the moped and motorcycles to pass through the border control which all went smoothly but then on the other side we were funnelled into narrow lanes with motorcycles and mopeds seemingly coming from all directions as we crossed the bridge. I felt the panic rising inside me and my chest felt even tighter, as I imagined an impact from behind any minute from a careless driver. The bridge was short, but it seemed to take an age to cross it and then suddenly everything changed.

The streets were quiet and empty, the traffic was structured and slower and the pavements and roadsides were spotlessly clean. We stopped at a petrol station which stocked a range of products so similar to the UK we were spoilt for choice, but the prices were distinctly higher than we were used to. What seemed an almost eerily quiet ride to the hotel was a relief after the chaos of the rest of Asia and the service was exemplary even if mask-wearing was still mandatory due to covid precautions.

To celebrate what felt like a massive achievement arriving safely at the end of the Asian leg we went out for craft beer and stone-baked pizza at a trendy place which felt very westernised. We had a limited amount of time to let our hair down though, as we needed to get back to the hotel to meet Julio, a friend of a friend who had not only received a raft of deliveries for us, including two new panniers but also sourced the cardboard bike boxes, packaging material and tape we needed for the flight. Opening the first drop boxes from the UK felt like Christmas and we found that Matt and Megan, who were the ground crew in the UK sorting our deliveries, had also included some of the Biltong they make as a side business. A new bike light, new bib shorts for Stevie, a replacement chain tool as well as more electrolytes and beard oil were all real treats and we finally had everything sorted by 11 pm before setting our alarms from 4:30 am to get to the airport in plenty of time.

A small misdemeanour with my routing (or rather a failure on Google Maps part to identify a restricted area/path near the airport) gave us a slightly stressful start, racing the taxi with the boxes to the airports. We managed to collect them safely, found an ideal packing area for the bike and set about disassembling the components. We had been under the impression we had managed to get upgraded seats as the cheapest band had been sold out when we came to rearrange them, but on checking in this turned out not to be the case. The lady behind the desk was disinterested and unhelpful and I was starting to feel emotional as we really needed good seats for this flight with the injuries from the crash and also the leg swelling Stevie had experienced on previous flights. We tried the ticket desk and a much more helpful man listened to our concerns and at least managed to get us bulkhead seats with plenty of legroom, even if it wasn't the business-class experience we had hoped for.

However, what followed was still one of the most uncomfortable flights of my life. Stevie was able to stretch his legs and sleep, but I felt my chest was restricted in the seat position and couldn't perform my usual party trick of curling up into a tiny ball on the seat with my ribs still causing me significant problems. We landed in Perth six hours later and I was exhausted and fed up. Customs with the bike was straightforward this time but we were glad we had been pre-warned that the biosecurity for Australia was strict, and we had to guarantee we had removed as much mud and dirt as possible. And then we had to declare the Biltong; the young girl at the customs desk looked concerned and scurried off to check with someone more senior and we were just preparing ourselves to have to give up on our wonderful Derbyshire gift when she came back and confirmed our friends knew their stuff and it was packed correctly to be allowed into the country. We soon emerged into the Arrivals hall in slight disbelief that we had made it to Australia, the furthest from home either of us had ever been. We had little time to take this in though as it was straight back to building the bike and repacking the panniers.

By this point, we had lost the whole day travelling and it was late evening and having anticipated we wouldn't be making it far I had obtained a contact here through the Tandem Club who was called Rob. Rob had not only invited us to stay the night but had been very flexible when our plans changed and also given us a route to his house in the centre of Perth, so once we had got everything assembled, it was straightforward to ride from the airport. It was dark and beautifully cool, a huge relief after the oppressive heat of Asia and it all felt strangely familiar with cycle lanes similar to those in the UK and road layout and signage much more westernised – I even saw signs for Welshpool which is where some of my family lives near in mid-Wales. Stevie was a bit reluctant about staying with strangers as we never knew quite what to expect but after the long day of flights, I desperately hoped things would go smoothly.

We couldn't have had a better welcome to the country as Rob and his lovely wife Julianne welcomed us with open arms and quickly had us settled in their beautiful modern house. I could have cried with joy when they asked if we were ok with lasagne for dinner (we were craving Western pasta) and when it came with a fresh salad we were overjoyed as we hadn't felt we could eat uncooked veg for over six weeks in Asia. They regaled us with tales of tandeming down under and were very passionate about their bicycle made for two. We asked a range of questions that probably seemed rather daft, such as whether the tap water was safe to drink, did we need to worry about crossing the Nullarbor Plain and what to do about road trains? They answered and gave us sound advice on our route too. A couple of beers helped wash down the substantial meal and as excited as we were to be having a conversation with people more culturally similar to ourselves than we had experienced in months, we soon had to call it a day and get some much-needed rest.

It seemed Australia was a new start, a new opportunity and with the triumph of getting out of Asia, thoughts of abandoning the challenge had passed and we were resolute to continue. At this point we were on day 76 with just over 7,000 miles on the clock, so with our ideal of 100 miles a day average we were almost six days down. But for some reason we didn't question this too much at this point; we knew we had a lot to do to catch up but we also knew that until we started riding in Australia, we wouldn't know how the challenges here would compare to Asia. We had left Asia with a bit of a sour taste after the multiple complications in India, Stevie being unwell for most of Thailand and the accident in Malaysia capping everything off. Our attitude was partly due to exhaustion from pushing the mileage every day and not having the time to understand and appreciate the cultural intricacies that real tourists usually enjoy and relish. It is more a statement of how hard we had been pushing and our states of mind than a reflection on the continent, but the feeling of everything being more complicated or incomprehensible in Asia would stay with us for a long time, to the point where even accents would trigger caution on our part. It is not a nice thing to consider, and I am not proud to confess it; but it is a truth and was a big hurdle in our trip. So many people who take things slower and have the time to enjoy such exotic cultures and wonderful places have truly amazing experiences, but we never did.

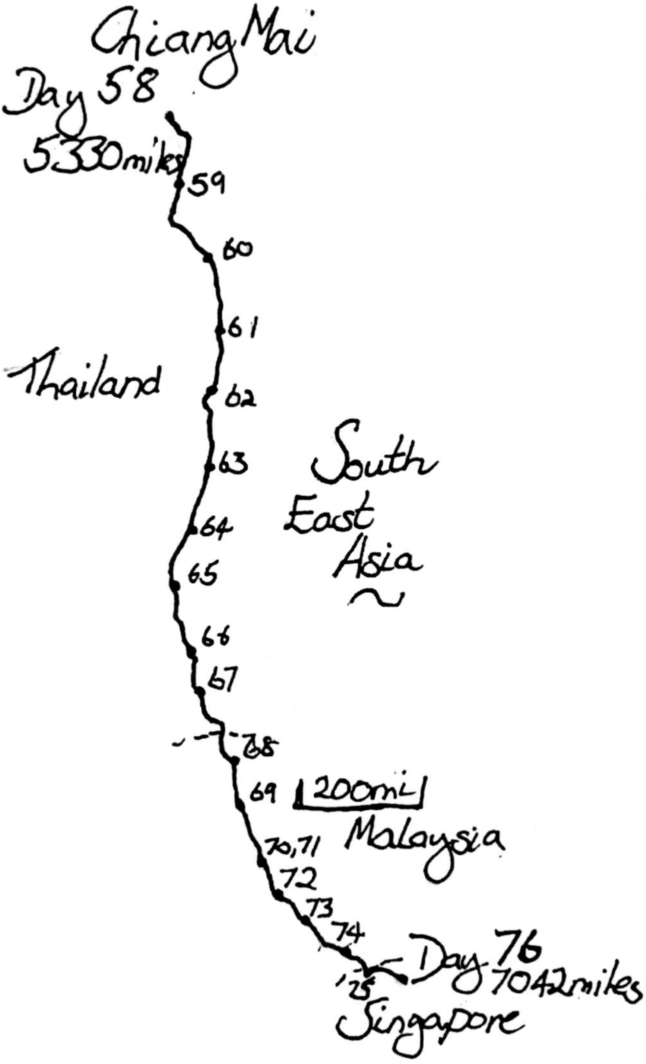
Chiang Mai
Day 58
5330miles
59
60
61
Thailand
62
63
South
East
Asia
64
65
66
67
68
69
200mi
Malaysia
70,71
72
73
74
Day 76
7042miles
75
Singapore

Aftermath of crash motorbike in background

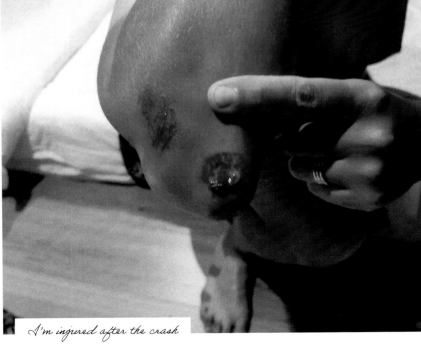

I'm injured after the crash

Skinny Stevie after the parasite

6000 miles down

Thailand

part four: australia and new zealand

Day 77-82: Perth, Australia to Norseman, Australia

WE SET off from Rob's full of a nutritious breakfast (including to my delight boiled and not fried eggs) and a food bag on the back bulging with goodies. He and his wife also offered to escort us out of the city along the best routes. It felt strange to ride with another pair and we were happy to stop at the Swan bridge to make a short video for the Tandem Club and to thank the local aboriginal tribe for welcoming us to their lands. We quickly entered the suburbs and Rob and Julianne bade us a fond farewell before leaving us to continue into the countryside alone. We stopped briefly at some public toilets in a park – another novelty of the western world, and I admired the different plants and birds. As we headed south down the main highway, eucalyptus trees lined the route and the fauna and flora were distinctly unfamiliar; it seemed everything was slightly different. The farmland was reassuringly the same as the UK though with rolling fields of sheep and cattle, many native breeds that I recognised from the UK. It was spring here, as opposed to late summer in the UK, and it felt strange to see lambs at foot for the second time in a year and the temperatures felt distinctly crisp after so much time in the tropical heat.

There was a pint of beer in it for whoever spotted the first kangaroo. As we rode through a forested area Stevie shouted, "Kangaroos". I almost didn't believe him at first, but there they were, disappearing into the undergrowth at a speed I had not expected, almost perfectly camouflaged against the grey tones of the trees. The delight of kangaroo spotting on our first day certainly lifted our spirits and I was excited about what else there was to come.

Our next authentic Australian experience was just around the next bend though in the form of a roadhouse and I knew from my research that these fabled places would soon become critical to our resupply and fuelling strategies. We opted for a proper cup of tea and pies, which the Australian roadhouses are well known for, and tried not to wince too much at the price, which would have been dear in the UK, but was a small fortune compared to what we had been paying in Asia. The temperatures dropped in the last few miles, and we rolled into Williams having topped the 100 miles for the day and feeling pleased with ourselves. The accommodation option was in a worker's cabin at the back of a busy hotel cum pub and was basic but suited our needs. We quickly turned the heating up, still unused to the cooler temperatures, and headed back to the bar for dinner. The main pub was packed full of locals, it seemed to me mostly farmers or those that worked the land and I felt content in the slightly raucous atmosphere which felt so familiar to home. We found a quieter room for dinner and huddled by a toasty wood burner. A local lady came over to chat and expressed concern about the cold temperatures and late spring, adamant it was far too late this year, and she was going to head north to get some proper sunshine. She was concerned it was evidence of climate change and over the next few days we would hear conflicting opinions as to whether this was the case or not, but it was certainly cooler than expected.

The portions were generous, and we wrapped up some remaining pizza in a napkin to eat for breakfast the next day to give us a head start on the road.

It was even chillier in the morning and Stevie had left it until then to get a shower which he regretted. I went to heat the pizza only to find someone else had got there first and there were neat little nibble marks around the edges. Not willing to waste it I trimmed off the mouse-sized bite marks and thoroughly zapped it in the microwave before tucking in.

It was just as well because we were straight into a nagging headwind which seemed to be coming straight from the South Pole. Everything seemed a lot more remote compared to Asia and facilities were sparse, but this made for good progress, and I had picked out a bed and breakfast about five miles from the last town. The headwind had sapped our speed a bit, so we were just about on the cusp of darkness but were happy to be rolling in for the night, or so we thought. We missed the small sign for the bed and breakfast on the first pass and going back we found a suspiciously unlit drive and a dark house. A dog emerged from a kennel and started barking defensively and we waited for someone to emerge or a light to come on, but to no avail and having knocked on all the doors we could find had resigned ourselves that there would be no bed and breakfast here tonight. With the next town a significant distance down the road we had the option of a chilly, hungry night or backtracking to Cranbrook, the last town we passed.

We reluctantly made our way back, desperately hoping the one pub or hotel in the village would be open. I left Stevie outside with the bicycle in the cold and dark and pushed through some heavy wooden door into an explosion of warmth and noise. A fire roared in the fireplace and there was a queue at the bar. When the lady serving asked what she could get me I felt a bit more than uncomfortable asking for a room instead of a beer, but she was quick to see our predicament and before we knew it, she had cleared out a spare room got us settled and we were sipping some rather pleasant local red wine over a plate of lamb chops next to the hearth. Her husband had taken over the bar and we talked about the way of life in Western Australia and our trip. He asked us to send him a postcard when we got to Canada and I'm ashamed to say we never did, but we were extremely grateful for a warm bed that night.

The headwind hadn't relented the following morning, and it was quite a battle south to Albany, despite it being a gradual downhill. Thankfully we turned left there and now our general direction would be eastbound until Melbourne, well over 20 days and 2,500 miles away. The countryside had changed from pastoral to vineyards but now had become uncultivated bush. Flocks of dusty pink chested Galah parrots squawked noisily as we passed, and feasted on seed at the side of the road. A couple of large black parrots took flight as we rode by, and I couldn't be sure that they weren't the rare black cockatoos as they rapidly disappeared into the foliage. Kangaroos too bounded in the bush and at one point across the road right in front of us. For tonight's stop, I had a foolproof plan: I had pre-booked a camping pitch and was rather looking forward to our first night under canvas since Europe. We stopped to ransack the local convenience store for supplies and cycled the last mile with me carrying a brown paper bag of tins and packets under my arm and a bottle of Australian red to help keep us warm. We were just in time to get the tent pitched and to see the sunset. Thankfully there was a wonderfully quirky indoor area to cook and relax once it got dark and we were soon ready for bed as we were starting to build the miles back up and every day was a long day.

A crisp morning at the campsite helped us get up and packed relatively quickly, which was just as well as we had another long day ahead of us with facilities only really at 50 and 120 miles so we really needed to push for the longer distance. The roadhouse at 50 miles was very basic and very much had a local feel and we felt rather out of place, but people often asked questions and were friendly. The rolling road, which turned out to be a steady climb, meant that we reached Ravensthorpe just at nightfall. Another busy hotel bar but this time our luck was out, and it was full of construction workers who had taken all the rooms, the motel was full as well, so we were relieved to get into the campsite. Pitching up in record time we raced back to the hotel to make it in time to make last orders for dinner. The bar was still very lively, verging on raucous and we ate our fill and headed back to the tent quickly.

Dawn revealed we had been lucky not to stumble into a small lake in the dark, but it made for a picturesque view for breakfast, with mist hanging over it and rolling onto the campground. I was relieved we had carried the camping stove and that Rob in Perth had sourced us some camping gas (and new sporks!) for a warming cup of tea – it had been one of the not-strictly-necessary items I had taken that Stevie wasn't convinced was just excess weight. The attritional rolling road continued, and it felt like we were dragging along, both lacking in energy somewhat, so we were relieved for a roadhouse at 50 miles. Some epic burgers should have provided the fuel we needed but Stevie was struggling to digest the meal. The lady there was very friendly though and reassured us that Gibson, our destination for the day, definitely had a motel and it would definitely have space for us with most workers pushing onto Esperance or Norseman. Buoyed by this thought we pushed on, undulating up and down over the snaking tarmac where every time we reached a summit, we saw the next one loom further down the road. The area was called Many Hills and certainly lived up to its name. I thought I had spotted a short cut, but this turned out to be a gravel road, so we aborted pretty quickly and took the next turn to cut off the corner instead of heading down to Esperance at the coast. It was still tough going and we now had a different sort of wind problem... Stevie had developed incredible flatulence! Which I can assure you is the last thing you need as a stoker on the back.

Getting to the Gibson Soak Hotel, this turned out to be just a pub and to our distress, the motel was closed, despite the assurances we had had 60 miles before. With no other options within a sensible riding distance, our options were limited and a wild camp on the football pitch was looking like our best hope. Having been under canvas for the past two nights this wasn't ideal as we needed to charge everything up and get showered. But now food was our priority, although Stevie wasn't feeling hungry, we needed sustenance to be able to ride the next day and ordered a couple of meals from the pub and a round of sandwiches each for breakfast.

We were leaning up on the bar where one distinctly local chap proclaimed, "Don't go to Ceduna, the blacks will nick everything you've got!"

Slightly stunned by his bigoted racism, we assumed he was referring to the aboriginal people as there was a black man playing pool next to us who seemed exempt from this prejudice. We decided to find more pleasant seats and conversation, and the other pool player, a worker called Tom, came over and we were quickly regaling the story of our trip. Hearing our predicament, he was determined to help and declared the "MacGyver of Gibson", a man called "Puss", would definitely be able to find us somewhere undercover to sleep.

Our dinner arrived and he headed to the house next door where Puss lived to see what he could do and arrived back with a large gruff bearded fellow, who did not look like he had the nickname Puss! But true to his word he was happy for us to sleep in his homemade gym, just as long as we didn't mind the mice and the toilet facilities being an outdoor shack used by the workers. We weren't fussy and were delighted by such a kind offer, Tom even shared his mobile internet with us so I could ensure we had the following night's accommodation booked. Stevie wasn't feeling great though and had struggled to finish dinner and I had my suspicions that he was showing similar signs to Thailand when he had flared up with the Giardia parasite.

There was little we could do about it at this point though, so we got our sleeping bags out and bedded down on the gym mats, making sure our breakfast sandwiches were safe from nibbling rodents!

The next day was significant: Stevie's 46th Birthday! I hadn't managed to sneak a present into our luggage, but had got his favourite Queen cover band lead singer to sing to him. He still wasn't on top form though and had had a bad night's sleep, which was concerning. Tom waved us off in the morning and stayed in touch for the next few weeks, even managing to get us a scoop with a local journalist to publicise our trip. We were extremely grateful for his help in such a tricky situation.

Today was a big day for another reason too, we were heading to Norseman, which is the western end of the Nullarbor Desert. The Nullarbor is infamous for its sparse facilities, the one road through the wilderness only intermittently broken by the occasional roadhouse and no shops or freshwater in between. Seeing as we had already struggled with the more remote areas in Western Australia the prospect was a bit daunting to say the least. Given we were now travelling in a more northerly direction we felt quite hard done by to have the wind in our face yet again, the direction having switched by 180 degrees. We made it into Norseman in relatively good time though and although it was a sleepy town, we finally had some wonderful accommodation at an old railway inn, complete with a massive whirlpool bath. The generous landlady gave us pots of Epsom salts to soak with when she heard how far we had ridden. We headed to the pub for a pint and birthday dinner or "chicken Parmi" which is essentially a large chicken schnitzel/steak topped with tomato-based sauce and cheese. We had been agonising about what to do about Stevie though as he was still unwell and struggling to eat and with an arid desert with few facilities and limited options for medical services (barring the flying doctors) we needed to be sure we were up to the challenge. We had another course of antibiotics he could start on, but he needed to get his birthday pint out of the system first. We felt we had little choice so decided to start the treatment, get him an early night, and would see how he felt in the morning.

Day 83–89: Norseman, Australia to Ceduna, Australia

We both woke up feeling groggy and not quite sure we knew what we were letting ourselves in for. The last petrol station had plenty of signs warning about limited facilities and posters of people who had disappeared into the bush; this didn't do a lot to build our confidence. Stevie was still feeling unwell, and we briefly debated staying in Norseman for another night and visiting the medical centre the next day, but seeing as he had already started another course of treatment we opted to push on, cycling past a large sign stating, "Limited water Norseman-

Ceduna: Obtain supplies in Norseman," which essentially covered the next 800 miles of road. But still, we rode on.

I had done my research though and knew that this would be one of the most challenging parts of our trip so checked and double-checked the facilities. For example, I knew the first roadhouse on the route: Fraser Range had never opened up after the pandemic and we wouldn't have any supplies until Balladonia that evening. We still stopped by the sign for refreshments on the roadside and were glad it had warmed up significantly but were not prepared to be swarmed by flies; another of the known trials of cycling in Australia! We got a bit of downhill and thankfully wind behind us to finish the day and a glorious sunset: the skies here seemed to be on fire as the sun dipped below the horizon and a multitude of pinks, reds, oranges, and yellow blazed across before finally setting to a myriad of stars. We made it to Balladonia just as the dusk fell and just in time for dinner too; we were learning that food service often finished early here and would be something we would have to factor in if we wanted a hot meal. The prices as well reflected the remote location, and we tried not to wince too much at the cost of bed and board as we had no other option apart from wild camping. Stevie had possibly seemed a little better throughout the day but was still struggling to eat what he needed and with his dramatic weight loss in Malaysia this was becoming quite a concern. We knew rest and recovery were vital so we got an early night, but not before watching an episode of the UK television programme "Escape to the Country", which was surreally based less than 10 miles from where we live.

The next morning followed another tumultuous night for Stevie, he had barely slept, being in discomfort, and was not fit to get out of bed when the alarm went off. I was desperately concerned we had made the wrong decision and would be turning back to Norseman but knew he would have to at least eat something even if he spent the whole day in bed here. I managed to convince him to let me go and buy some breakfast and all he fancied was cereal, so I paid a small fortune for tiny packets of muesli and Weetabix (which isn't like UK Weetabix at all) and a couple of pints of whole milk. I returned to our room fully expecting him to be back asleep so was shocked to find him dressed and to all appearances ready to ride.

If not for his problems, today should have been one of the best days of our trip, not only was the wind still behind us; blowing from the west but we would reach a big landmark: the 90 mile straight! This piece of road is the longest straight bit of road in Australia, with no turns or corners, just 90 miles of dead-ahead riding and the weather was perfect for it.

It was 113 miles to the next roadhouse at Caiguna and we should have flown through, but with Stevie weak from sickness, we were having a hard time of it, and he was feeling dizzy and wobbly when we stopped. We still posed briefly at the famous "90-mile straight" sign but the only other stop was a roadside picnic area where a couple of cheeky birds begged for crumbs of biscuits. Aside from that, wildlife was sparse and there were a few flocks of Galahs, but not a lot else to see. The flies were still persistent and I'm sure the same three rode most of the 90 mile straight with us on Stevie's back. The word "Nullarbor" means treeless, but this wasn't quite the case, as actually it is covered in low scrub and bushes, very different from the idea of a sandy featureless desert. This fauna stretched as far as the eye could see with very little in the way of features or undulations and the enormous brilliant blue skies with the sun beating down overhead made it feel quite exposed. This made for fairly monotonous riding, especially as Stevie wasn't at his best, and it was a relief to reach Caiguna Roadhouse for the usual motel room and dinner. Stevie had had an awful day and had raised his game to even get on the bicycle that morning so I fervently hoped he would be feeling better tomorrow, but was also disappointed we had missed out on the triumph of celebrating conquering the 90 miles straight.

The next morning, I panicked when I thought the wind had turned against us, until I figured out this roadhouse was on the other side of the road from the previous two nights and in fact, we still had tailwinds.

There was another treat in store today as we had a lunch stop at Cocklebiddy, 65 miles down the road. Budgerigars outnumbered humans as residents here, but there was at least hot food and cold drinks and with Stevie's appetite returning I was keen for him to get in as many calories as possible. The wind was still strong from behind giving us the helping hand we needed. At one point I failed to secure my windproof around my waist and it dropped to the ground, only to have overtaken us with the wind, by the time we stopped to collect it. The warning signs for various species of wildlife were sadly unfounded and we saw no evidence of the kangaroos, camels, or emus depicted; apart from the occasional desiccated carcass on the side of the road. We were glad of every turn and corner though and I was desperate to start giving navigation directions again, a complete contrast to some of the more complicated sections of the route in Europe and Asia.

Suddenly the road dropped down before us, revealing a massive flat plateau where the ocean had covered many years ago. We were descending what would have been a sea cliff and to what would have been the ocean floor, now dry, arid, and covered in bush. We were to stop partway down the descent though, as with Stevie still recovering and we were keen to sleep in a bed again and Madura made it a slightly shorter day at 98 miles. We felt we deserved an early finish to rest and recover a bit, despite the extra expense. We'd been unable to book a room in advance and had hoped to get away with just turning up so were disappointed when we found the motel rooms full (although we suspect only a small proportion of them were open due to short staff). At least they had a campsite with the option of a hot shower and dinner. We paid to pitch up amongst a host of campervans and motorhomes who were also traversing the desert. Not willing to risk the same situation for the following nights in the Nullarbor, I called through to the next two roadhouses for the following three nights, only to find out they all said they were fully booked too. This left us in a bit of a predicament and feeling a bit put out that our early finish had been taken up with pitching the tent and a cold shower block, we were feeling a bit down. We did have a comfortable night under canvas though. It wasn't until the following morning that we hit the next stumbling block: the clocks had changed. Having crossed the whole of India without a time zone change I had almost forgotten it would happen here and even more bizarrely for us, used to living in a country with one time zone, we were now 45 minutes ahead of Western Australia so had lost 45 minutes of the day already! We knew we needed to at least make it to Eucla at the other edge of the low bowl 114 miles away and would be able to camp there if there wasn't a bed. The challenge was set, and we started out trying to maintain the pace above 13 mph. A brief stop at Mundrabilla Roadhouse had us shovelling sandwiches down to get back on the road as soon as possible, we were certainly in the zone today!

There was a 42 mile time trial left, and we picked up the pace getting close to 20 miles an hour as the wind dropped, determined to make our destination in time for tea. Just as it was dusking and with the final climb out of the bowl visible in the distance Stevie exclaimed, "A big cat just ran across the road!"

He said it so suddenly, it took a minute to register and then from behind his back I saw a large bounding animal sprint across the road and into the bush at a speed that rivalled ours. Stevie wasn't as knowledgeable about Australian mammals as I, but he was quite correct that the animal definitely had a feline bounding gallop and appeared to have a long tail. It was sandy in colour and covered the ground easily and quickly, so it did not appear to be an escaped pet. I racked my brains at the time, but was fairly sure that there was no such native carnivore in Australia and doubting my lucidity after so many days in the desert asked social media too but to no avail. The creature remained a mystery and to this day we cannot explain what it might have been (but it definitely wasn't a kangaroo!)

We thankfully made light work of the last climb and rolled into Eucla not only in time for dinner, but also to find that someone hadn't turned up for their room and that if they still hadn't arrived by the cut off time the room was ours (for a fee of $160 of course!) Our luck was in, and we settled into the most luxurious room we had had on the Nullarbor with promised sea views for the morning. We had a pannier explosion and got clean, and hand-washed everything while we had a chance and then got settled for a comfortable night. Our big effort to arrive in time for dinner had paid off in getting us an early night.

The following morning the brilliant blue of the sea was tantalisingly visible over the edge of the cliffs. Stevie took the opportunity to do a bit of bike maintenance and we had a hearty breakfast to set us up as we now had our longest stint without facilities planned. It was over 120 miles to the Nullarbor Roadhouse, we had decided to stock up at Border Roadhouse just nine miles down the road and wild camp that night to split the difference before pushing to Nullarbor the next day. Border Roadhouse was much better stocked than Eucla and after six days without it, I finally had Wi-Fi to update the world, and ended up doing a local newspaper interview too. Stevie made use of the hot food, coffee and toilets, and before we knew it, we had lost much more time than we intended. In another setback, the clocks had changed again by 45 minutes, so it was now 11:40 am and we had done nine miles! The likelihood of hitting 115 miles in daylight was rapidly diminishing, especially as there was wind against us.

We pushed on regardless, pulling over only for the thunderous road trains (lorries made up of three carriage-long trains transporting goods across the length of the country by road rather than rail). We had been informed they could make emergency stops but it cost thousands of pounds of brake pads to do this and although they would often swerve around us on the relatively empty long roads, we had an issue if two were coming from opposite directions, up and down the road. This meant we had to bail into the gravelly soft shoulder, as we also had to do when the "oversized" trains came past which carried loads that seemed so ridiculously wide I don't know what they did when they encountered a normal train coming from the other direction: houses, boats, swimming pools, you name it there's nothing that the Aussies won't put on a back of a lorry!

The only other time we pulled over was at a picnic spot overlooking the Southern Bight Ocean where there was whale spotting at this time of year. With the time pressure, we couldn't venture close enough to the coast to do any whale watching, but instead ate some sandwiches and pushed on down the road. The afternoon flew by and too soon we were in for another tremendous sunset. We got wrapped up against the cold and got our lights on, now even more cautious of the road trains.

"Road train!" I would call from the back as soon as I detected the lights or the rumble. It was hard to crane around all the time though and there was one that seemed to be approaching too rapidly without moving over to give us room.

"Get off the road!" I screamed at Stevie, panicking it hadn't seen us. We skidded to a halt in a spray of gravel and the train passed like thunder, honking its horn at the same time. With the disorientation which came with darkness, I couldn't figure out if I was being over-cautious or if it truly had been a close shave, but I was suitably rattled. Our average speed had dropped with the darkness, and I was struggling to stay focused. We had only just topped 90 miles instead of the 115 I had hoped for, but it was clear there was little point pushing on at snail's pace, especially with the increased danger from the trains. I was relieved when Stevie agreed to pull into the next rest area. We quickly set about getting the tent set up despite the plummeting temperatures. It was instant noodle surprise for dinner, topped with our imported biltong. By the time we were fed and wrapped up in our sleeping bags, it was already 10 pm so we were happy to fall asleep listening to the rumble of the trains on the main road.

We survived the night in the desert and I was woken up by the birds, but they don't sing nicely here, they just make noise! Bundled in down jackets we got the kettle on and the tent down promptly with only a couple of Tim Tam biscuits to get us going, intending to push on for a hot breakfast at Nullarbor roadhouse.

Today felt like a completely different ride compared to last night but the wind was still in our faces and our speed barely making 10 mph. The incentive of breakfast was enough though and the waitress looked horrified as we devoured two of their epic "Nulla breakfasts" followed by cakes and muffins! Full of breakfast the thought of 90 more miles into a headwind didn't seem as appealing so we considered a change of plan to stop at Yalata Roadhouse 60 miles down the road, leaving a big, but doable, push to Ceduna and out of the Nullarbor tomorrow. We mentioned our plan to a couple of the people we spoke to at the roadhouse (everyone was always keen to know where we're going) and no one voiced any concerns about stopping at Yalata, even those having come from that direction.

The wind dropped throughout the day, and we made better progress than expected and were looking forward to an early finish and a bit of catch-up after our wild camp. Yalata was near an aboriginal reserve which was still heavily signposted to exclude visitors as a Covid-19 precaution. As we approached the gas station, motel and campground, we quickly had a bad feeling: it was completely deserted. Dogs barked from some shabby-looking caravan at the back of the complex and we were almost relieved that no one came out as it did not feel like an especially friendly place. Having investigated that campground, there was no running water available, and it was easy to make the decision not to stop there with no water, no food, and a distinctly bad feeling about the place.

So, we needed to push on to Nundroo, another 32 miles down the road, and by this time it was getting dark. Nundroo had been one of the roadhouses I had called a couple of days ago and they had said the motel was full, but if we could at least get water, that would be a start. There was nothing for it but to get on with it, so I plugged a Disney playlist into one ear and listened for road trains with the other, ready for the slightest hint of rumble or lights to get Ste to pull over into the gravel. Having put a positive spin on things and relieved not to be stuck at Yalata the miles started to go well. We had one brief stop and I gazed up to a dark sky full of millions of unfamiliar constellations with the ephemeral haze of the milky way stretched across it: the Nullarbor was a truly special place.

We hesitantly pulled up at the roadhouse, blinking in the bright lights of the petrol station as we dismounted after a hard stint. The door was closed, and we feared the worst until a man stuck his head out, "Can I help you?" he inquired.

"Are you open?" I asked, dreading the answer as it was gone 9 pm and a lot of places had closed at 7 pm.

"Yes, of course," he replied, seeming a bit bemused by our question. Stevie was feeling brave from the positive answer and dared push it a step further.

"Do you have a room and hot food?"

"Yes, we have a room, and I can do you schnitzel and chips," he offered to our amazement. Our gamble had paid off and we had a very comfortable night in a bed and managed to stock up from the shop as well before tucking into dinner.

The next day our spirits were still high despite a strong headwind, and we encountered Penong, the first piece of civilisation that wasn't a roadhouse that we had seen for six days. Taking a break in the café felt like a novelty and it was an interesting people-watching experience to see who else was on the road. We stayed tucked in a corner and managed to get away without regaling our whole story for once. Back on the road, the headwind had become attritional, and it became clear we weren't going to get past Ceduna today, a frustrating end to our time in Nullarbor. The landscape was changing already, trees were appearing, and the vegetation was getting greener, there were signs of wombat burrows too on the side of the road, but we didn't spot a live one. I'd booked a motel on the far side of Ceduna to try and at least get as far as possible today and it was basic but fine for our needs. I was delighted when the kind owner offered me a lift into town to pick up dinner. As we drove in it became clear it may not have just been his kind-heartedness, but also a concern, as it seemed a rough place, with homeless people huddled in doorways next to empty bottles of alcohol. No one was walking alone in these streets. I remember what the horrible man had said at the bar in Gibson and realised that his racism was directed at the less affluent people in this town and sadly there were obviously some deep-seated issues. Even back at the motel, there was a ruckus, and we couldn't figure out if the party were guests, staff or unwanted visitors, as their heavy aboriginal accents were hard for us to understand, but there was enough noise and commotion to make sure we had locked the door before bed.

But we had made it, we had crossed the Nullarbor desert and considering our trepidation on entering it with Stevie's illness it had been a huge hurdle to overcome but we were looking forward to finding out what the rest of Australia had in store in the coming weeks.

Day 90–95, Ceduna, Australia to Adelaide Australia

Now out of the Nullarbor, we were crossing the Eyre Peninsula for the next three days, travelling pretty much directly east. Advice from the Tandem Club had been it would be more scenic to divert down the Peninsula, but we feared we didn't have the time for extra mileage having had a few less than 100 miles days in the Nullarbor. The Easterly winds had not abated though and Stevie was cursing about who had checked the prevailing wind direction! We had hoped to camp more as well, but the wind was not just strong but icy and we were struggling to get our average speed into double figures. The temperature dropped well into single figures with reports of -2°C at night. This resulted in us having to spend more of accommodation, so to compensate somewhat we raided the shelves of the first supermarket we had passed in a week, purchasing a "Mighty Foodland" cool bag which was to become our larder on the back pannier rack for the rest of the trip, now space in the replacement front panniers was limited.

The fact we had reached day 90 and were still well short of

9,000 miles was barely talked about and the days were dragging; the incessant wind making us feel like we were getting nowhere. Another night was spent in a crappy overpriced motel, where initially we were delighted that they served takeaway curry but were quickly disappointed by small portions of mostly salty sauce. The final day on the peninsula had a depressing start, the petrol station shop seemed to intentionally not sell anything we could cook in the room for breakfast despite there being a microwave, so we were resigned to buying it from the café. We'd gotten used to the prices being much higher than in the UK, but when Stevie was still waiting to get his food after I had finished my portion, we were getting more than a bit frustrated. We chased up the food to be told it was just coming but then heard an ominous scraping noise from the kitchen... As well as breakfast Stevie had ordered a side of raisin toast and when this arrived it was obviously the cause of the scraping noise. Resembling thin triangles of charcoal, it had been burnt to a crisp and given that we were paying more than you could buy the whole loaf for, we were not impressed. It was so bad it was funny! But we were also getting delayed more and more and waiting for another round to be lightly toasted made us later still. By the time we had finally got away from the horrendous motel and passed the "Halfway Across Australia" sign, we were still struggling to feel positive. It felt like we had been here forever and should have made better progress.

As the day went on the winds shifted slightly and became a crosswind sweeping great plumes of cloud into the sky, the pressure was lifting, and it finally felt like the bike started to move. We were approaching a feature called Lincoln's Gap, a pass between two sharp-sided hills on the otherwise featureless plains. The scenery was becoming more interesting again, or maybe I was just able to look around more with my face out of the wind. Suddenly a flock of emus appeared from nowhere sprinting across the landscape, spooked by the bicycle. Later in the day, Kangaroos appeared, a welcome sight after the desolate Nullarbor where all we had seen was roadkill and flies. We tried to pull into the town of Iron Knob for lunch but found it silent and to all appearances deserted, although there were signs people currently lived there. Now with some landmarks on the horizon, we were able to make better progress to Port Augusta, the first proper big town since Perth. I relished the chance to sweep the supermarket for fresh food and we enjoyed a dinner of pasta and salad instead of anything deep fried for a change.

The microwave and toaster were put to full use the following morning and it was good to fuel up cheaply with scrambled eggs and beans on toast to sustain us up Horrocks Pass, the first significant hill of the country and since Thailand! There was still a headwind, and it was a slow drag to the base of the climb where the green hills rumpled down like green fabric, finger-like protuberances beckoning us up. I was excited to see some different terrain and peered around Stevie at the rocky outcrops and gullies at the side of the road, spotting unknown birds and skittish lambs in the bushes. And then a descent! The tandem finally stretched her legs after weeks of flat work and it felt wonderful to move for free. On the other side of the pass, we quickly entered villages with art studios, cafés and bakeries and the options and number of buildings almost felt overwhelming after so long with nothing but bushes on the side of the road. There were plenty of nods to times gone by and a very traditional sense to the area, making for some very pleasant stops and cycling. One resident wasn't so pleased to see us though, a whoosh of feathers and an angry squawk and something rattled off Stevie's helmet. We both ducked as a blur of black and white feathers deployed a second attack. The magpies of Australia are quite well known for their strong defensive streak, and it was nesting season. They are quite different from European magpies, not corvids like the UK version, and have a strong dislike of cyclists who invade their territory. This is to the extent that there have been injuries and accidents due to the attacks of these birds and some cyclists ride with stick-on eyes or pointy bits of cable ties stuck up from their helmets to try and ward off attacks. Thankfully our assailant lost interest quickly once we were out of range, but I was now on alert for the rush of feathers that indicated another assault. My next excitement was a town called "Laura" and much to Stevie's annoyance, I attempted to take a photo of every sign with my name on it to make an Instagram reel later.

We faced accommodation challenges again and having got lucky. finding a bed for the last few nights it appeared it wasn't to last. Having decided to head for the smaller town of Blythe instead of Clare we were already at 120 miles when we found ourselves standing shivering outside a very dark and closed hotel with nowhere else in the village open. Riding the eight miles to Clare was still doable but would add distance onto the next day and we had a more pressing time commitment then. We opted for the village picnic area instead and camped next to a barbeque shelter with picnic tables, making do with a cold dinner of peanut butter and honey sandwiches which Stevie lovingly prepared for me. At least we had an early night, and the café was open in the morning, although the waiter did fib about the sandwiches being freshly prepared!

Feeling surprisingly refreshed for a night under canvas the day continued to improve, the wind got behind us and the weather was warming up, a wonderful contrast from the tough stint on the Eyre Peninsula, and it was starting to feel like I was actually enjoying riding the bicycle again. It was downhill to Adelaide as well and a brief stint on the main coastal road that we had been avoiding confirmed that we had made the right decision heading up through the villages, as it was far too busy with road trains.

The houses built up and we began to see familiar names, KFC, McDonald's, Subway, Dominoes, but we weren't ready to stop yet and powered on through suburbia. The buildings got taller and soon we were surrounded by what seemed towering skyscrapers, blocking out the vast Australian skies we had gotten used to. Feeling confused by the number of people and the stream of visual information we wended our way through the centre of the city, which on reflection, would have seemed peaceful and half-empty compared to UK cities, but we were used to our isolation in the outback at this point. Emerging through the other side of town we started to climb up through quieter Eucalyptus woodland and although signs warned of koalas crossing, we saw none. The traffic was surprisingly patient as we ground our way up a twisty single-lane road and we spotted someone videoing us at the top before we descended to our destination for the night.

Alex and Trish had a history of helping record-breaking tandemists and in 2016 had hosted the "Tandem Men" John and George who had set the original record in 290 days. They then followed up by hosting "Tandem WoW", the female record holders in 2020 who set a new fastest record at 263 days. Now they had tracked us down and invited us to stay and given it was our first hosted experience since Perth we were keen to take them up on it, especially as there was a strong rumour of a hot tub and beers. We were pretty pleased to make it there in good time, even after literally taking a trip around the houses in the estate they lived in. Their house was massive and beautifully modern and after we had stowed the bicycle safely in their garage we were shown around and soon installed in the hot tub with a beer each. After living rough on the road, we could barely believe it and Alex, being an avid cyclist himself, was full of questions about our trip. Having little comforts like a full wash of clothes, music to listen to whilst we chilled out and spending a bit of time not either riding the bicycle or doing logistics was a huge relief and it is hard to explain how much we had missed many of these simple things that we took for granted. All topped off with a massive meal of spaghetti Bolognese; we were delighted as we were still craving a more nutritious diet than the fried fodder of the Nullarbor. A few bottles of red were cracked open, and we stayed up later than we should have, but were just so delighted to interact with like-minded people who understood what we were trying to undertake. The evening was over all too soon and after filling us full of a hearty breakfast we were gutted not to be able to stay another night, our time constraints as ever forcing us back on the road. We did have a chance to get some significant photos though; it was a landmark day today as finally; we would be reaching a massive milestone: 9,000 miles. And it was day 95.

A bicycle made for two: it's a romantic notion, the image often used on wedding invites and in kitsch gift shops with inspirational phrases like "Life is a beautiful ride", but what is it actually like to share propulsion of the same vehicle? I can't think of any other common examples unless you count a pedalo, where two people are responsible for moving the same machine and it is certainly not like being a passenger in a car. The first thing to know about tandems is they do not go anywhere unless both people are pedalling, or if they did it would be very slow! They are much heavier than a solo bicycle and often need strong competent parts to deal with the extra stresses of coping with the weight of two people. This makes them notoriously hard to winch uphill but does mean the descents can be a delight and if you get them cruising on the flat, they will often fly past a solo bicycle, and we have picked up many a "wheelsucker" on group rides keen to benefit from our slipstream. Apart from the forces needed from both people pedalling there is no option for one person to "have their feet up on the back" as the majority of tandems have a timing chain which links the front and back pedals, turning them at the same pace. So, when Stevie pedals, I do. In our case, the timing is belt driven and we have a Gates carbon belt drive which we were swapping every 4,500 miles between two to ensure equal wear. This means I have to always have half an ear out for a direction from Stevie that we will be changing down gears or chainring to make sure I don't carry on putting force through the pedals and crunch the gears or give him an awkward jarring of the legs. We are often asked if we swap places, and aside from the over a foot of height difference, it would be too physically challenging for me to hold the bike on the front. I'm not one to resign myself to my physical limits easily but with over 50kg of bicycle, plus the weight of Stevie as well as my weight it would be too much for my upper body strength to handle safely. There is also a degree of skill, especially when crosswinds and front panniers are involved, and Stevie is an experienced and extremely proficient captain.

So where does this leave me on the back? It is hard to judge input so it is my job to make sure I am putting enough effort in, and Stevie is adamant he can tell when I'm distracted or busy on my phone as the power drops. Able to take my hands off the bars more easily I benefit from being able to move more freely so I can carry out tasks like unwrapping food, checking directions or locations on the phone and signalling at junctions. The challenges of tandem riding come not only from the logistics of manoeuvring and transporting such a large bicycle but mostly from the dynamics of riding in a synchronised way with another person. I have no control of direction, speed or cadence and Stevie relies on me to uphold my side of the bargain by putting the effort in. Tandems have been called "the Divorcer" before and I have heard it told that whichever way a relationship is going you will get there faster on a tandem!

But tandems are not just for romantic couples and pairs like the Tandem Men and Tandem WoW have demonstrated a huge commitment and amount of teamwork to complete the records they did when their marriage wasn't at stake as well if their team failed! Living in such close proximity to a partner where you experience all the flatulence, all the mood swings and all the other realities of life is quite something and it takes a very special pair of people to go the distance, joined by the frame.

Day 96–103, Adelaide, Australia to West Wyalong, Australia

Setting off with full bellies and a full "Mighty Foodland" bag from Alex and Trish's we felt like we had had days off instead of an evening and welcomed the undulations and twists and turns in the road which was adding interest; we even spotted a kangaroo darting along the fence. Despite having had our fill at breakfast, what was meant to be a brief toilet stop descended into a full-on pie fest when we got a whiff of the bakery in Meadows that Alex had recommended. The Aussies are passionate about their pies and the variety was astounding-shrimp, pizza and Thai green chicken to name but a few! Feeling rather pleased with ourselves we still needed to push on to finally reach the 9,000-mile mark, it felt tough going along the flat again and although technically we were now only four and a half days down on the 100-mile-a-day target instead of the six days we started Australia with, it still felt like we had so much more to do. I couldn't even contemplate what it would be like to ride the same distance again, Australia felt like it was going on forever and Canada would be even longer! I tried to stay positive, but I was tired and fed up with the continual stress of the logistics, finding food and accommodation, keeping abreast of times and distances, and always thinking one or two steps down the road.

We had a short ferry to hop over the river at Wellington and then road to the small town of Coonalpyn where a motel that was too raucous and busy didn't suit our mood. We should have been celebrating but I felt worn out and grumpy and then we mis-ordered dinner, ending up with a schnitzel and salad between two. I sloped off to bed feeling out of sorts and not myself.

The next day I had a splitting headache and was still feeling under the weather but there was nothing for it but to get back on the bicycle. With cross tailwinds, the ride cheered me up a bit though and with familiar breeds of sheep and cattle, Dorsets, Herefords and Simmentals interspersed with vineyards, it was familiar and yet not. Parrots and parakeets screeched from the trees; yellow-crested cockatoos, dusty pink-breasted galahs and ruby red rosellas along with many I couldn't identify announced their presence noisily, and I was starting to miss British birdsong. Feeling determined to get back on track from a financial perspective I had spotted a camping option at the local showground at Naracoorte and convinced Stevie to save money on a motel. Calling in advance to prevent yet another accommodation mishap, the lady on the other end of the phone seemed a bit confused that we were travelling by bicycle.

"But where will you sleep?" she asked, and I reassured her we were carrying camping kit with us. On arrival, it was getting close to dark and threatening to rain. Despite my optimism Stevie was not convinced, especially when her husband led us to a rather sodden pitch next to a large motorhome. Unheated showers were enough to convince us to change quickly and go in search of food and I suspect we ended up spending as much in a restaurant on food as we would have if we had stayed in a motel and bought a supermarket dinner, but I tried to skirt around this subject, particularly when the rain set in as we got back to our dark tent.

The following morning, I was packing up when the husband came over for a chat.

"Did you know your Queen has died?" he asked. I had at least managed to pick up on this piece of news, although we were struggling to keep up with who the UK Prime Minister was! It felt a bit surreal to be so far distanced from UK events and to be hearing news about our country from the locals who knew more about the political situation than we did. It was to be a day of delays though and an early stop to fuel up at McDonald's took longer than intended, our quick loo break at 30 miles turned into a full-blown pie stop and then the second McDonald's of the day was meant to be just for a drink but ended in Big Macs. I was quite happy for Stevie to be eating everything though as he desperately needed to put the weight on after his two bouts of sickness. He thought he looked like Chris Froome, the professional cyclist and had renamed himself the "racing snake". I saw a higher risk of injury and illness from compromised immunity and recovery...

We lost another 30 minutes crossing another time zone into Victoria and as the road narrowed through the forests, we were continually on the lookout for road trains as small dark kangaroos skipped through the shady trees. Unsurprisingly, we were later than we would have liked to Heywood and with the supermarket shut and the petrol station not stocking anything to make a meal from, we were relieved to find an open pizza joint. The young ladies running the show were quickly interested in our trip and asked question after question, we sheepishly blagged some milk off them for our breakfast and then when our pizzas arrived, they announced they were on the house! We were happy to pose for a selfie with them for that! A small motel room explosion to dry out the tent and I couldn't disagree we had done better with the budget tonight whilst eating free pizza in bed.

The pizza cold made for a solid breakfast too and packing up from the motel room we were to find bitterly cold winds but blowing in the right direction. It blew us along the rolling Great Ocean Highway and, aside from another magpie attack in Warrnambool which had Stevie diving for cover and me in stitches of laughter, it was smooth going. The unseasonable temperature convinced us to push the distance to Colac instead of camping and we were relieved to find some quieter roads without so many trains. It was a bit of a surprise when one old farmer pulled us over on a back road to warn us to watch out for road trains and we were a bit embarrassed to turn down his offer of a bed at his farmhouse and dinner cooked by his wife, trying to explain why we needed to push the distance. Stopping in Colac put us in a good position to reach Melbourne the next day and this was not only another big tick in Australia, but also where we turned north towards Brisbane.

We were making good progress towards Melbourne, which was welcome as we were to be hosted there, and I was feeling particularly pleased with a bit of rerouting I had done along some country lanes to miss the busier roads...until it ended in a motorway! We had almost forgotten that there were roads out there, which bicycles weren't allowed on, but the signage and speed of traffic were clear, and it took a frustrating backtrack around the houses to get back on track. We entered the suburbs of Melbourne just in time for it to start to drizzle and we had to accept that for the first time in Australia, we would be donning waterproofs. More routing misdemeanours trying to get on the Federation Trail we had been recommended cost us more time and patience, but once we were on it, it proved a great traffic-free route into the city, apart from having to dodge the rabbits in the dark, stunned by the shine of our front lights. The rain had truly set in, and we were pretty cold and miserable arriving late at the ferry port to find the sailings had finished hours ago and we would have to cross the city in the dark to get to our accommodation. We weren't too worried about our arrival time as our hosts were out for the evening, having had something planned for months, and the babysitter was to let us in. As I finally managed to navigate the last few intersections and bridges of the unfamiliar city in the dark downpour, we rolled up to their address bedraggled and exhausted. I was quite taken aback when a man opened the door, as I had been told the babysitter was a lady, but he welcomed us in and helped us stow the bicycle. And then it all became clear our hosts were having an even more epic night than us!

Liz is the older sister of a school friend, and I had probably last seen her in my school days and had never met Shane (hence why I didn't recognise him when he answered the door). They were getting married in a few weeks and were due for their first night out together since the birth of their daughter, just over a year ago, to see their wedding band. Hence the babysitter. But the babysitter was now flat out on their carpet suffering from vertigo, their little girl full of cold and their precious evening off had been cancelled! Quite surreally, we were shown in and ordered fish and chips while waiting for an ambulance, which turned out to be the Royal Flying Doctors when they arrived!

They checked her over and took her in as a precaution, but it made for a very odd night. Liz and Shane were real troopers and still managed to feed us, ply us with some Australian wine and share cycling tales, with them both being avid cyclists it was great to hear about some local rides. We felt extremely guilty to have rocked up in amongst so much chaos but are eternally grateful for their hospitality.

Negotiating our way out of Melbourne was much easier the following morning and the skies had cleared to sunshine. The city was gleaming towers and seeing so many shops, theatres and restaurants still seemed unusual. We were quickly lapped in the backstreets by a postman on an e-bike and in some ways, everything felt very modern and familiar, but somehow not.

It was steady going heading north and the roads were rolling but thankfully free from road trains, although we almost got caught out the next evening approaching a wooden bridge at dusk, with gaps between the slats just wide enough to trap a tandem wheel. There was a bit more wildlife along the route though and we saw cockatoos and kookaburra perched watching and waiting, but it was more than a bit unnerving when the sun set and we saw the dark shapes of kangaroos hopping in the bush on the side of the road. They were pretty erratic and would cross at a moment's notice, we had no doubt who would come off worse if they piled into the tandem, but there was little we could do, except hope they had the sense not to!

The next day provided a very welcome wildlife encounter though as after hours of gazing wistfully at the eucalyptus trees my search paid off.

"Stop the bike!" I shouted because a few days ago I thought I had spotted something similar, and we had ridden on past too fast. Luckily there was a side road and I managed to convince Stevie to turn in. And there he was! Half asleep, completely unfazed by our presence, but a ball of grey fur with two bright black eyes gazed down at us from his wedge in the branches. I was delighted to spot a koala in the wild, as I had expected to see more wildlife in Australia, so it was a real boon. We of course didn't stop for long, but I was glad Stevie let me stop for long enough to get some photos.

Unfortunately, things didn't improve from there, Stevie had become suspiciously windy and grumpy again and his appetite wasn't great. Now experienced at spotting the signs I couldn't quite believe he seemed to be suffering another bout of giardiasis, despite two courses of treatment. We still ummed and ahhed about what to do. Pausing in Jerilderie we had the dilemma of having a very short day and stopping to go to the health centre there or pushing on to our stop for the night, which was a wild camp at a rest area off the main road. Heading out of Melbourne I had been hopeful of not only reaching Brisbane in good time but also making up some more mileage too. Having cut the route shorter in India we had lost miles there so if we rode the planned route straight back to Berlin, we risked coming in under the 18,000 miles required by Guinness, so needed to add some distance whilst still abiding by the rules regarding travelling too far in the wrong direction of longitude. But if we weren't on top form and were going to lose time seeking medical attention, we risked being late for our flight from Brisbane and this would likely mean not only rescheduling that, but also rescheduling the flights from New Zealand too as we were there such a short space of time, we didn't have the leeway to lose a day or more.

Stevie was conscious I wanted to push on for these reasons, so we stocked up on instant noodles and tinned fish and rode off into the sunset, reaching the rest area in time to pitch in the light. It was pretty good as wild camps went with a picnic table and toilets at the other end of the off-road layby. Another motorhome was near the toilet block, but we were otherwise alone, and I soon got pitched and got the noodles on the go. I convinced Stevie to eat as much as he could, and we cosied up for a night under canvas.

The next morning, I scrubbed my eyes open to the dawn light through the tent, the birds had started now and typical for Australia it was not with tuneful birdsong but squawks and shrieks. The night had not been restful. Stevie had been up and down, uncomfortable and tossing and turning and then the full moon had excited the neighbouring herd of young cattle who had sounded like they were at a rave all night. With Stevie finally slumbering I let him sleep and tried to get as much as possible packed up and ready to go before stirring him. He was not in a good way and having already become stick thin from his last two bouts with the parasite was lacking reserves to fight it a third time. I was concerned the medications weren't working but knew we would have to get to a medical centre to get the drugs he needed. We did have the option to backtrack to Jerilderie, but that would be lost time and mileage with it being west of us, so the best option was to make it to Narrandera, a mere 40 miles down the road.

Next came what were probably the worst 40 miles of the trip. With a bitter headwind and Stevie weak and wobbly we inched along, barely seeming to make any progress and having to frequently stop. Counting the miles, desperately worried not only for the trip but more for Stevie, we finally reached the town. The medical centre was wonderfully efficient considering our unusual predicament and they quickly got us triaged by the nurse and to sit and wait for the doctor. The nurse had been very reassuring and was sure, given Stevie's history, the doctor would prescribe the medication he needed.

The doctor called us through and I explained the situation, having better medical knowledge than Stevie, but was careful not to be rude enough to suggest what he needed as I appreciated how annoying this can be when the roles are reversed. The doctor silently examined Stevie and asked a few questions including if he had been sick at all. He had been a bit nauseous earlier with a bit of reflux in his mouth, but the gut pain and bloating were our main concerns.

Concluding his examination, the doctor solemnly sat down and proclaimed his diagnosis.

"I think you have reflux." he stated, "Yes, you have been in India, but this parasite isn't very common, and you have had some treatment and I do not think this is the cause and we must treat your reflux instead."

Having made his declaration of diagnosis he turned back to his computer to write a prescription and it seemed there was to be no discussion or debate.

"But I don't have reflux." said Stevie, "And it's the same signs as before and we have consulted qualified doctors previously."

But the doctor remained staunch and was not to be dissuaded. Somehow it seemed worse that he appeared to have Indian heritage and we couldn't help but feel he was being very defensive that Stevie's illness was not caused by a parasite picked up from there. We left having paid for the consultation to go and collect some medication for reflux feeling deflated when the pharmacist handed over the prescription. Stevie asked how long he needed to take the medication and she responded, "Until the reflux stops." We couldn't help but point out that he didn't have reflux and left her looking confused and us even more so.

It had been a draining day so despite only 40 miles on the clock we found a motel to try and get Stevie some rest and I decided it was time to try and get a second opinion. Dr Rich concurred with my suspicions that Stevie's symptoms didn't correlate with reflux and the medication we had been issued with was actually at risk of making matters worse not better! Unfortunately, Stevie had already taken a dose... The recurrence of the problem was the most concerning thing and he offered to get in contact with a friend, who not only had a lot of experience with tropical diseases but had also worked in this area of Australia a few years ago. It was massively reassuring to have this sort of medical back up when we felt we were in such a pickle and as much as I am a strong advocate of respecting a professional opinion, our confidence in the doctor we had seen had been undermined, so we were relieved to be able to seek advice elsewhere. Whilst we worked on a solution to where we could get a prescription for the medication we needed and whether we would need to stop for tests, I tried to encourage Stevie to take on as many calories as possible, his preference seemed to be mostly for cereal and milk, so as well as some toast and cheese, he managed this for dinner.

The next day he felt a bit better from a night's rest, but still weak and at the first small town the medical centre was well and truly shut so we went to the café instead for creamy hot chocolates and cheese toasties to warm up from the cold damp weather outside. A shortcut out of town backfired when it ended in a deep ford, and we had to backtrack a distance to get back on route. The next stop was to push onto Wyalong to try and get there in time for the medical centre's opening hours and it was a tough stint into a headwind again. Just catching the doctor there in time for the last consultation was a huge relief; he seemed to take us a lot more seriously and issued the medication we had been told we needed. He was interested in our trip and despite it being the end of the day asked quite a few questions before making a call to the receptionist to tell her to waive the consult fee! We were massively grateful and our faith in the Australian medical system was restored.

Brandishing the much-needed prescription we triumphantly entered the pharmacy nearby, but our good mood was soon ruined when not only was the pharmacy out of stock of the medication, but the whole of Australia was also, due to import issues.

Feeling stuck again it was time to find another motel and sleep on it, at least we had managed a more respectable 90 miles but with 730 miles to go and six days to do it the chances of making our flights were looking grim.

You before me.

I heard of this concept from one of a pair of trans-Atlantic rowers when she was discussing her mental strategy for undertaking such a gruelling and epic challenge as a team of two. Admittedly it's a bit different when you are husband and wife as opposed to friends as a divorce would be a lot more awkward to sort out if the whole challenge and relationship fell apart, but I thought she had a great concept. The only way for them to succeed as a pair was to cross the finish line together; and the same was true for us. There would be no new Guinness record if only one of us got back to the Brandenburg Gate, not to mention one person cannot ride the bike any significant distance!

This lady came up with the idea that for the team to succeed her priority had to be to get her teammate across the finish line, no matter what. And if her focus was on her teammate and how to help her succeed, her own success, and therefore that of the team would happen by default.

A completely altruistic idea of "you before me".

At this point in the trip, when Stevie was starting to suffer so much, not only with the third bout of sickness but also now developing saddle sores from the severe weight loss he had suffered (we suspect he lost over 15kg at his thinnest) and general fatigue from handling the tandem for over 100 miles a day; I was already in charge of the logistics, but now more than ever, it became my priority to try and look after Stevie to the best of my ability for the sake of our trip and the record. So, if this meant I had to go to the shops after the days ride and get him something to eat I did, if I had to research the pharmacies and medical centres along the route to find the medication he needed I did and if he needed to go through the shower first and then relax in bed and air his sore bum, I took second go. I can't pretend I was the perfect model of the caring wife all the time as I was becoming increasingly tired too, but my focus was becoming increasingly on what I could do to keep Stevie comfortable and able to keep riding. This also helped me worry less about my own woes by focusing on something else.

Day 104–109: West Wyalong, Australia to Brisbane, Australia

It felt like we had little choice the next day but to get up and keep riding. We tried Forbes and Parkes along the route to try and find the medication we needed but still to no avail, it seemed there truly was a national shortage and I was frustrated with feeling helpless. The roads and drivers were not the best too, with some floods and epic potholes and less than considerate motorists. It was over 30 miles from Parkes to Peak Hill where we hoped to stop, and I knew we would be arriving too late to find any dinner, so would have to carry it from Parkes. Stevie was less than impressed by this idea, annoyed with having to wait while I shopped, and the extra weight. I knew anything I bought would be too heavy, but was determined to get us something nutritious, so ended up draining the water from a can of chickpeas in Woolworths car park. It was a relief to get to the motel after another long day and we had somehow managed to get 117 miles on the clock, but still no medication for Stevie. He seemed to have stabilised a bit though, whereas the previous times he had deteriorated rapidly until the treatment had started. Dr Laura was still on the case of trying to help us track something down, but she was struggling too, despite her contacts in the area. I had a restless night worrying about the implications of this and whether it was just too much of a push to try and make the flights from Brisbane, and therefore the flights from New Zealand as well.

The following morning Dr Laura did have some news, but it wasn't regarding medication. It had occurred to her that giardia infections can cause damage to the gut wall and they then can cause temporary lactose intolerance and given Stevie wasn't getting worse without treatment, it had occurred to her that this might be the case instead of a re-infection. Ideally, he would have had faecal samples done, but with us moving through the country so quickly it was challenging to arrange this, so we had been working on a presumptive diagnosis. Suddenly it all seemed to make a bit more sense; even the second time in the Nullarbor, Stevie had craved cereal and milk and now he was most keen to eat milk-based products and we suspected his inability to digest the lactose was making him crave it! Unfortunately, we had both had large bowls of milky cereal for breakfast, but now we had an idea what was wrong, it was a massive relief that we could do something about it.

This proved easy enough to begin with, the touch screen system in McDonalds making it easy to order McMuffins without cheese and I popped to the local shop to stock up on anything I could without milk products in it. Tim Tams, a type of Australian chocolate biscuit, had become popular with Stevie but was out of the equation for now and replaced with ginger nuts and bananas.

The horrible roads continued for the morning until we peeled off onto Newell's Highway, which was much more pleasant, with comparatively more wildlife in the form of kangaroos and emus. I had decided to take this route and I was initially pleased as the more pleasant farmland was lifting our spirits, but as we approached Binnaway, I became more concerned as I had found the hotel to be full when I had rung ahead earlier and we were booked into the old Railway Barracks. With only the phone call as confirmation, I couldn't even find their location on Google Maps. When we arrived, we waited outside the hotel that smelt temptingly of food but was also spilling out locals who had had one too many shandies onto the streets. I called our contact to come and let us in. The wait seemed to take too long, and the locals were getting rowdier, when she finally turned up and seemed surprised to see we were on a bicycle despite me having mentioned it twice on the phone.

The barracks were out of town further than we expected and were comfortable, but left us with a dilemma for dinner: either riding back to the hotel, calling and trying to negotiate a delivery or making do. With Stevie's new restricted diet, he wasn't feeling the most enthusiastic about food and was also tired and fed up from the last few stressful days. I cajoled him to eat some of the bits we had before he collapsed in bed to try and sleep. I was soon to follow, my head still whirling with the stressful events of the last few days, deep concern for Stevie and worry we would not make it to Brisbane in time to fly. The decision we had almost made by default, not to postpone the flight, now weighed heavy on us and was putting more pressure on poorly Stevie to ride instead of recover. My brain automatically seeks a distraction, and my imagination ran wild with the creepy empty railway barrack we were housed in, and the ghost of the past, haunted my dreams...

What really happened at the Railway Barracks...

It was only in the time after we left that things seemed to piece together... our memories are strangely vague... almost dreamlike... and maybe we are wrong. Maybe the exertion is getting to us...or maybe, sometimes, things cannot always be explained...

Laura often booked accommodation ahead, especially when options were limited so when she spotted a hotel in Binnaway, saving Stevie and her from a ridiculously epic day to Coonabarabran, she gave them a call...

A man picked up the phone, sounding vaguely disgruntled it had rung... "do you have a room for tonight?" she asked.

A long pause which suggested the question wasn't straightforward and a "Nope, sorry". Feeling persistent, Laura asked if there was anywhere else?

A sucking of teeth and, "there's the railway barracks..." with a wry chuckle. OK great thought Laura and got onto Google maps to track down plan b.

Unusually, nothing was apparent, so she called back to get more information, but only a telephone number was gleaned. Not to be put off a good night's rest Laura made the call.

"Yes, yes," a friendly woman said, "it's $100 a night, just give us a call when you get there, but make sure it's before dark and one of our volunteers will let you in!"

"Ok," said Laura, "we'll do our best!" Knowing that it was going to be a stretch to make the distance but not seeing another option.

"Yes, before dark! Yes..." said the lady and the line went dead. Well, it's better than nothing Laura said to Stevie with a shrug, and they peddled on.

It was a long day and not far off dusking by the time they got to Binnaway and the wind whipped leaves around the streets as two adolescent girls rode undersized bikes in circles with speakers pumping out a dubious choice of music.

"Watch out for the magpie," they screamed and looking up there was a pied bird fixing them with an intent gaze from the telegraph wire above. Before they could beat a hasty retreat in case it attacked Laura's phone rang.

"Are you here yet dearie?" A voice crackled down the line.

"Yes, we're here," answered Laura, feeling vaguely surprised-she hadn't left a number earlier, but it must have shown up on the caller's phone.

"I'll meet you at the hotel," the lady said.

The hotel was in full swing having had a night of "money darts" and as they pulled up a trio of locals rolled out of the hotel. After asking the usual questions: where were the pair from? Where were they going? Where had they cycled from? Where was the motor? They asked where they were staying...

"The barracks?" One exclaimed, "you'll not sleep well there! It's haunted!"

"Yeah," his mate followed up with, whilst sloshing his pint into his shoe, "some little girl. She like appears in the corridors... woooo" and burst into giggles with his tipsy mates.

"Nope." A voice says from the shadows under the eaves. A lighter spark illuminating a gaunt weathered face lighting a cigarette, "it's the youngest of the three sisters. She never left."

The lads go quiet and then shuffle back inside, ricocheting off the door posts and each other as they go, but the gentleman follows in a more dignified manner leaving Laura and Stevie alone on the suddenly quiet, dark, empty street. The wind picks up and rustles the leaves, creating shivers.

"Maybe we should try again for a room here," says Laura, fearing their host may not arrive.

"Evening dearies," a voice suddenly says and they both jump, having not perceived anyone approaching from down the street. A lady in a floral dress and piercing dark eyes peered at them. "You'll be wanting your room no doubt." She stated, rather than asked.

Not in the mood to question Australian country fashion sense on such a cold night they both agreed.

"Go back down the road, take a right, then over the tracks, then a left and I'll leave the light on," she directed and strode off down the street. Mounting the tandem again and switching the lights on they thought they would catch her up, but it was almost a mile to the Railway Barracks, and they saw not a trace of her on the road but, true to what she said, the light was on when they arrived. The front looked smart and recently done up, but she quickly beckoned them to the rear of the building.

"Main door's this way dearies," she said, unlocking it with a large mortice key. They wandered in and the lights came on revealing a great space – communal dining area, kitchen and 11 bedrooms. They were able to wheel the bike in too, which was a bonus.

"I'll leave you to it then," said the lady. "I'm Lila by the way, great to meet you."

"What about payment?" Stevie asked.

"That's fine in the morning dearie" she said with a dismissive wave of her hand.

Trying to be efficient and stay on top of the record attempt Laura remembered the witness book just in time. "Would you mind signing it?" She asked, and for one moment the lady looked like she would say no, but then with a shaky hand, put her details in. Then bidding her goodbyes she swept out of the door leaving them to their own devices.

Wandering around their home for the night they investigated the strangely chilly bedrooms laid out down a long corridor before getting back to warmth of the communal areas. The dining room had books and photos about the history of the barracks, and the railway line which ran through Binnaway.

Old photos showed three sisters and their daughter who used to run the barracks and a separate photo of the youngest daughter with a magpie perched on her shoulder. She was apparently a favourite amongst the railway workers, often helping with the mechanical tasks. Laura took some photos of these on her phone to add to the blog of the trip.

They had neglected the issue of dinner somewhat and spotting a menu for the hotel tried to call for a takeaway. Despite a full bar of signal, the line wouldn't connect just making a crackling chugging noise. Of course, there was no Wi-Fi either, or roaming Internet and they were completely isolated. Trying to make the best of matters, they rustled up what they could from the food bags and were soon feeling tired after a long day. The strange chill persisted despite the heaters being on and Laura wandered around wrapped in the blanket from the bedroom.

"You look like an old lady in that!" Stevie said wearily. "I think we should change the chain tomorrow morning. I know it's due, but it won't take long. Can you just get the new chain out please?"

They both went to bed, and inevitably Laura was sound asleep in no time having forgotten all about the chain.

They were sleeping soundly but Stevie got up in the night to use the loo. On the way back he spotted Laura, wrapped in blankets again, down the end corridor.

"What are you doing down there?" He mumbled sleepily, "go for a wee and come back to bed" and wandered back into the room to Laura's soft snores, thinking no more about it.

The next morning Stevie was first up to put the kettle on and found the new chain out in the kitchen. Laura must have got it out in the night when she was up.

A while later Laura emerged, "I can't find the new chain anywhere!" she complained.

"It's here, you got it out last night when you were wandering around," Stevie said.

"I didn't get up in the night," said Laura, confused.

"Well, I saw you wandering about!" Said Stevie and eventually they had to agree to disagree, as Laura was convinced that she slept through, and Stevie was convinced that he saw her up and the chain was out and ready.

They changed the chain, got breakfast, and packed up. Trying the back door, it was now firmly locked and the heavy key nowhere to be seen, only a small modern one which opened the front door.

While Stevie was finishing up Laura went for a wander outside and admired the new frontage and various artefacts from times gone by. A curious magpie followed her around.

They were just ready to leave and wondering what to do about payment when a Ute pulls up with a yapping dog in the back.

"Oh, so you did make it," an Aussie lady calls from the driver's seat. "When it got dark, I thought you'd stopped elsewhere, and it was only when one of the neighbours said they saw lights on we realised you turned up. How'd you get in?"

"Another lady let us in," said Laura feeling a bit confused, "I forget her name now."

"That's strange... Carol and Sharon are out of town, no one else should have a key." Laura paid up and the lady still looked uneasy.

"Did you see any magpies around here?" She asks warily.

" Yeah, one was following me around all morning".

Without another word the lady wound the window up and drove off in a cloud of dust. They both decided it was about time they got going too and headed back to the main road.

After a couple of hours, they chatted through the whole experience and a lot of things didn't add up. The call, how she got to the barracks ahead of them on foot, the back door, the bicycle chain being out... but all easily explainable. As they tried to figure out who she was, Ste remembered "she signed the book! Check that!"

On getting the book out, the signature was there, the date unclear but the spidery writing was just about legible, and the name "Lila" was indistinctly etched. Checking her phone for the photo of the picture of the younger sister Laura had taken, it had inexplicably disappeared...

Back in the real world, the next morning somehow things seemed a bit brighter, the sun was shining, and we had had a relatively long and good night's sleep. An early stop for footlong subs fuelled us up after having had a meagre breakfast at the barracks and a long, uninteresting road got the miles in, so we only had 30 miles left by the time we stopped to pick up supplies, and a cheeky McDonald's, in Narrabri.

Another spectacular Australian sunset followed with the whole sky afire with glorious hues of orange and red as we reached Bellata in the evening. I was trepidatious about the night's accommodation, as it was a camping option at a golf club and remembering how well the last wild camp had gone down, I fervently hoped this would be more comfortable and restful. A rather unengaging young man was behind the bar in the club and my heart sank a bit, worried that things weren't going to go plan but it all proved very simple, and we were soon pitched near the 18th hole on soft grass and back in the bar for a pint and some wonderful home cooking. It turned out to be a great set up and very cheap and we were happy to get tucked up in the cosy tent for a good night's rest.

Waking just before dawn we packed the tent away to a glorious magenta sunrise and tucked into porridge and tea before getting on the road. This camp spot had definitely worked out! We were well set up to put in a solid performance; and we needed to do about 350 miles and three days to get to the airport. A solid 112-mile day put us in good stead, but we still had a long way to go. We had a bit of a surreal evening in a boutique motel room watching the Queen's funeral on the TV, feeling very distant from the events in the UK on the other side of the world.

The next morning, I thought I'd cracked it and spotted a shortcut to shave some miles off and confidently directed Stevie the opposite way from the original route. We did well initially, flying along some nice roads and I was feeling smug having cut down the distance to give us an edge. Then we turned into a side road... which had a sign saying dead end.

"Keep going, I'm sure it will be fine." I said with misplaced confidence, and we continued as the road turned into a lane and we crossed a bridge sending a couple of small kangaroos bounding from the bushes. I was still feeling happy that we had successfully cut the corner off at this point as the road was single carriageway and the surface was good. I felt that if we kept going like this we were in for a good day and an early finish. Then the road started to get rougher, and the surface deteriorated to a gravel track. I was starting to get apprehensive and I could sense Stevie's doubt emanating through the frame as a grassy strip started to appear down the middle of the road. I checked Google for the route I had planned and cross referenced it with Ride with GPS and Komoot to try and establish if my detour was viable. I could see the tracks marked but the surfaces looked dubious, and I was starting to get more and more sceptical. We got to a crossroads and my heart sank; straight on was a field, right was a dirt track overhung with bushes and left was a six-bar gate with a big sign saying, "PRIVATE NO ENTRY".

We were meant to be going right, but without needing to ask, I knew that Stevie would not be riding our precious tandem down there.

The main road we could have been on was tantalisingly close and I could almost hear the traffic, but that would be a left turn and I had the sense that trespass wouldn't be well tolerated.

We ground to a halt, and I shame-facedly had to admit our situation to Stevie. Unable to go forwards or to either side we would have to go back. It was about seven miles off the main road, but this would mean at least 14 miles lost and I still wasn't sure we wouldn't have to retrace back to Goondiwindi, where we had spent the previous night.

Unable to bear the backtrack and humiliation once back on tarmac, I persuaded Stevie to push on to the next turn and hoped that this would prove a more rideable option. We had just turned onto the side road, and I breathed a massive sigh of relief when a pickup pulled over. The driver was very friendly, but slightly confused about what we were doing in this neck of the woods. He did however confirm the road was rideable and having lost time to the "detour" made a very kind gesture of leaving us some water out, down the road on the driveway to his farm, as we were running low in the heat. We thanked him profusely, bade him well and set off up the road.

This was a much more promising prospect: fully paved and relatively free of vehicles. We were relieved to be making progress in the right direction, but the temperatures were rising, and it was a massive relief that we had some more fluids available up the road... if only we could find it! We reached a crossroads as described and spent precious time furtling in the bushes and getting savaged by some vicious mozzies before realising this probably wasn't the spot. Pushing on and feeling hotter and thirstier I was desperately hoping, but also had a sinking feeling, that our water drop was not going to pan out. An unexpected chain suck dampened our spirits more and I felt certain we were doomed to a bitter end of dehydrated exhaustion on this tiny baking backroad. Just as I had given up all hope a driveway with a sign which looked familiar appeared and I barely dared hope for our salvation. We pulled over and spotted a cool box behind the sign and, on raiding it, not only discovered precious icy cold water, but also a stash of Tim Tams, that national biscuit of Australia. Such kindness from a stranger on the road buoyed our morale and we made a good pace to rejoin the main road we should have been on. It was still a long day to our last motel in Australia and I treated myself to a final "chicken Parmi" before the last stint to Brisbane the next day.

The final day should have felt like a triumph, but it all felt rather routine: get up, get fed, get dressed, get on the bike and ride.

We were inevitably into a headwind straightaway and caved after only 18 miles when the Golden Arches beckoned yet again. We were determined to push on after fuelling up, but the road was rolling, and the headwind was incessant. The traffic built up and we were soon thrown into suburbia as the population density increased. I had taken great care to plan our route to the airport after the previous misdemeanours. We entered the outskirts and the rain set in. The navigation got more intense and lightweight carbon commuting bikes whizzed past as we picked up off road cycle routes through the city. The artificial lights felt confusing through the rain, and we were battling to the end point, desperately stretching and straining for the finish in the dark downpour.

We knew we were late, but we had the resignation of those that have pushed so hard for so long to get to this point, whatever it took, that any time would be a success.

We rolled into the airport hotel to an unexpected round of applause and cheers. Matt and his long-suffering daughter had been waiting hours for us. Matt had offered, even before we started the trip, to assist us with the boxes in Brisbane; having helped world record cyclist Vin Cox previously. They had everything we needed and took some photos before leaving us to get packed up. Matt seemed to understand without being told that we still had a lot to do, and it was getting late. It was a shame we couldn't get to know him better, but we were immensely grateful to him for making the process of getting the boxes so smooth.

We quickly established the car park under the hotel as the best place to disassemble and box the bike and Stevie soon got to work. I got us checked in, arranged getting to departures the next morning and started washing clothing in the shower. Another rather unpleasant job, because in the dark and rain, Stevie had stepped in dog poo and it was ingrained all around the cleats on his cycling shoe. It took a lot of getting out, but we certainly wouldn't be allowed on the plane with a shoe stinking like that!

Despite getting boxed up quicker now we were more practised, it was still late into the evening by the time we finished, and all the restaurants were shut so we had one last Australian splurge on room service, wincing at the price of a sandwich and beer. It had been a very expensive leg, with the cost of living higher than the UK and our options of what to buy and eat limited by our route and location. There was now the added issue of Stevie's lactose avoidance, and I was unable to convince him that they had remembered not to butter the sandwiches, so he went to bed tired and grumpy. It was now midnight, and the alarm was set for 5am.

We should have felt triumphant having battled so hard, but we were both just exhausted.

Day 110–120: Brisbane, Australia to Auckland, New Zealand

A groggy start and the trials of getting us and the bike checked in and through security felt tough. We discovered, to our frustration, that we needed to collect the bike boxes and check them back in at Wellington, as the flight to Dunedin was classed as domestic. Arriving in Wellington had a strange sense of reverse déjà vu, knowing we were aiming to be back here in a matter of days, having ridden the length of the South Island and crossed the Cook Strait. The flights took all day with a five-hour layover and the second one was delayed, dragging things out even longer. When we were asked to unpack the bicycle and get the tent out for a customs biosecurity inspection, I thought it was going to be the last straw for Stevie, but the customs officer was friendly and made things as easy as possible, helping us get the boxed taped back up again.

Finally landing in New Zealand at 10pm local time the bike still needed to be built as there were no hotels near the airport, so we had to cycle to get somewhere to sleep. What we hadn't banked on was that the actual airport was so small it closed overnight, and an initially friendly security guard got more and more impatient as we reassembled as quickly as we could. A child's Postman Pat ride played an incredibly irritating tune every 5 minutes until I got fed up and unplugged it.

Eventually, we headed outside to finish fitting pedals and saddles, shivering in the damp cold air, having got used to a bit of heat again at the back end of Australia. Cows bellowed in a nearby field, and it certainly felt like a strange remote location for the airport, with us being unable to discern our surroundings in the dark. Finally, we set off for the 15-mile cycle into town to find our accommodation. In another wonderfully altruistic gesture, an old school friend of mine (and actually the sister to Liz who we had stayed with in Melbourne) had offered us somewhere to stay, despite being away at a conference. Her partner was working late at the hospital (they are both doctors) so we had been left instructions to let ourselves in, help ourselves to dinner and whatever else we wanted. What we hadn't counted on was the flight being so delayed so we were a bit embarrassed to find her partner waiting anxiously for us, knowing we should have arrived a couple of hours ago. There was a tremendous home cooked curry waiting in the fridge though and a wonderfully warm and cosy bed so we could get some much-needed rest before exploring New Zealand properly the next day. I agreed to set the alarm later to give us a bit more recovery and when it finally went off the following morning, we were feeling quite a bit better.

In this instance our lie in would not be putting us behind schedule due to the time we had to cycle through New Zealand. When planning the trip so many months ago I was conscious that not every leg would be the same in terms of difficulty and in this case the relatively short distance of just over 880 miles made the decisions about which flights to aim for crucial. If we had ended up a day behind in any other leg the likelihood would have been we could have made it up (it was only because the crash was so close to the flights in Malaysia that we hadn't managed) but with less leeway in New Zealand and the complication of the ferry between the two Islands to factor in I needed to make sure we had every chance of getting the flight at the other end. Therefore, we had 9.5 days to cycle the whole length and planned to get the ferry late on the fifth day to preserve the daytime for cycling. This gave us a 93 mile per day average, well under the 106 miles per day average planned for the overall trip. The 106 (as opposed to 100 miles for 180 days to make the 18,000 miles) was to account for six flying days and four days off the bike for whatever reason beyond our control: this turned out to be a very good guess on my part as we had three full days and two halves!

What this doesn't account for is the "buffer". We had assumed that if we rode into the Brandenburg gate on 18,000 miles exactly it would (a) look a bit suspect, and (b) be open to further critique and analysis as to whether we had our distances correct; if it turned out we had done 17,999 miles I'm pretty sure Guinness wouldn't be counting laps of the Pariser Platz!

So, we knew we had to do extra, but there was no clear guidance or consensus on how much of a buffer we would need. Following the packing of the bicycle at the airport palaver, where asking the question definitely hadn't helped, I was reluctant to go to Guinness about this as even if they said one per cent that would equate to an extra 180 miles which would be close to two days cycling! When I had set out the plans initially, I had assumed we would accumulate the extra mileage as we went, going to and from accommodation, taking diversions etc. But having lost a massive chunk of mileage first in Asia and then cutting the corner off in India meant that we were still well under target at 10,675 miles on day 110, with my spreadsheet plan expecting 10,961 miles at this point. 290 miles down meant potentially almost three extra days of cycling if these miles didn't get factored into longer days, we risked the 180-day target we had become obsessed by.

180 days was what we said we were going to do, and we were prepared to give everything we had in terms of physical and mental endurance to meet this target.

With the pressure mounting to get the extra miles in, I was looking at route extensions in New Zealand and Canada to try and get us back on track, the hope being that if we could at least hit 100 miles per day distance at the end of Canada, we could then worry about the buffer for the final 17 days in Europe. But there was another reason I had been planning to drop the daily mileage in New Zealand: aside from Europe it was the hilliest leg of the trip and given it was early spring, the weather and daylight hours threatened to be some of the biggest challenges. Not an ideal place to add distance, but I had started to plot routes anyway in the hope we could claw back a small amount over the next week and a half.

This was the point where the day-to-day planning and analysis became more and more pressing as I totalled distances, checked, and rechecked how much we had to go and how far we could get to in a day; continually reassessing how far to push things and what might be possible.

The morning sunshine streamed through the window, and we rose groggy, but refreshed, to help ourselves to breakfast and let ourselves out of Gwen's comfy abode. If it had felt strange spending so little time with Matt at Brisbane, it felt even stranger not even being able to thank Gwen in person for such a wonderful stay.

The glorious sunshine revealed what we had missed last night though, the large bay that surrounded Dunedin glittering blue, and tall hills towering around, looking lush and green compared to the arid flora in Australia. Seagulls wheeled above and we picked up a cycleway out of the city, feeling like everything was a lot more familiar. We were soon climbing though, and our legs creaked and groaned with the unfamiliar effort of dragging the laden tandem up the hill. It was surreally spring-like as we passed green grazing fields with sheep and lambs; the grass and trees looked so similar to the UK, compared to everywhere else we had been. The mist descended as we climbed the pass, and it could have been many roads in the more remote areas of Wales or Northern England. Quiet country lanes led us back down and out of the mist into blazing sunshine again and we were back at the beach with waves crashing on the shore. With the late start it was dark by the time we reached a backpackers' place in Oamaru. I took advantage of a shared kitchen to run out to the supermarket and stock up on suppliers and oven pizza for dinner. With Stevie still being off the lactose it was easier to find him vegan options in the larger shops and also helped keep the costs down compared to eating out, as well saving time in the evenings.

Recovery time was key as we were not only still tired from the flying, but Stevie was really starting to suffer with saddle sores over his "sit bones". We are no strangers to saddle sores but what started out as a spot was developing into more of an ulcer and I was suspicious that his dramatic weight loss over the past month had contributed to what was usually a bombproof bum. Getting clean and dry of an evening was becoming key to try and stop these progressing, but with about 10 hours a day in the saddle it was a process that was hard to reverse once it had started.

The morning was overcast, and we felt as glum as the weather; we were never catching up on sleep and weariness was set in our bones. Many friends and followers kept suggesting wonderful places to visit, but we had no choice but to get our heads down and keep pedalling, keenly aware we were missing some of the wonderful sights and attractions New Zealand had to offer. The highlight of the day was yet another motel but one with a stove top so we could yet again rustle up some fresh food from the supermarket before passing out in bed.

We spent some time that night carefully setting the alarm; the clocks were changing for spring, and we thought we had got it all sorted by leaving Stevie's phone on aeroplane mode to ensure it didn't update. It took a good 30 minutes the next morning to realise our planning had backfired and the phone had somehow still updated without a connection, and we were up an hour earlier than intended. With no time to lose though, we tried to take advantage of the early start and push for a better day. We glimpsed the snowy peaks of the mountains as we approached Christchurch and the urge to come back and explore one day was great, it had definitely been easier to ride past places that weren't such a pull to visit and stay longer. Cycle paths worked wonderfully, getting us through the city of Christchurch efficiently, and after another brief stint along the coast we headed inland to stay in a very quirky backpackers accommodation, formed of old train carriages around a central kitchen made from an old waiting room. I chatted to a young Spanish girl who was staying in a much cheaper dorm room longer term while taking jobs at the vineyards. It sounded like a great way to really get to know New Zealand and I was quite envious of her working holiday.

Hot porridge on a cold dark morning got us going into a stunning dawn where the sky was alight with colour, and it certainly felt like we were somewhere near middle earth as the scenery got more dramatic. With daylight hours now an issue we were pushing to avoid riding into the dark in the evening so early starts were a necessity. I had plotted some extra mileage as well, taking us off the main road on more circuitous backroads, but this plan quickly fell flat as we immediately rounded a bend to see a deep sharp sided valley with the road diving down and up the other side with what appeared to be a near vertical slope.

"I don't think we could ride up that even if we wanted to," Stevie said, frustrated. I shame-facedly admitted that I knew it was a hillier route, but didn't realise it would be that hilly. With Stevie muttering about us not being on a sightseeing cycle touring holiday, we backtracked to the main road where at least we could make better progress. We had a rather upmarket but tasty second breakfast in Cheviot, which had dry stone walls rather reminiscent of Northumberland, and having seen hedgehogs at night and heard skylarks about the fields, it still seemed strange that we were on the other side of the world. A slow steady climb up into the hills made us grateful we hadn't taken the scenic route earlier, but the scenes were still getting more dramatic on this route with snowy peaks in the distance towering over the green hillside surrounding us. A plummeting descent back down to the coastline, the back of Stevie's head framed by the mountains, before the waves were suddenly crashing to my right. There were sea lion colonies barking on the rocky beaches next to the road, but we had no time to stop; with a stiff headwind we were forced to be as economical with stops as possible to try and get to our destination before dark.

The final stretch up the coast felt vaguely triumphant as we had conquered a tough long day to get there, and we were within the last five miles when we got offered a lift by a man in a pickup. Obviously declining, it was only when we arrived at the Bed and Breakfast, we discovered that it was one of our hosts. Knowing that going into full details about our trip often caused confusion, I had mentioned we were arriving on a tandem, but had failed to mention that we were, in fact, racing around the world. They had become concerned when it was getting closer to dark as they didn't know our level of capability or experience. The village was more of a hamlet, and we were slightly disappointed that the seafood and lobster restaurant across the road was closed that day, but I don't think our bank balance was. Instead, the wonderful B & B owners rustled us up an entire roast chicken, salads and potatoes all washed down with a cold beer. They were intrigued by our trip and extremely helpful and friendly, making us feel more like friends than paying guests. Our efforts had set us up well as we had 60 miles to the ferry the next day and were on track to catch the evening boat to arrive late in Wellington without losing out on precious daylight riding time.

But it is never as simple as that. Feeling maybe slightly

complacent about a shorter day we started slightly later than the past few days and were quickly straight into a block headwind. A headwind can make or break a day and if I was to say our average speed on a downhill ride was 9.8mph and Air New Zealand was cancelling flights due to the winds it will hopefully give an indication this was not just a bit breezy...

Feeling drained with the effort of getting there, it was still a relief to check in and safely stow the bicycle on the car deck before we found seats upstairs. Unlike the cross-channel ferries, there was plenty of space and we had a table to ourselves to enjoy some New Zealand lamb and red wine, the extent of our touristic activities so far, before passing out with heads on the table for a few hours. The crossing was smooth despite the winds, and we arrived late at night, but still with Andrew waiting to meet us. He worked for a local wheel building company and had kindly offered to host us overnight after I had put out a plea on social media realising the logistics of finding a hotel in the early hours would be challenging. He was even happy to have an early start with us and guide us out of the city, along cycleways and lanes that we wouldn't have had a hope of finding by ourselves. Finally waving us off at the top of the hill. we had made great progress out of the city and achieved a major point in the trip: Antipodal point number 1!

The relationships of land masses on our trip had resulted in this being well over halfway and we would still ride a significant distance after passing the second point in Madrid, Spain months later. Another descent to the coast and I had decided to heed local advice from Andrew and ditch some of the more ambitious diversions I had routed at the beginning of this leg. Local knowledge goes a long way especially from someone who understands the challenges of riding a tandem. Trying to make a solid start we were pushing on to late morning for our first stop, but nothing was forthcoming in terms of a café or shop. I was getting hungry and frustrated as I felt we were going on too long and when the first café didn't take our visa debit cards and we didn't have cash, it took 45 miles into the day to get somewhere to eat. Relieved but annoyed at having wasted time, my mood at least improved with some food, and it sustained us to our first stop in the North Isle, and our second attempt at a Warm Showers on the trip. After the disaster in Turkey, I was apprehensive, but they were fellow cyclists this time and had a separate annex for us to sleep and offered to cook us dinner, so I was sure it was a good option, not only for our budget. Stevie was less convinced, his saddle sores were becoming more problematic and with constant fatigue he wasn't feeling like socialising in the evenings, but the booking had been made, so we followed a side road off from Marton to their smallholding, complete with pet goats and cows. Lor.raine and Neil certainly gave us a warm welcome and although Neil was recovering from a leg operation, he was excited about his own plans to cycle tour in India next year. We tried our best not to give a biased impression of cycling in the country as we were well aware our experience would have been very different if we had taken more time and been more selective about where we travelled.

They seated us at the table for dinner and after we sat and talked about our trip, I was enjoying some different company. I hadn't realised that Stevie was feeling the need to be polite and in fact was suffering on a hard seat with his sores. When we eventually retired to bed he was tetchy and unimpressed with having no downtime to himself; it was a tricky balance, as the kindness so many people showed to us was instrumental to the success of our trip, but as the same time we were increasingly in our own little bubble and especially when feeling sore and tired it is so hard to stay positive around others and want to interact.

The following morning, we were treated to a tremendous breakfast and half a dozen farm fresh boiled eggs, but through no fault of our hosts Stevie's cycling shorts had failed to dry and, as he was now having to wear both pairs, it compounded his misery to have to put them on damp. I decided it would be quite some time before I opted for another Warm Showers experience on this trip, we just weren't in the right frame of mind.

It was another tough day ahead as well, with a serious climb up to the highest point we would reach on the North Island and, with our destination being part of a ski resort, we knew we would have our work cut out.

It was steady climbing from the off and after a second breakfast at the oxymoronically named Flat Hills Café, it became increasingly rolling with fewer sharper ups and downs breaking up the long drags. We took a break in Taihape and picked up Josh, a touring cyclist who was having a tough time on the road too. We helped motivate each other for a bit as the climb continued, until he continued a more direct route to Taupo, and we skirted around the massive snowy peak looming above us. On quieter roads now we admired some exceptional feats of engineering as a massive railway viaduct spanned an impressive gorge with river rapids below. Reaching the National Park just as it got dark, we settled into the ski chalet/hostel that I had pre-booked. It wasn't particularly warm, but we still slept well before we ventured out into a cold, dank, grey dawn; the mist had set in, and the snowy peak was invisible this morning. But finally, we were going down! The pleasure of the descent was only ruined by one particularly irate lady screaming "Get off the road!" from her car window as she overtook us. Quite where she thought we should be wasn't clear!

More than a bit perturbed by her level of rage, we carried on regardless and warmed up in a café for a two course second breakfast. We left in the rain, and I had my head down in the drizzle for the first few miles before I realised something was wrong... my helmet wasn't on my head. Cue, an unnecessary retrace back to the café, where it had thankfully been put to one side, but a frustrating loss of time and miles, nonetheless. We had done tremendously well at not losing many things given our nomadic nature on the trip, the chain tool in Turkey being the most notable, and for example I managed to go the whole trip with the same two hair bands. When you have scant belongings, you take good care of them.

The rain did nothing for the views over Lake Taupo and yet again we were made to feel we were missing out on what was clearly a popular holiday destination. Riding past the steaming hot springs on the roadside did nothing to warm us up either. The main highway we had avoided yesterday was busy, and unfortunately after the outburst from the lady earlier we suffered more aggressive driving as we skirted a narrow and rough hard shoulder. With some roadworks thrown in as well, Stevie's patience was being tested to the limit as he had to concentrate on keeping the bicycle and us safe from the multiple hazards. The rain kept coming and as much as it warmed up slightly as we descended, we were soaked through. Stevie's skinny frame was struggling to stay warm enough. We rounded a bend and there was an SUV pulled over with a woman waving to flag us down. Feeling confused why someone would be stopping us in such awful weather we hesitantly pulled to a halt.

"It's my boyfriend," she stammered hysterically, "he's having a fit and he crashed the car!" I had to think fast. Why she had flagged down us, not another motorist, I'll never know but the SUV was just nudged against the verge and as much as her boyfriend was only just conscious, he was breathing and there was little else I could do to assist on the roadside. Stevie was already shivering while holding the bicycle and I had to be logical in ensuring one casualty didn't turn into two or three in these conditions. I set the lady to flag down another vehicle for assistance using our high vis vest and told her to seek help from the garage across the road too. Once someone pulled over, we had to offer profuse apologies and get back on the bike and ride to try and warm Stevie up.

It was only 10 miles to our motel and he was still shivering trying to get his sodden gloves off. I knew we'd have to get him warmed up quickly and still full of adrenaline I got him inside, put the heating on full and left the panniers on the bicycle telling him to get into a warm shower while I braved the downpour one last time to get our dinner from the supermarket. I shopped as quickly as I could; I had microwave dinners in motel rooms down pat at this point and made a break for it with a treacherous paper bag of food back to the motel. As I got into the room, I was greeted by a giggling stark-naked Stevie who was very proud he'd got all the bags in by himself, but was now undoubtedly hypothermic. Not impressed, he'd ignored my instructions; I bundled him into the shower and then bed while we gradually warmed up, testing the room heating to max. It wasn't necessarily that cold outside, but we had yet to source our winter kit, having missed a delivery to Dunedin and now aiming to pick up more clothes in Auckland, we were treading the line a bit in terms of having enough layers in the worst of the weather.

The next morning, we were somewhat better prepared for the downpour, which was still ongoing, and after a slightly surreal chat with the motel manager about some lady called Liz Truss, who was apparently now Prime Minister and had turned the UK economy on its head, we set off trialling out some new pairs of marigold gloves we had stopped to get from the shop. This is an old audax trick, as being waterproof, they can help with hand warmth by trying to keep under gloves dry, but it had been a bit tricky to find some big enough for Stevie. The roads and the drivers were equally as unpleasant as yesterday, and I had read in a couple of places that New Zealand drivers weren't very tolerant of cyclists and it was disappointing to find that this was true, with frequent honks, shouts and swearing from motor vehicle drivers. It seemed quite exceptional given the friendly demeanour of everyone we met off the bike.

Entering the small town of Te Aroha, I was a bit more nervous, as it seemed a very small community with signs that it wasn't as affluent an area and certainly not somewhere tourists often went. Visiting the supermarket there the accents were so strong, English was basically incomprehensive, and I believe some native dialect was being spoken as well. I was tense riding out of town and jumped when some youths hanging on the street corner shouted at us, but it was not the aggression I'd feared but was in fact encouragement as they seemed to cheer us on! I had misjudged this place on its image and felt that I had been rather narrow minded.

We were heading to the coast again now and what had started as tailwinds spun around us seemingly coming from all directions at once and the grey sea merged indiscernible into the sky. The wind settled in front of us for the last stint to an Airbnb for our last night in New Zealand.

The following morning, I heaved a huge sigh of relief to see sunlight through the curtains, we had had enough rain for now! It also felt like it gave us a good chance of getting ourselves and the bike to the airport dry, as packing up wet again would be a pretty miserable experience. We almost got stuck by a landslide early on and thankfully the bike could squeeze through before we rode up over a headland to cut a corner off on minor roads. The forest here felt practically tropical with dense lush vegetation, and I was enjoying the scenery as we came to the top of a rise. Stevie had just positioned the bike to descend in the middle of our lane with no traffic coming up behind, when a car driver approaching on the other side of the road hurled abuse at us for not being in the gutter. Now we wouldn't necessarily expect a car driver to understand the necessity to pick a descent line for a laden tandem, but given we caused this driver absolutely no inconvenience and were nowhere near the side of the road he was driving in, it was almost laughable he had got himself so upset!! His language was vile, and it felt confusing that he seemed so put out and upset to see a bicycle on a road which was not only a back road but also marked as a cycle trail. It was truly weird the attitude some people here had to cyclists. Putting the unpleasant experience out of our minds we had a pleasant ride where we skirted the coast for a bit, making the most of the now blue sea and sky views. A rather upmarket and pretentious brunch had the owner scowling at our helmets placed on the table (a habit I had picked up to prevent any more misdemeanours with forgetting mine) leaving us with mixed feelings as we rolled into Auckland, dodging the showers.

We stopped outside departures and started to strip down the bicycle, awaiting our boxes. As Stevie was taking the pedals off, I got a call and scuttled over to a large SUV and by the time Stevie had turned around I was there with two bike boxes and another precious box full of extra clothes and kit! He was confused by the seamless nature of the process, but this event had been planned for months, before we even departed on the trip when "KeyWee" Rob had got in touch; keen to help, as he is a fellow audax rider and was very excited about our trip. Rob had then acted as our second drop point, receiving a number of deliveries, and sourcing the crucial boxes and packing material, but an unfortunate clash of timings had meant he was out of the country when we were due to depart. He had then arranged for his housemate Chris to drop our supplies off for us and given the parking restrictions at the airport this was done in a drop and go fashion to avoid incurring any parking charges. I have still never met "KeyWee" Rob, although I feel like I know him after multiple conversations and messages leading up to this logistical feat and am massively grateful to him and Chris who got roped in too. It just would not have been possible without the help and assistance of all these wonderful people.

Pack the bike, check it in, check ourselves in, navigate security, customs and find the gate... it was all feeling familiar now and soon we were settled on our longest flight- 13-hours to Vancouver.

It was day 120 and we had 11,586 miles in the bank.

So, 60 days and 6,414 miles (plus buffer) to go...

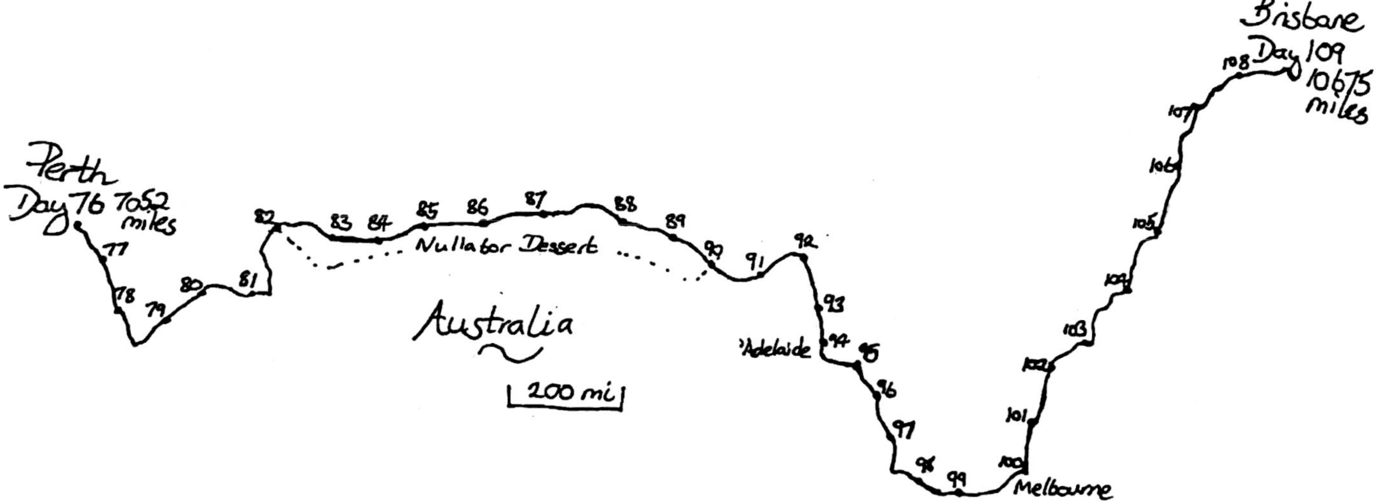

Brisbane
Day 109
10,675 miles

108
107
106
105
104
103
102
101
100
Melbourne
99
98
97
96
95
94
93
92
91
90
89
88
87
86
85
84
83
82
81
80
79
78
77

Adelaide

Nullabor Desert

Australia

200 mi

Perth
Day 76 7052 miles

The Haunted railway barracks

I spotted a koala

Halfway there Adelaide

Feeding Stevie up

Rare photo of me with the bike

Camping in the Nullabor

Roadtrain

How far to Berlin

The classical 90 mile striaight photo

Cold in Aus after SE Asia

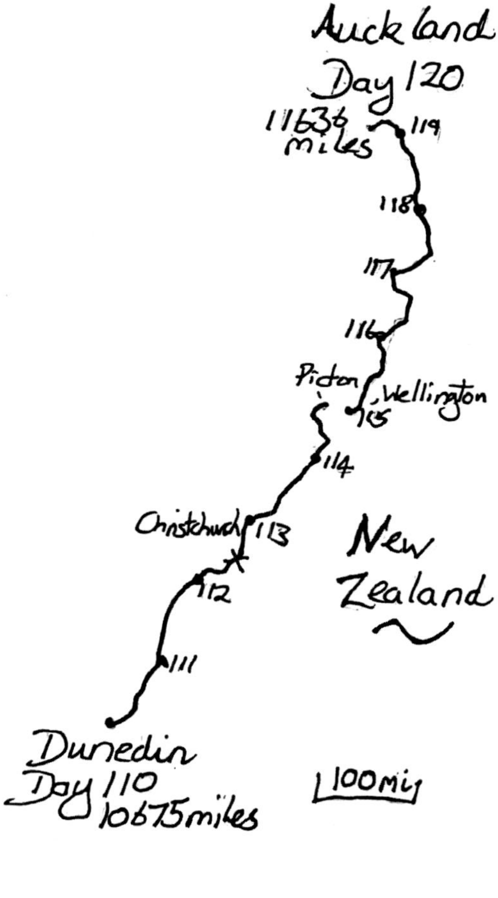

Auckland
Day 120
11634 miles

119
118
117
116

Picton
Wellington
115
114

Christchurch 113
112

New
Zealand

111

Dunedin
Day 110
10675 miles

|100 Mi|

Worse weather in North Island NZ

Beautiful South Island NZ

part 5: canada

Day 121–127: Vancouver, Canada to Olds, Canada

WE STUMBLED off the plane bleary eyed and jet-lagged, as ever never quite having as much rest on a flight as we had hoped. Stevie's ankles were swollen and we both felt none the better for such an unusual amount of time sitting down. We stuffed the panniers with the cold weather clothes we had collected in Auckland including some thicker layers from Huub and full road shoes to replace my SPD sandals from Exustar.

It was then a bit of a surprise to find it was over 20°C in Vancouver. Stevie was concerned I had made an error with the climate and was not impressed by our bulging bags, but I tried to reassure him that it was unseasonably warm. After yet another bike building session we headed out to the city, picking up some food supplies and Lidocaine local anaesthetic gel on the way. Stevie's saddle sores were worsening and given that there was no time to heal, he had resorted to using a topical local anaesthetic, usually used on haemorrhoids, to be able to sit in the saddle. This was a big concern with so much time and distance to go but these sores weren't going to heal up in a week, he had little choice but to ride through the pain.

We didn't have far to go from the airport to a very warm welcome at Moray and Jose's house, who were the aunt and uncle of a good university friend Elle, back in Scotland. It was a bit surreal to exchange stories on what felt like the other side of the world, but they wined and dined us and even got all our clothes through a much-needed machine wash!

Feeling fresh the next morning I was ready to tackle Canada. It took a bit of focus to get us out of the city but I didn't do too bad a job; apart from one slightly dubious off-road path through muddy puddles. We crossed some immense bridges with rafts of logs floating in the rivers below from where they had been transported downstream. This seemed a much better idea than the logging lorries which we had experienced worldwide, often thundering past us.

As the landscape opened up, the Rocky Mountains loomed ahead of us, looking like a beautiful but impassable wall of peaks and rock.

Our first destination was Hope, the small town at the foot of the Rockies, famous for being the setting for the Rambo, First Blood film. The town certainly felt like it fitted the bill with a slightly eery edge to it and empty streets surrounded by the imposing peaks. We arrived in the dark and a drunk man shouted incoherently, slumped on the pavement, as we tried to find our motel. The motel was basic, and it took more negotiation than we were used to, to get the bicycle stored safely, and then a worry they wouldn't open up in time for us to retrieve it for an early start the next day. The prices were certainly not any cheaper here compared to New Zealand and Australia and I went out to the shop to get dinner to try and save on takeaway costs.

The streets were quiet, but one man was walking behind me

and crossed at the same time I did. I started feeling nervous that he was following me and questioned whether I had been sensible to venture out alone. When I turned into the supermarket, he did too, and my concern grew as he looked like he was travelling or living rough. As he followed me down an aisle, I headed to the checkout wondering whether to ask the staff for help; but then he approached and pleasantly asked if I had been riding the tandem bicycle he had seen earlier. My concerns were unfounded, and he was just genuinely interested in why we were there on the bike! But it was a good reminder that I shouldn't be taking my personal safety for granted in places that were unfamiliar.

We started early the next morning, with the sun still rising, the imposing peaks a reminder today was going to be a tough day as we left Hope and started climbing... and climbing... and climbing! It was steady for the first 20 miles and then ramped up for the next with heavy lorries chugging on their exhausted brakes as they came down the other direction. Looking back down the road gave a sense of vertigo as it plummeted back to where we came and reaching the summit after four and a half hours the work wasn't over yet, as what had appeared to be a flatter section on the route profile, turned out to be much more rolling and a hard push for our tired legs. Our only option at the right distance for the day had been an eye-wateringly expensive log cabin Airbnb situated in a picturesque location next to a lake. It would have been the perfect place to spend a week or two chilling out, but we arrived late and in the dark, and the priorities were getting clean, getting fed and getting to bed. I was massively frustrated when the Wi-Fi wouldn't work so I could plan for the next two days, and the host seemed confused as to why I was so desperate to get online when most people visiting were there to disconnect. We were in the log cabin for a total of 10 hours, making the most expensive night's accommodation all the more disappointing and it was another dawn start, to try and beat sunset the following day.

We felt we had rolled out of the airport and hit the Rockies with a bang, but at least had a morning descent to Kamloops which picked up the speed a fair bit. A McDonald's stop provided the Wi-Fi I needed and we were able to push on through the valley, still much higher elevation than we had been but with more peaks surrounding us on all sides. Endlessly long freight trains passed us, and the driver would wave before at least 15 minutes' worth of container carriages rolled past, this was obviously Canada's solution to moving stuff across the country, as opposed to the road trains in Australia and we were grateful not to have to share the roads with the lorries.

Stopping in a small town we picked what appeared at first glance to be a trendy retro café for lunch, but actually turned out to be completely lost in the midst of time and delightfully traditional with a hearty bowls of homemade chilli and chunks of freshly baked bread without a grain of quinoa or smash of avocado in sight!

The mountainous terrain continued and each day we felt we were battling the daylight, trying for earlier and earlier starts; the balmy 20°C in Vancouver was a thing of the past and bitterly cold mist usually surrounded us for the first few hours as we would leave our accommodation bundled up in layers. The climbing felt relentless and being on my period too, I felt drained of energy, struggling to get enough recovery and sleep every day. Last month it had barely occurred at all, presumably due the physical toll on my body but now it was back with a vengeance, throwing cramps and unhappy guts into the mix too and I felt weak and feeble in the face of the soaring mountains.

No matter how hard we tried there was no way to increase the pace of winching the 50kg plus bicycle up the climbs and we just couldn't seem to gain time. Unnecessarily slow service at a posh café in Revelstoke had Stevie fuming; it cost us over an hour of daylight riding time. We were tired and barely able to appreciate the beauty of the mountains around us. As we reached the summit of Roger's Pass, with snow on the peaks and majestic glaciers on the mountainside, I felt dissociated from the beauty. It was so tough that it seemed bittersweet to be surrounded by such amazing views. This was the literal high point of our trip in terms of elevation, but that felt so hard to comprehend given how far we had come and still had to go. A plummeting descent through snow tunnels left me feeling overwhelmed by the incredibly dramatic landscape and the brutality of the ride.

A change in time-zone left us up at what still felt like 4:30am for yet another comparatively expensive, but underwhelming, night's accommodation.

Consoling ourselves with a two course Mc Donald's breakfast we started out on the road toward Banff tentatively as we had been seeing signs for road closures, but they also stated the road would reopen today. As we took the turn and headed up the start of another climb my heart sank as the barricades were clear and it appeared they were late opening the road up, but surely, they would let a couple of cyclists through?!

The answer was a flat no.

The young lady in charge of the barriers was staunch in her decision and told us we would have to wait until midday. We had little choice but to settle down in the sunshine for an hour and a half. Stevie tinkered with the bike whilst I updated the blog and sent irate messages to the Canadian highway authority on Twitter about the misinformation on their signs (they actually replied and apologised!). At midday exactly and not a moment before we were let through the barriers, but so was all the other traffic. Unfortunately, we had been unable to convince the barrier lady that it probably wasn't the best idea to let us all go at the same time; with already frustrated motorists now stuck behind a heavily laden tandem in the roadwork section it did not cheer anyone up. If she had only given us a 10 minute head start it would have avoided a lot of stress and aggravation for all.

We were now racing the dark and getting to Field at 4pm we were only halfway through the day's distance. A brief stop at a trading outpost, which didn't really sell anything edible and had an owner that was determined to get Stevie to fix his bike, had his patience fraying and it took one poor application of peanut butter to his bagel to descend to complete sense of humour failure. Somehow though we managed to hold it together and push on, even though the days destination seemed impossible and the clock ticking too fast. I plugged in some Disney music to my ear buds to raise my spirits and the dreaded last climb of the day actually turned out to be much shorter and more achievable than we had feared. On as much of an emotional roller-coaster as we were on the road rollercoaster, we descended past Lake Louise to Banff, with the incredible scenery just getting better and better. We'd made an massive effort and the sun was just setting, giving the snow-capped mountains a beautiful pink tinge, and then as we rounded a corner, a spectacular sight of the large peak behind the town with a bright full moon emerging behind it. People were parked in lay-bys taking photos and I felt privileged to have the chance to see it from the back of the bicycle, a truly magical moment.

Getting into the town was surreal, it had a friendly, relaxed, party vibe with bars and restaurants in full flow and everyone seemed ready for a night out when we were just ready for bed. An opportunity for a full stocked supermarket with plenty of fresh food was welcome and it was curry and rice with added veggies for tea in the microwave. We'd been piling in the calories recently, partly in an attempt to try and fatten Stevie up a bit and partly as comfort food for the tough days in the mountains. Getting in the most luxurious shower we had had in a while I had a shock when I turned around and saw myself in the mirror... Despite the hard effort that my quads assured me had been happening on the bike I had most definitely put on weight since Asia! Bundled up in more and more clothes I hadn't noticed the change and given that I had been focused on trying to get Stevie to stop and eat at every opportunity, I had ignored the fact that this often resulted in me eating too. But sadly, the calories required by a 6'3" man are significantly more than a 5'2" women and I had most certainly got the balance wrong somewhere along the way. With the pressures of the logistics; finding accommodation, calculating distances and feeding Stevie I hadn't had the mental capacity to focus on myself too. This left me feeling defensive and grumpy about my obvious weight gain and when Stevie commented too, it didn't go down well. The fatal combination of a husband commenting on a wife's weight and tiredness and hormones in the mix did not make for a happy end to the day! But at least I now knew I would have to be careful not to keep up with Stevie on the calories consumption front and not buckle the back wheel!

Body image, weight and sport, especially cycling, is always a tricky one. Stick thin professional cyclists like Chris Froome give an image that is not necessarily relatable to the general cycling population. These riders are carefully managed, at the peak of their performance, but also on a knife edge between injury and illness. Issues such as REDS (relative energy deficiency syndrome) are becoming better recognised in sport and the impact that this has, not only on susceptibility to illness and injury, but also on performance. Skinny doesn't equal faster. There is an argument that power to weight ratio does have a massive impact, but there is a fine line between going faster and taking things too far and that absolute power is actually a more important factor.

We don't all need to be Tour de France riders. If you consider the best endurance riders/athletes out there: Mark Beaumont, Jenny Graham, Emily Chappel, Jenny Tough, Meghan Hacklin, to name but a few; they are built for endurance. Strong body frames that would not fit the traditional picture of a "skinny" cyclist but all have undeniably been at the top of their game and have all achieved incredible things. This is partly due to the fact that endurance almost always necessitates you not going into negative energy balance as this is when injury occurs and you are at higher risk of illness. Exposing yourself to these issues is detrimental to any endurance ride, and self-management is key when you don't have a team of professionals surrounding you. I lost a lot of weight when I started cycling, but I fear I was treading the line then, as it didn't make me any faster in the end and I struggled with becoming obsessive about calories. Prior to that the 5:2 fasting diet had worked well when I had been overweight after an injury, and eating very little for two days a week retrained my body to learn to be hungry and not submit to cravings. But with a more active lifestyle this wasn't possible, and it also had led me to binge on less healthy food on the non-fasting days, skipping veggies in favour of biscuits. Nowadays I aim for a more consistent approach, fuelling for long days and big efforts but keeping to the "eat food, not too much, mostly vegetables" approach otherwise. Learning about my weight and food intake is still an ongoing process, and effort, and there is no magic solution but I feel in a much better place to make sensible decisions (and not panic about weight gain!) than I was several years ago.

Oh, and pizza, I will always eat pizza!

· · ·

It was another chilly start the next day as we headed out of Banff, with mist hovering alongside the road and over the rivers. We peeled off Highway 1 on to Highway 1a, for the first time since Vancouver having a more minor road option. It was a lot quieter with less traffic and stopping briefly we turned around to see an amazing sight of the Rocky Mountains behind us: at last! It felt like we had conquered them, and it was a huge sense of relief to be rolling onto flatter terrain. We skirted Calgary to avoid the traffic and headed slightly north to Olds, past dusty fields of crops. Having lost more elevation there was a feeling of late summer and we felt a contented sense of achievement, having made another big step towards the finish line.

Day 128 – 131: Olds, Canada to Davidson, Canada

A delightfully boring day on the road! Just flat rolling terrain towards Edmonton, no dramas, no hills, no headwinds. It felt good to decompress somewhat by just turning the pedals and getting the job done.

Picking a hotel on the outskirts of the city we were flattered when the kindly manageress gave us an upgrade after we asked if we could have a ground floor room to store the bicycle. On entering the room, I could have cried with delight, not only was there a massive open plan bedroom with a full mini kitchen including an oven (which meant we could have pizza for tea!) there was also another separate bedroom with a massive jacuzzi bath! We had become accustomed to motels in Canada having two double beds in each room which was great to spread our kit on one, but this suite was just amazing. A long soak in the tub was just what I needed to soothe my aching legs from the mountains.

I felt like a new person the next day as we set out to a

glorious red and orange dawn painted across the sky. It was Thanksgiving today in Canada (earlier than the US equivalent) so the roads around Edmonton were thankfully quiet and yet again we had the opportunity to make good progress. Lakes started to appear on the side of the road with flocks of waterfowl psyching themselves up for migration, swooping up, down and around. There were tall mounds of sticks and mud in some of the lakes and I excitedly figured out these were beaver lodges, and we even glimpsed some bison; great shaggy brown hulks in the distance. Given the warnings we had been quite happy not to have seen too much wildlife so far, especially bears! I had intended to pick up some bear spray in Vancouver but had never gotten around to it and given the attritional nature of the ride so far in Canada, camping hadn't even crossed our minds.

The wind picked up from behind and we were soon being blown along, making a strong 80 miles before a proper break at a Tim Hortons, which were becoming a welcome alternative to McDonald's for fast easy food. As I ordered, Stevie was cornered by a group of ladies out for coffee who wanted to know what we were up to. One lady was completely bowled over when she heard about our trip and exclaimed so loudly that soon the whole restaurant seemed involved in our story! We were taken aback by their enthusiasm but having been rather isolated, keeping ourselves to ourselves through the Rockies, it was a wonderful reminder what we were doing was exceptional and we needed to celebrate our achievement so far. The ladies asked a wealth of questions, which we took turns in answering between bites of lunch, followed us on social media, took selfies with us and the bike and then pushed a couple of notes into my hand.

"Thank you so much," I said. "I'll make sure that goes towards our charities."

"You will do no such thing!" The lady exclaimed, "That is for you! To get a nice dinner or somewhere to stay! I want you to spend it on yourselves!"

A wonderfully touching gesture that showed recognition of the monumental effort we were making and a massive boost to morale.

Absolutely buzzing when we got back on the bicycle, we managed speeds frequently exceeding 20mph for the rest of the afternoon and finally the tandem was stretching her legs and flying!

The next day felt like the day we never thought would come, we were so used to the struggle: the uphill battle to keep the distance, keeping the bike moving, keeping the pedals turning. We had stopped believing in the tailwinds days we had fantasised about at the beginning of the trip. Even looking at a wind speed well over 20mph and gusting over 30s on the weather apps we still didn't dare believe and I couldn't imagine booking a motel any further than 120 miles. But as we mounted the bike the wind picked us up and carried us, but with our legs still spinning the pedals. A rather indulgent diner style breakfast buoyed our spirits more as for once a sit-down break didn't seem to have put us behind. And then the tandem galloped past the lakes and little villages dotted along the route, the scenery flying past, and it soon became clear we would be well beyond the conservative 120 miles; I dared set our sights on North Battlefield at 138 miles.

We reached the turn at 4:30pm, still far earlier than expected but as we rounded the 90-degree bend WHAM! The crosswind hit, and we slowed to a crawl with a rather nerve-wracking last few miles over a very exposed bridge. The gusts were so strong they sent the whole bike and us sideways and closer to the edge of the bridge and I was ready to bail from the stoker seat at a moment's notice!

North Battleford felt like a slightly rougher area, the motel I had chosen based on price had two double locking doors and a screen in front of the counter; the bar it was attached to seemed unusually rowdy for this time in the early evening. We were determined to make the most of an early finish though and ordered a curry whilst getting through the showers. With Stevie tired from a tough day of bike handling and also needing to treat and air his saddle sores, I volunteered to pick up dinner. Scurrying past a girl drunkenly crying at reception I braved the street, keeping my head down, moving fast and not making eye contact. Thankfully the town was quiet, and I retrieved dinner and made it back to the safety of the room to tuck in.

The next morning, we left early before anyone was up and skipped breakfast to pick up brunch on the road. My confidence was increased now, and I had an ambitious target for the day in mind, albeit with a backup plan, but as the wind was in our favour again we needed to make the most of it. However, any slight deviation from the wind being on our backs made the handling dangerous, with crosswinds threatening to push us into the traffic. The high speed was an added complication to holding the heavy bike, but we needed these miles desperately. We reached a sweet spot just over 25mph where the front panniers started to cause a speed wobble and needed to be swapped around to prevent this at our brunch stop. On leaving the roadside services it took us two attempts to get back on the main road as the wind was so strong it gusted us off the first time, it was more akin to sailing than bike riding!

Only slowing slightly for the traffic in Saskatoon we were on track for my stretch target of 159 miles to Davidson, with an average speed exceeding 20 mph for the day. We were delighted with our progress, but it had made me think of all the days where our average speed had been closer to half that and I had a worry niggling about our route back through Europe. I had planned this part based on the record-breaking route that Ian Walker took as part of his North to South record through Europe, as I knew he had thoroughly researched this route for speed instead of scenery. However, as we were landing in Lisbon and needed to get to Berlin, our route would only take in part of his and I had routed the bits at either end myself. I was aware this resulted in this "leg" having the most elevation per mile of the whole trip and as our resilience dropped and our bodies became increasingly weary, I was concerned we would be grinding along at snail's pace. It had suddenly occurred to me that I hadn't even considered Jenny Graham's route (adapted from Mark Beaumont's) and a quick check of the elevation showed me that there was quite a difference in height gained, and I wasn't sure what had possessed me not to look into this earlier!

I first came across Jenny Graham when some of the cycling ladies from the Peak District posted about a talk that she was doing with Emily Chapell at Buxton Opera house. Stevie and I made the trip up for the evening and not knowing quite what to expect were quickly thrown into Jenny's amazing story. Stevie already knew quite a bit about Mark Beaumont's rides but being less obsessed with round the world cycling at this point we didn't know the details of Jenny's ride. With tales of sleeping in drainpipes, defeating the elements, and being terrified of kangaroos and bears, I was engrossed in the dynamic Scottish lady's tale; told with the right mix of humour and modesty that made her feat seem all the more amazing. I was in awe and at this point couldn't even comprehend what it would be like to undertake such a challenge.

But something stayed with me from that talk, and it wasn't until a lot later that cycling around the world would seem less like something other people did and more of a challenge we could undertake. Once we'd decided to do it, Jenny was one of my first points of contact and I clearly remember waiting for her call in a pub in Horton in Ribblesdale in the middle of walking the Pennine Way. I was a bit star struck that she would actually take the time to talk to me and pass on advice, but she is such a down to earth character she gave me confidence in our plans. I followed up with a fair few random text and voice messages, especially around the intricacies of the Guinness Records rule book and when the opportunity to meet her in person, on the premise of getting her on my podcast "Stoked to be here" came up, I jumped at the opportunity to meet my heroine. And so, we ended up with my basic dual mic and phone recording the chat in a friend's hotel room above a pub in Inverness where she had kindly met me. It was fantastic to hear about her trip first hand and she was as much of a laugh in real life as she is to listen to on the many podcasts I had downloaded with her in. This may sound a little obsessive, but I have also listened to all of Mark Beaumont's cycling podcasts and a wealth of other round the world, record breaking and endurance cyclists (usually while on an off-road ride or run). Our start point of the Brandenburg Gate was a nod to her spectacular self-supported record-breaking ride, completing her circumnavigation in 124 days. She continued to cheer us all the way around and had some helpful tips when our routes aligned such as Mount Gambier not being a mountain! However, it was only when I got back and read her book Coffee first, then the World I truly understood what she had achieved. I had always been impressed by her self-supported ethos, which was far stricter than ours, where I knew she didn't accept any external assistance that wasn't publicly available. But, reading about the situations where it would have made the trip easier and smoother to bend these rules, which were self-imposed by her not Guinness, who doesn't differentiate between supported or self-supported, was truly inspiring in terms of integrity and determination. What Mark Beaumont achieved with his 78 days circumnavigation is an exceptional feat I am not sure will ever be repeated, but what Jenny achieved with no external support; a record still unbeaten even by a supported athlete is a whole different level for me.

If you're enjoying this book, I recommend you go and read hers!

So, having reassessed my options I was sat up late, trying to reroute over 1,800 miles through Europe on my phone. Stevie was suffering and exhausted, and we bickered when I tried to get his input. This was not the deal: I was meant to sort the logistics, and he was meant to be resting. It ended up with him saying he would route the way back up Europe himself with an atlas and road signs, but in the end after a few nights of me trying to stay awake long enough to get the route fixed I had something I was prepared for us to ride. It was definitely worth the effort in the long run and Jenny even gave us a tip about where not to get on the autobahn by mistake! I put a post out with an update as I knew that there were some members of the tandem club keen to track us down and hoped no one would criticise my poor initial routing and open up a whole can of imposter syndrome worms.

Day 131 – 145 : Davidson, Canada to Sault Ste. Marie, Canada

We hunkered down on the leeward side of the building to pack the bike. The wind had dropped slightly but now brought with it a bitter cold and we sensed our flying streak was over. We had been told, repeatedly, since getting to Canada that it would snow next week and annoyingly asked what we would do about it when it did. But it was hard to explain to people the pace we were moving at, and we had been told the same story for over a week now, so were taking the locals' weather forecasts with a pinch of salt; but today there was a definite drop. Having missed a parcel of warmer layers in New Zealand I tracked down a Walmart where I got a reluctant Stevie to stop to get some extra layers. I lucked out with leggings, mittens, and a wonderful thick snood that I could essentially hide my entire face behind. We weren't so lucky for Stevie though, and there wasn't a pair of thick mittens suitable in the whole store; he really suffers with his hands in the cold and seeing as it is him working the gear shifters, it was more than a bit disappointing not to find anything to keep the cold from his hands. But having taken enough time, we had to cut our losses and leave.

A McDonald's break down the road approaching Regina gave me the chance to assess our accommodation options, I had a few in mind given the previous days progress but wanted to keep our options open and hadn't booked ahead yet. We had a 14-, 22- and 44-miles option from where we had stopped at 95 miles. Having felt confident approaching Regina when we turned slightly coming out of the city it quickly became apparent, we weren't going much further at all. The wind had picked up significantly, rolling across the open prairies; it was now gusting from our left side. This at least meant we weren't being blown into the traffic, but with the gusts well over 30 mph, it was getting rather scary, and I just wanted off the bike. We got to a motel having risked not booking only to find it shut, the contact telephone number not working and no sign of life. Sensing another accommodation misdemeanour, I tried calling the middle-distance motel, only to have no answer there either and I was certainly not confident about reaching the stretch distance in these conditions. We also hadn't sourced any dinner and with the temperature dropping it would be a cold and hungry night to wild camp. In the end we ended up doing a rather dodgy back track seven miles back down the road to a hotel on the outskirts of Regina and with the cross-headwinds in our face I clung on to the back trying not to panic as we were severely buffeted. Stevie, as ever, did a fantastic job handling the bike in such tough conditions but it was a seven-mile ride I would never want to repeat.

We were relieved to get to a large hotel with plenty of space and a microwave in our room which allowed me to do the supermarket sweep for dinner. Feeling the need to recover and reassess a bit, I left booking the following night's accommodation until the following morning... but this turned out to be a mistake.

As Stevie packed the bike up, I tried first one hotel to find it full, and then the next on Google maps was a retirement home and the third possibly a pub but certainly with nowhere to stay. Panicking slightly, I looked at other options until I had a brainwave and tried Airbnb... only to get refused by the first host! There was one option remaining, but it took us off route: heading more north than east. Stevie was impatient to leave as we were losing time on the road, but it was too cold to plan this from the back of the bike so I plumped for it and did a speedy reroute, hoping they would accept my booking. We now had a 127 miles day instead of a 107 we had hoped for with a frustrating out and back which wouldn't count towards our total. It was the coldest day yet and Stevie had come up with a new hand preservation strategy, using his down booties on top of his gloves. I had lovingly bought him these in a striking hot pink colour, not anticipating they would be on show to the wide world beyond a tent... but they did the trick and helped insulate against the cold levers. Finally making a late start, we psyched ourselves up for the challenge, determined to make good time, despite the setbacks, and get in before dark. But it was not to be. Less than 10 miles down the road there was a twang and the gear cable had snapped. This wasn't the greatest disaster because we were carrying the extra-long spare that we would need to reach from one end of the tandem to the other, and it was a familiar fix for Stevie's mechanical skills. But it is not such an easy fix on the side of the road with close to zero temperatures and quickly numbing fingers. He got straight on it though, expertly threading the cable through and by pure skill managed to set the gears correctly on the first go, getting us back on the road in record time. It was easy to take for granted the diligence Stevie was putting into keeping our machine going and he regularly referred to her as the third member of the team. He was continually checking, oiling, cleaning and generally staying on top of the endless jobs that came from riding a bike day in day out for thousands of miles.

We set off again, but the going was tough, and it felt like we were getting more and more isolated as we headed north. I had a bit of a shock when a large grey lump on the road turned out to be a dead wolf, presumably victim to a road collision, but it made me even more happy not to camp. The accommodation had been confirmed, so it was now a race to get there in the light but not looking like one we would win with the crosswinds. It is miserable fighting against the wind when you know you can't win, and I had the Disney tunes on again for motivation. By the time we had got to the town, ordered and eaten burgers for dinner, and got washed and cleaned it was midnight; we decided to have a lie-in until 6:30 am the next day.

The next day's start was stiff and sore after the big push last night and retracing our steps felt like far too much effort at the start of the day. It was still bitterly cold too which made leaving the warm comfort of the Airbnb flat even worse: what I wouldn't have given to have had a day of R&R there. A remote café served us plates of eggs and pancakes to raise our spirits and one lovely lady offered us a room for the night, but it was far too early to stop. Another man repeatedly warned us about the cold and that "it was a very long way" to where we were heading, seemingly unable to comprehend how far we had come already.

The endless expanse of the prairies was getting to us a bit, tired as we were and with nothing on the horizon for miles, it wasn't making for stimulating riding. We did make it to Yorkton in time to go glove shopping for Stevie again and found him a thicker pair of gauntlets for the continual battle of hands versus cold. Little did we know this was only the start of the cold weather and running the forecast through Epic Ride Weather (an app that maps the weather along your selected route, showing wind direction and the expected temperature and rainfall for the time of your ride amongst other things), we had a "feels like" temperature of -10°C to start, barely hitting 0°C at the peak of the day. All the layers went on and I was bundled up on the back and well hidden behind my snood. It was completely dry though, with no hint of snow or frost but somehow this made the temperature feel sharper. A minute with hands out of the gloves and we lost feeling in our fingers. Finally, we hit some trees which thickened into a forested area, small lakes were dotted along the roadside, and to distract myself from the weather I watched the beaver lodges carefully until I was rewarded with a loud plop and saw a semi-submerged head creating a wake through the water. No chance of getting a photo in these temperatures but I was still delighted to have seen a wild beaver!

Diverting north had made me lose track a bit, so when I realised the time zone had changed again as we entered Manitoba, it was a blessing and a curse because it was now light until later, but also, we had lost time that day.

This part of the world felt very isolated, and we set out on mostly empty roads the next day into the freeze again, Stevie was suffering on the front as we now had a headwind too and he was soon having to pull over to get his down jacket on. It was a worry as we didn't have any layers left so barring wrapping ourselves in sleeping bags there was little more we could do against the cold. It was sapping the strength from us so when the café we had been relying on didn't exist, or at least it did but in a different location (I had checked it on google maps and reviews on Facebook to ensure it was current and open), we were in a pickle. We at least had some supplies from a tiny roadside store, but trying to eat on the side of the road in these temperatures was not an inviting prospect and with Stevie struggling to stay warm I knew I had to keep him fed.

There was a strong Ukrainian influence here and we passed row upon row of cemeteries, peaceful and austere to match the weather. The relief of finding an unexpected café was immense and hot food and drinks gave us hope we could continue into the icy temperature which didn't feel like they had increased a degree all day. The sleepy town of Winnipegosis was our destination, and I feared another accommodation disaster as it was so quiet, but we managed not only to get a bed but be in time for wood fired pizzas in a proper sit-down restaurant. Stevie wasn't as happy, preferring the solitude of a room and able to air his sores, but I was delighted to sit down in a social setting, even if we were the only ones there.

I had a sense that we couldn't rely on facilities now, so we were prepared the following day when the first stop was 65 miles down the road. The wind was in our faces again and this was made even more frustrating as this was part of the route that I had adjusted to add distance, so we were now heading south, but still into the wind. The 65 miles gave us some focus and as often happened when things got tough, when we had a goal, we knuckled down as a team and strove towards it. The reward was a double sandwich and soup for both of us, followed by cake and then M&Ms given to us by the kindly café owner (who was probably worried we were starving to death having scoffed so much food!)

The wind swung to crosswinds, but the light was dropping rapidly, I at least felt confident we had booked accommodation online so had a bed for the night, but it would be a tough roll in to get there. It felt absolutely isolated and the sun set gloriously over the lakes and forest until the last glimmer was just visible over the water as we rolled up to the pre-booked lodge... only to find no lights on and the door locked.

I couldn't believe it.

This trip was starting to feel more like a 'finding accommodation challenge' than a cycling challenge and as much as we hadn't planned on being so reliant on a bed inside, the state of Stevie's derriere and the temperatures were necessitating nights under a roof- not to mention the bear risk. I tried all the doors, attempting to stay calm, then tried the phone but to our dismay could just hear it ringing behind the shut bar. The website said the bar was open until 8pm (I had been banking on getting dinner here too) and it was only 8:05pm when I checked. There was nothing and no sign of life. Stevie went to scout out a wild camp spot. I was reluctant to give up though; I knew he needed the recovery more than me and a cold night in the tent would do nothing to help us make good progress the following day.

Wandering around the back of the building I happened upon an unexpecting labourer staying in one of the rooms. He was very helpful, even offering to shoulder barge the door to the room we had booked or set the fire alarm off as this seemed the only way to get in touch with the owners. We politely declined and were just preparing to settle down in the corridor which had been left open, and was at least warmer than outside, when another man stuck his head out to see what the commotion was about. He was extremely distressed to hear about our situation and kept saying, "Well what are you going to do? What are you going to do?"

This didn't entirely help my attitude to the situation and I was resigned to make the most of the corridor, but then in a great act of altruism the new man declared he had a spare bed in his room, and we should sleep there. He would certainly not have us sleeping in the corridor!

Feeling slightly apprehensive about sharing a room with a stranger, we could hardly tell him the corridor was a luxury compared to some of the places we had stayed, so we graciously accepted. It turned out Dave was a food safety inspector, on a work trip to inspect various establishments in the area and was able to give us a rundown of where was safe, or not, for a 50-mile radius. He also generously offered us some fried chicken he had in the fridge and was able to assure us he had inspected the premises it was cooked on himself, so perfectly safe. We only had a few other leftovers for dinner so were grateful for a bit more food and he was extremely interested in tales from our trip, but after a long day we were fading fast and soon squeezed into the smallest double bed ever. Dave had warned us he often fell asleep with the TV on and got up early, but what he hadn't made clear was this meant the TV was on all night and the volume then went up at 5am! Earplugs and eye masks went some way, but we spent the whole night feeling vaguely uncomfortable and not relaxed about intruding into his space, so it was a very groggy start the next day. It was bitterly cold again as we set out into the endless rows of silver birch trees, only glimpsing small sparkles of water through the woods as evidence of the massive lakes that were surrounding us. We were finally beelining it to Winnipeg, having diverted to gain some mileage, but the forecast wind behind was proving slow to turn and it continued to feel like a struggle. When it finally turned late in the day, we were keen to make the most of it and made what felt like a relative sprint to the biggest piece of civilisation we had seen for days. It felt like a milestone and a huge relief, and I celebrated by over-ordering an Indian takeaway and some blueberry flavoured beers, which seemed to be the local speciality.

In complete contrast to the previous few nights' accommodation, this was a busier motel and breakfast was included, but as always slowed down our progress getting on the road the next day. It is always a Catch 22 of whether starting on a full belly keeps us going further or whether the faff of waiting for food and delays in packing up actually sets us back; I suspect the latter.

It was surreal to be surrounded by skyscrapers instead of trees briefly, but we were soon out of the city and on the Trans-Canadian highway, which sounded like a promising way to get across the country; there was even a "Centre of Canada" sign which made us think about how short and long it felt since seeing its equivalent in Australia. The roads started out flat but then became more undulating as we passed small lakes, but we pushed on to make the 6pm check in at the next motel. Greeted by the resident deer we had a friendly welcome from the staff too and having a rare moment of feeling like we weren't in the race in a bustling pizza restaurant that evening, our spirits had risen somewhat after the tough times in the prairies and the endless flat forested roads after.

It was a relief to be on rolling roads again and I was delighted to be sneakily trying to peer around Stevie's back to see what was around the next bend. We were treated to more diverse forests than the endless birches; rocky outcrops, and shimmering lakes as we had reached the Canadian Shield, a massive rocky plateau in the centre of the country. It had been just the boost we needed and were delighted to get to Dryden by dusk. It was a small quiet town when we arrived and Stevie, desperate for rest and saddle-sore recovery, was quick to go through the shower and to bed. I decided the easiest thing was to venture out to find our supper and spotted the nearest supermarket on Google maps and set out on the dark streets. It was silent on the streets, and I felt the need to stay aware of my surroundings; the walk was longer than I anticipated and I jogged in my flip flops, without trying to look like I was in a rush. Stevie had been waiting anxiously when I got back but I'd been reluctant to have my phone visible in the night to let him know my progress. It was another instance of the nightly dilemma of how to get food: eating out was not practical due to an expense, saddle sore recovery and time, and we were eating lots of unhealthy fast food in the day so didn't want too many takeaways at night. By going to the local supermarket I could buy what we fancied and we could stay inside the motel room that evening and stock up for breakfast the next day. There was often somewhere to buy groceries within a mile or so, but on foot this was a long walk there and back after pedalling all day. It was a relief that night when I got back and shut the motel room for the night.

Opening the door, the following morning was not a joy: it was raining. We had almost forgotten it could rain with it having been completely dry since landing in Canada, even with the bitterly cold temperatures. But now we had a distinctly set in drizzle. To dampen our spirits further I had found out the ferry from St. John's we were due to take across Fundy Bay was closed for maintenance on the day we were due to travel, and I would need to do yet more rerouting. I could have felt bitter that all the hours and days spent on the route prior to the trip were going to waste but actually, I was a lot quicker at drafting routes than I had been and much better practiced at spotting flaws in the programmed route Komoot and Ride with GPS came up with.

We were back in the wilds again too and it took 65 miles to get a footlong from Subway before ending up at a very isolated motel where we were the only occupants. Once the rain had cleared the views were stunning though and with no Wi-Fi there was little that I could do about rerouting, so had a quiet night. The next day was to be a big push to Thunder Bay as with facilities becoming sparse again, we needed to keep an eye on our progress to ensure we found accommodation each night. The weather, although damp, was much warmer though and I started to think that camping would open up more options in terms of where we stopped and our daily distances. Just about to bring this up with Stevie as we left the last petrol station for the day, I had a shock when I saw a large lump of black fur on the side of the road. The young black bear was tagged in both ears, and I suspect had been out raiding the bins before being fatally hit on the road. We quickly decided that despite the cost and inconvenient distances, we would rather stay indoors from now on; it was a shock to see a bear in real life, even though it was sadly dead.

A big push into the headwind that had us arriving late in Thunder Bay, made even later by another time zone change. Trying to save money I had not booked the most expensive hotel and this backfired fairly quickly with a room that smelt like a damp Alsatian might be residing under the bed. I got to work on rerouting and Stevie worked on the bike for its final change of the crossover belt of the trip. It made for a late night, and it barely felt like we'd gone to bed when the alarm went off, followed by a clap of thunder; a horrible irony of being in Thunder Bay!

Although we'd already ridden through many thunderstorms this trip, getting out of bed exhausted, to get soaked in another one, was just too much of a stretch that morning, so we rolled over and reset the alarm to allow the storm to pass. When the rain had finally stopped battering the windows and settled into a drizzle, we had 120 miles into a headwind to our planned accommodation option dilemma... the only other option was a mere 70 miles down the road, nowhere near the distance we needed to do. But we had to be realistic about what we could achieve and with the increasing lethargy as the trip went on, we knew we would have to cut our losses and our day short. Even skipping the inspiring Terry Fox memorial on the way out of Thunder Bay. The rain was quick to come back as we reached the shores of the immense Lake Superior. I used what might be the worst public loo in Canada. We were struggling with the motivation to ride, and had a couple of rare quiet minutes admiring the vast expanse of water.

We both agreed that we would stop early and hopefully have tailwinds tomorrow, but the ride was still a stiff one with one unhelpful man at a village store on route refusing to believe we were out riding in the windy wet weather and repeatedly telling us we were mad: this didn't help matters and it was a good thing we were stopping before our sense of humour failed entirely. An annoying amount of faffage ensued, trying to get dinner, before heading to the motel to dry everything out, refresh, reroute and rest Stevie's knee which had been playing up a bit. Every heating surface in the room was quickly covered in drying kit and I made the mistake of putting my Exustar cycling shoes on the radiator – a simple error, but I was tired and couldn't bear the thought of soggy feet in the morning. It should have been no surprise when the glue had melted, and they needed to be taped together in the morning!

It was a dark start that morning to try and make up time and distance, but there was something more positive about riding into dawn than dusk. Lake Superior was as impressive and seemed even bigger than the day before with waves breaking on the shores. The rolling route took us up and down and we eventually stopped in the native community of Pays Platt, which was an interesting experience because being British we are not used to having an aboriginal population and culture to consider. We were slightly off put by a man who stopped to fuel up and told us the familiar story of "It would snow next week and what would we do then?" He seemed unable to grasp that we would be hundreds of miles away and we had to agree to disagree that we would survive the blizzard he was sure would come.

The dark mornings were to become the norm now to try and avoid riding tired in the dark at the end of the day. With sparse facilities and lots of places closed for the season, I was constantly checking our resupply options and worrying about where we would eat and stay, I even convinced Stevie to buy a thermos bottle, concerned we weren't drinking enough of the icy cold water on the bike. An A&W burger restaurant was a real treat.

The maximum distance I found between facilities was 100 miles and things were as sparse as the Nullarbor desert, something I hadn't truly anticipated. Woodland wee stops were accompanied with me frantically scanning the trees for bears who might catch me going wild and the Thermos was a welcome addition as the temperatures plummeted again: but thankfully no snow.

Lake Superior was endless, but beautiful; tough riding, but scenic, with granite crags and what seemed an ocean with sandy beaches glimpsed beyond the pines, often sparkling in the sun belying the bitterness of the temperatures.

Finally, after four days in the wilderness after Thunder Bay, we came out the other side of the shield to Sault Ste. Marie.

Day 146–155, Sault Ste. Marie, Canada to Montmagny, Canada

We had stopped on the outskirts of the city and treated ourselves to a nicer motel and curry the night before, so were well set up to skirt around early the next day, being careful not to end up in the USA across the bridge without a visa. The scenery was changing again now, autumn colours were a lot more vibrant, and facilities were a lot more frequent which was a massive relief as it took the pressure off me a bit. A traditional breakfast of eggs, bacon and poutine at a roadside café cheered us up more. The traffic felt busier than we were used to and we were thankful for an official bicycle trail giving us more room: we hadn't seen much evidence of cycling in Canada, but this was probably more to do with the season and places we had been. It was a long day in the saddle to get to Spanish, but one of our regular followers pointed out that with the past few days' effort we were now averaging over 100 miles a day for the whole trip: a big win after the setbacks we had had in the first half and a massive reassurance that there might be hope yet of making the 180-day target.

We had an amazing amount of support on a daily basis around the world and far too many people for me to recall individually, but every single day there were people cheering us on online and it meant the world to us. I say us, but Stevie is not into social media and found it easier to be in his own bubble, so stayed blissfully unaware of most of it until we got back. Whereas, I lived a double life of daily suffering on the bike and trying to generate daily social media updates that were interesting, didn't just consist of us moaning and quite frequently omitted any information we thought might unduly concern close friends and family. Quite a large proportion of the followers were people we had never met or known before our trip. Tandem Club members Colin and Diane I had met virtually via my podcasts and Jane and John had come to our leaving do but both these couples were devoted in sharing our posts to Tandem Club members every single day!

Possibly even more impressive were the stats followers out there... It was only when we got back that we realised how many people had generated their own spreadsheets around our stats and mileage and one of the most dedicated statisticians was Peter Madley, the first one to point out the greater than 100 miles/day average achieved. Peter was much more on top of our stats than I was and had some great insights into our trip, as did other regulars such as Gerald Davidson, Andy Thomas, Michael Kennedy, Charles Kendall, Scott Bolton, and a whole host of others. Looking back at it now, I cannot believe the people that checked in on us day upon day, gave us messages of support and were truly along for the ride!

Today we were pushing to get to a place I had hoped to stay: Massey! I had in my head we would at least get hilarious photos of one "Massey" and one "Massey-Pugh" near the town road sign, but it was not to be, as leaving Spanish in the dark we entered a deep dank freezing mist that just wouldn't lift. When we got to Massey it was all we could do to dive into the services to get hot coffees and try and defrost poor Stevie's hands and beard which had suffered the worst exposure on the front. It wasn't the coldest we had been but, combined with the damp, ice was forming instantly on our exposed surfaces and we desperately donned layers in the service station loos. We had little choice but to head out again into the freezer, and it took until 11am for the mist to burn off leaving us immersed in a strange otherworldly light as the sun battled to shine through. Taking a back road to avoid the traffic quickly backfired as the road surface deteriorated into potholes and gravel and horrible linear cracks in the surface. Stevie's hands were still numb and incapacitated with several layers of gloves and there was little I could do to convince him that this should have been a reasonable route choice from the information I'd had from the maps. We were both hungry and tetchy by the time we got to Sudbury, and I was fantasising about what kind of takeaway I wanted most for lunch: surely not another subway, but maybe even a McDonald's would be on offer!

My routing thankfully avoided the busy centre, but this took us flying past a range of fast-food establishments as well and I couldn't believe it when Stevie didn't stop. Then we were back on more cracked and pitted back roads, and I was desperately trying to find a happy balance between these and the busier Highways; everyone seemed to be in a rush now, much more than we had experienced in other parts of Canada and a few close passes soured our mood more. Having failed to stop in Sudbury where there would have been facilities, Stevie was now desperately hungry, and I was frustrated he hadn't just picked somewhere earlier. We were rapidly heading out of town, and I sensed disaster if he ran out of energy and bonked (a technical term in cycling for sudden and utter exhaustion), and we were over 80 miles into the day without a stop.

I have never been so happy to spot a Tim Hortons as we left the edge of town, and a good feed went some way to improve our grumpy moods, but I was fed up with the continual logistical struggle (and having missed the opportunity for a McDonald's) and Stevie was suffering increasingly with his saddle sores and the niggling knee pain he had been getting. I thought I was sorted for the evening though as we still had a fair way to ride but I had pre booked an Airbnb, so I knew we'd have somewhere to sleep in what was yet another remote village. The hosts seemed lovely and had even offered to go to the shop for us when they figured out that we wouldn't arrive before it closed and there was nowhere else to get food for miles around. It was a long day (130 miles) but a thankful tailwind for the last stint and we rolled up a bit tired to say the least, after a bit of an emotional roller-coaster of a day. Tim welcomed us in, and it was obvious he knew a bit about cycling himself so was excited to hear about our trip. His wife Denise was lovely, and it turned out to be the couple's first-time doing Airbnb and they couldn't do enough for us. Having already got us basic supplies from the shops they immediately decided we wouldn't be cooking but joining them for a beef brisket dinner, washed down with a couple of beers; completely above and beyond what you would expect from Airbnb hosts! They were deeply interested in our trip and Tim brought out a wonderful retro custom-built bike he had to show off. I was delighted to have a chat and relax with someone outside of our immediate round the world bubble, not so much that I was sick of the sight of Stevie; more that it was just feeling so intense being in each other's company all the time with no link to the "real world" and it felt a modicum of socialisation did me the world of good. Not so for Stevie, I hadn't realised his knee was quickly seizing up from sitting at the kitchen table and being too polite to protest; the evening was not what he needed at all, it resulted in us feeling in rather different places when we got to bed.

Still treating us like royalty we had freshly baked bread for breakfast and still full to the brim "Foodland" bag on the back when we left, which would definitely see us through the next few days. Having made a good start as the mist burnt off a lot earlier this morning we were confused to be flagged down on the side of the road. Carrie and Len had been following us virtually and had decided to track us down in real life; the first people to cheer us on the road! This, combined with a pizza vending machine for lunch, was a real boost to morale as was rolling through Parry Sound with a myriad of little lakes, apparently each with its own beaver lodge.

I was nervous though, as we were in another Airbnb tonight and Stevie's tolerance for social interaction was still low. We had little other choice so I knew I would just have to do my best to make sure he got the recovery time and space he needed. His knee was, if anything, worse and becoming more of a concern. We caught Sue, or Barefoot Sue, as she is known, just on her way out for a swim in the lake! She is a wonderfully quirky personality, having written a book about the Camino Santiago and living up to her name by forgoing shoes entirely for decades: no mean feat in somewhere as cold as Canada. I thought it was a bit chilly for a dip at the time but have since seen pictures of her using an axe to dig out a swimming hole in the frozen lake behind her house. On hearing about Stevie's knee, she offered him her ice bath, but he wasn't convinced, so she instead came up with a topical CBD product. Leaving us to help ourselves to a delicious daal and rice for dinner we did our best not to devour the whole lot and I'm not sure if she regretted telling us to eat as much as we needed; another wonderful kind gesture and above and beyond expected Airbnb hospitality. We managed a better evening of getting Stevie rested and had a comfortable night, but our burst of social accommodation wasn't over yet.

Andrea had been in touch pretty much since we landed in Canada and was an avid tandem rider and follower of the trip. She had been insistent that we would stay with her as she was pretty much on our route and I had had to emphasise that the timings may not work out: but they had: we were 106 miles away.

We slightly shamefacedly put on two pairs of socks and cycling shoes in front of Barefoot Sue's glorious toes that morning and set out into much more reasonable temperatures than we had been having. It was Halloween and all the houses were decked out for the occasion, much more so than in the UK and it gave me something to distract myself from the worry about Stevie's knee and the third night of hosted accommodation on the trot having had our own company for so long. A lot of people were warning us off the main highways at this point, some suggesting we would be lucky to survive riding them! But for the sake of Stevie's knee, we needed as smooth a ride as possible, and although busy they usually had a good shoulder and were nothing compared to some of the scrapes we had had in other parts of the world. The rain set in for the afternoon and by the time we arrived at Andrea and Stephen's we were distinctly soggy but were cheered in from the road which was a novel experience. Being used to cycling in all conditions themselves, they knew exactly what to do with two bedraggled cyclists and newspapers came out for our shoes, stinking clothes went straight in the wash and we were soon showered warm and being fed yet more delicious home cooking. They had been following our adventures since our Land's End – John O'Groats trip in 2020 and had given us some valuable route advice then. We tried a series of potions and lotions for Stevie's knee too and, as much as we could have stayed up much later talking tandems, we resigned ourselves to get an early night to maximise recovery.

We had a bit of a fanfare to set off in the morning as it was day 150, hopefully only 30 days to go and we could hardly believe we had been on the road so long. With clean clothes and full bellies, we set off but were soon into some stiff rollers when we were convinced that Andrea and Stephen had guaranteed us a descent... but what a fresh legged experienced ultra distance cyclist would consider a mere blip, registered differently to a road weary tandem pair with one dodgy knee and over 30kg on the bicycle. The autumn colours were even more vivid here and wild turkeys ran out across the road as we dodged tiny black squirrels carrying nuts as big as their heads. A brief bakery stop had us meeting more riders: we had obviously entered realms where leisure cycling was more popular and one elderly couple called Jim and Mary were into their 70s but still enjoying a morning spin and were ecstatic to hear of our trip. We had to push on though, as I had booked a motel about 120 miles down the road and time was ticking fast. A lakeside ride helped pick up the pace a bit, but it soon became clear I had been overly optimistic and for the first time on our trip we would miss a night's pre-booked accommodation. I had a replan and then we settled for Belleville for a quiet night in and more rest for Stevie's poorly knee. There was a lot of pressure to try and catch up the mileage but I had to accept we would not make Ontario the following day. It was a guessing game how well Stevie's knee would be doing and how far we would make it; it felt like the race to Halifax was now on and the pressure of the flight was weighing on our daily distances. This was becoming an inevitability of our trip.

The weather was idyllic though and, aside from me sitting on some "poison ivy" when I went for a pee (it's a different plant in Canada and took me a while to figure out the burning rash on my upper thighs), a good day for riding. Stevie was doing a great job pushing on, but I knew he was suffering and in the motel room in the suburbs before Ontario I had to accept, we were definitely in a pickle with his knee. It was massively swollen and all the medications, topical treatments, ice, and elevation were not working: it was getting worse.

Looking like he had an extra kneecap on top of his normal one my heart sank: was this causing permanent damage? We both knew the cure was likely to be rest but this would surely take weeks and, even if we could afford a couple of days off the bike, this wouldn't be enough.

It was such a hard dilemma; we were so close and yet it felt like on the brink of disaster. I took a video and messaged our wonderful physiotherapist Simon, but the verdict wasn't good. He was concerned that the swollen bursa behind Stevie's knee cap was infected and would need sampling and antibiotics. I had a contact near Ontario so got busy asking them for suggestions of doctors and medical centres and also harassed Dr Rich again too for any suggestions; I was on the verge of sampling the swollen area myself with the sterile hypodermics and syringes I was carrying if it sped the process up. We just desperately needed to know what to do for the best!

In the meantime, another ongoing issue had come to a head too... In Canada, most beer bottles are twist caps, so unlike the UK, you don't need a bottle opener. But when it comes to cans of food, Canada almost never has a handy ring pull, so you need a can opener and we had not thought to bring one! Having risked severe lacerations opening several cans with the small attachment on the multitool I was getting fed up. When I found myself in the kitchen utensil aisle that evening and realised I had a basket full of yet more inaccessible cans, I couldn't resist. I knew it wasn't the lightest can opener available and if I was dedicated enough, we could probably have picked up a camping or travel one for a fraction of the weight, but I was tired and more concerned about whether Stevie's knee would explode than the extra grams.

The same could not be said of Stevie.

Prior to this trip he had dutifully weighed every item of his tool kit, making his own lightweight chain whip and cutting down a tension spanner to use with an adjustable wrench. His attention to the details had been extreme; carrying a large plastic handled tin opener was not part of the plan. I offered to compromise and relinquish it, as soon as I was confident that we could either access tins or do without, and this seemed to placate him somewhat; but the controversy gave me a perfect cover for the much more serious issues we were having with his knee. I firstly, didn't want to upset concerned friends and family by revealing the extent of the injury and secondly, did not want to open us up to what could be a massive influx of well-meaning but unfounded and conflicting advice by opening the floodgates of social media. So instead of feeling like I was covering up the distressing time we were having by writing innocuous posts for the socials, I diverted attention to "Tim" the tin opener and the ploy worked a treat, with someone even starting the #savetim! Misdirection a success, I could focus on the matter in hand and getting Stevie's knee sorted.

The following day we had been given enough confidence with the medical advice we had received to keep going. There was a consideration for stopping at a medical centre, but after the bad experience in Australia we had decided to bite the bullet and try treating Stevie's knee with the medications we had and cross fingers and toes it improved. It was a flat day to Ottawa and then along the river as we headed into Quebec. It immediately felt very different from the rest of Canada with a change in the architecture, lots of cyclist and bicycle paths not dissimilar to France and we got a great view of the parliament buildings as we sailed through the city. Tim was sticking out of Stevie's back pocket all day having had a near miss of being left for the hotel cleaners, and it felt like I was being taunted with the view of him in front of my nose all day. It was no coincidence that my shopping that night consisted of no less than four cans to open.

We lucked out with a spacious motel room that night and we tried everything to get the swelling down – ice packs from the shops, topical anti-inflammatories and heaps of pillows and cushions. The next morning, we tried to convince ourselves the swelling wasn't as bad, it was very hard to tell, but Stevie was bravely soldiering on. The spacious motel room was as good an excuse as any to do the last big bike maintenance jobs and get a bit more rest for the knee while we could. The last chain and cassette of the trip went on, jockey wheels were replaced, and Stevie generally gave our wonderful machine a once over. Doing all the maintenance himself was another big job and I am immensely proud his skill had kept us from needing any external assistance; and it saved us a lot of time and money as well. I took the time to finalise route options, check distances and try and anticipate the rest of the overnight stops in Canada. I was becoming more and more neurotic about making sure we had enough buffer distance, but also enough time to ride it, as I knew our options in Europe would be more limited. Finally getting on the road I didn't feel as stressed as I usually did by leaving late, more a sense of gratitude and relief we were still riding; 24 hours earlier I had been almost convinced we would have to stop for an undetermined amount of time for Stevie's knee to recover and 180 days would be well out of the window.

We accepted it would be a late finish and booked our motel just past Montreal that night, but it would be another big tick going past another major city. The weather was good and the roads along the river gently rolling through the sleepy French-Canadian villages and peaceful countryside made us feel like we were three weeks ahead of ourselves and in France already. It was certainly a culture shock to have to select to translate the touch screens in the McDonald's!

Dusk was setting as we reached the immense Jacques Cartier bridge, across the now much wider Ottawa River, to head through Montreal. Stevie was not impressed to be getting caught up into a city at this time of the day and I had hoped we had been more in the outskirts, but the skyscrapers and city lights gave it away as we approached. We barely gave any thought to the fact that we would be back here on a connecting flight in just over a week, so focused we were on each day's progress.

Finally navigating out of the city and to the motel in the dark we were tired but overall pleased with the day's effort and what we had achieved, but I had the longest walk yet to try and round up supplies. This time though, I enjoyed the warm night air on what felt like peaceful friendly streets, and had a good haul from a service station manned by what seemed to be a gang of teenagers, before wandering back sipping a beer discreetly.

The nice weather was still holding the next day, and we could almost remember what it felt like to be on holiday, except we still had to push the pedals. We deviated from the river and into farmland with a grain tower, which reminded us of Australia, and dairy cattle which reminded me of home. Large hydro-power stations were dotting this part of the route with thundering torrents creating energy to be captured for the nearby homes and businesses. There was a sense of calm in Quebec in contrast to the power of the river and we were still finding it more French than France. In one Tim Hortons a young lad leisurely rode in, had a chat with the staff, purchased a large box of doughnuts and rode off on his bright red trike to deliver them without a care in the world; it felt more like a scene from a local French patisserie than an international fast-food chain.

That evening we had a stunning descent back down the river, me in my short jersey sleeves, with the warmth still radiating from the ground. The fields were dusky shades of red, orange and amber and the summery feel was at odds with the Christmas decorations going up around. I felt a true sense of peace that was so rare on this trip, I tried to catch it in my mind's eye and hang onto it for if times got tough again. That evening we could have ridden forever, until the end of the Earth.

That night's stay was a quirky venue, up there with some of the best in Australia and New Zealand: a hostel in an old convent which could easily have inspired another ghost story. The tall grey building housed basic rooms, a formal reception area and a strangely modern and eclectic bar where a tattooed manageress spieled a torrent of what sounded like abuse in French at her hapless partner, to the point we feared we would not be getting a room. After about five minutes of the tirade, she stormed off slamming doors, and her partner turned to us and politely offered to show us to our room without any further explanation.

We didn't have to be asked twice.

Stevie's knee was now definitely showing evidence of being on the mend, but his saddle sores were a different matter and we suspected that the subtle changes in his seat position had set his knee off in the first place. He now had ulcerations on both cheeks, with exposed flesh open and weeping. A constant supply of barrier cream was needed, and we would have to pick up more that morning. Also, the local anaesthetic gel was essential for him to get on the saddle in the morning, but he would still sometimes scream in pain as the raw nerves made contact with the pressure points, and it was always a race once he had the gel on to get in the saddle before it wore off. Already in two pairs of bib shorts there was little else we could do to relieve his pain or help the sores heal when he needed to sit on them every day.

Crossing back over the river again that day we were set up for the last push north before heading east towards Halifax.

Day 155–158, Montmagny, Canada to Perth-Andover, Canada

Our spell of luck with the weather continued as we had blue skies and tailwinds blowing us up to Rivière-du-Loup. We watched with relief as the rainclouds raced ahead of us across the vast skyline and were pleased to see them disappear into the distance as we turned right and east for a steady climb up out of the river valley at last. The river was immense now, looking more like the ocean, and the views over the bay impressive. The climb went well and our luck was in as the wind followed us, blowing us gently uphill and I was feeling pleased we were on target for the day, especially now I had a set plan in mind of how we would get to Halifax over the next five days, potentially squeezing in a bit of extra mileage as well.

We gratefully started 14 miles of mostly downhill to our destination that night in Cabano and had high hopes of getting there in good time. Even a diversion for roadworks barely slowed our pace and it was a great end to what had been a really good day.

Until we went to turn the pedals, and nothing happened.

Being on the back I was confused as Stevie tried to change gear, but nothing seemed to be happening; I hadn't been paying attention to the bike at that point, my pedalling on autopilot, but now my legs were spinning too fast. Stevie pulled us over on the side of the busy road to check the bike and briskly went to work seeing what was wrong. Having given me no insight into his thoughts about what could have happened he straightened up and said:

"We can't ride the bike anymore."

It felt like a death sentence pronounced. Icy fear went through me, and I had so many questions I didn't know where to start:

What did he mean we can't ride the bike? Why can't we ride the bike? How do we fix it? Is he saying it can't be fixed?! Will we still make the flights? Is the whole ride over? How are we going to get to the motel? Will we have to camp? What on earth is so wrong we can't ride?

Before I could frame all those questions with the rising sense of panic I had, Stevie explained the free hub had gone. He said something about pawls and springs losing me quickly with the technicalities, but essentially the part of the bike that disengages and allows us to freewheel (let the wheel spin without the pedals spinning) and then re-engages when we pedal had broken; so we turned the pedals and nothing happened. We couldn't move the bike forward.

Our experience at staying calm in a crisis kicked in quickly and, first things first, was our own immediate safety. Down jackets came out, hi vis vests donned over the top and lights went on the bike as the road was too busy for our liking to be stood on the side.

Next priority was our safety ongoing: we needed somewhere warm to spend the night as it was now getting dark and the temperature was dropping. Food would be ideal too, but not essential. We had the option to camp and our sleeping bags should be sufficient in these temperatures, but it would not be the most comfortable with limited facilities.

Next on the list was the bike, not the record. She was our only means of transport, carrying everything, and we needed to get her safe and fixed. It was too soon yet to formulate a plan, but we knew we would need somewhere for Stevie to inspect the freehub and, more likely than not, some form of mechanical assistance. The replacement part itself was specialist and not something that a regular bike shop would stock.

And finally, there was the record, if we locked up the bike

and got a lift to the nearest town we were out of the game and equally if we didn't make more distance tonight our flights from Halifax would be jeopardised too. It wasn't our prime concern, but certainly cemented the decision we were rapidly coming to, to push on.

We had 11 miles left of the day, mostly downhill. Even if we walked most of the way we would be there in about three hours, but with some freewheeling hopefully much less. So, we did what we do best and got back in the saddle.

After a few miles of rolling gently downhill we were stopped at more roadworks and an irate lady managing the traffic yelled in French at us, our pleas (in French) that we didn't understand were ignored and she just repeated what she had just said; which we think was telling us we weren't allowed to ride on this road and it was too dangerous. With no way to explain our situation, even if we could pedal, and with nowhere else to go, we decided to politely ignore her and went for it the next time the traffic lights changed. Rolling as far as we could before pushing was working out well and we made steady progress downhill, walking for at least 3 miles and arriving less than 2 hours later than we would have been. It was a huge relief to get to a warm hotel room and I left Stevie disassembling the rear wheel while I went to hunt out dinner. When I returned, he had the freehub out and was able to show me the pawls inside which are tiny levers pushed out by springs to hold it in place one way and release when it turns the other. Three out of the four springs in the hub had completely disintegrated.

Stevie worked some more on cleaning it up and assessing the damage, he was amazed it had lasted so well with springs that must have gradually deteriorated and had figured out we must have been surviving on the centrifugal force holding the pawls out alone when the spring had disappeared. He cleaned it up, and figured out by using a bit of grease and oil to keep the remaining pawl moving freely, it could then engage as the wheel spun without needing the spring. This enabled us to see if we could limp a bit further with this hub in place, while we tried for a replacement. I was able to work my Google maps magic and was delighted to find a hardware shop next-door which would open at 8am. I also sent out a social media plea for anyone to help us sort the spare part we now desperately needed; there was no way we would make it to Berlin with the freehub in that state, but there was a chance we would get a little further.

Overnight the social media troops rallied, and I awoke to a flurry of messages of support and assistance. Pete at the Tandem Shop was on the case and ready to post a whole new back wheel out to Portugal, if only I could find someone to receive it. Andrea from a week or so ago was hunting around all of her tandem club contacts and our contact in Halifax was on the case as well. I had also sent messages to the manufacturer of the part, Hope International, and their supplier in Canada, to see if there was one in the country. Ironically, the closest one I could find online was in Vancouver, but then I started to get more information.

It turned out some poor gentleman at Hope International had woken up to a rather full inbox; all messages seemingly regarding some crazy tandem couple and a freehub... I should point out at this point, that we were testing their parts to destruction, and no one would normally ride a back wheel close to 16,000 miles through all conditions without planned service or maintenance, so it is actually amazing that the part lasted as long as it did!

Having obtained the grease and oil the next morning, and done the best we could, it was all we could do to get on the bike and hope it worked. And it did! I was still fieldling the logistics around the replacement and intermittently sending messages and taking phone calls on the back to try and see what was possible. Then halfway through the morning we had some fantastic news: the amazing people at Hope International were going to airmail the part to Halifax!

We couldn't have asked for a better outcome; if we could get it there and we didn't have a disaster in the meantime, it wasn't beyond belief that we could get the part brought to us and continue our trip abiding by Guinness World Record rules. The relief was immense, and I set about arranging for local bike builder Mark who was due to meet us at Halifax to accept delivery of the part.

We felt like we had turned the whole situation around and were back on track and the bike was even behaving for now too. It was brilliant news!

And then we got a message to say hurricane Nicole was going to hit.

Day 158–162: Perth-Andover, Canada to Halifax, Canada

We could barely believe it the next day when I got a message to say the freehub was already in Halifax and we couldn't thank Hope International, NRG Enterprises and Mark enough. It was 9th November, and we were due to fly out on the 13th; Nicole was due to hit on the 12th. So, nothing was a given and we were in spitting distance but yet again it looked like a dramatic finish to the leg. In contrast to a few days before I was now trying to shave off mileage from the route instead of adding it on and I had a sense of desperation about making the last flight on time. If we could just do that, we stood a chance of making the 180.

Our focus was set, after barely being able to commit to getting back on the bike in Malaysia and then weeks in Australia where we couldn't even contemplate an end point, never mind our ambitious 180-day goal we were now resolute. We'd both been through and were still going through so much, that to slip now would make it feel like it had all been for nothing and every time we had raised our game over the past five plus months meant nothing if we didn't race for a sprint finish now! I say sprint, over 100 miles a day never felt like a sprint.

The fatigue was real now. A lot of people ask us if we "got on" all the time on the trip, undoubtedly expecting tales of blazing rows and threats of breakup. In fact, it was quite the opposite, almost like we had lost the capacity for intense emotion... and I'm an expert sulker!

Stevie's temper was fraying more readily with the constant pain he was suffering from the saddle sores and knee pain, and I worried about his mental state too. We had both become introverted and drawn in on ourselves; almost as if any extreme of emotion would ruin the status quo and we just didn't have the capacity to cope with that. We functioned like clockwork robots, each doing their own jobs with a sense of routine that needed little interaction with the other person and we often operated in an automatic fashion. I tried to be empathic and caring about the trauma Ste was going through with the sores, but I was worn down and felt like I had run out of things to say; and there just wasn't anything to say, he still had weeks of suffering left. There was no intimacy, no closeness and very little expressed in the way of love and care; we functioned independently. The baseline of support and a shared goal was always there, but we slept apart trying not to disturb the other and cause more discomfort by changing position in the night. There we no hugs or kisses, no softness; we had been hardened by the road and it seemed the only way to the finish now, because any chink in the armour, any break to the routine and we could lose everything.

. . .

We had the wind behind us for a change, but it was an icy cold Northerly, reminding us we weren't out of the woods in terms of snowfall yet either, Nicole would bring warmer weather from the south, but even one day of snowfall could jeopardise everything at this point. We pushed on, playing a continual gamble of main roads, which were now busier, versus back roads which resulted in tree trunks across the road and a rather dodgy swaying suspension bridge. The next day was still bitterly cold and raining, but we didn't care too much anymore, as long as the snow held off and the bike held out – she was still running on a freehub operating by centrifugal force and just one pawl spring out of the four, but I was trying not to dwell on this.

Snacking on the side of the road we pushed onto Monkton that night and onto Nova Scotia: our last province in Canada. There were obviously strong links with home here with place names like Truro, Oxford and Colchester and it felt like another subtle shift in culture, like those we had experienced all the way across Canada. We were too tired for much reflection though and it was to be the second day in a row we didn't sit down all day (apart from on the bike obviously), having lunch hovering around the bike at a picnic spot with no picnic benches. I cracked out the Riesen chocolate toffees to try and give us a sugar boost, but it felt like we were fading fast. A bit of coastal riding felt very surreal, it had been so long since we had seen the sea, but the company of Lake Superior for so many days had helped us not feel landlocked. With the evening sun shimmering over the bay, it was pretty, but I felt distant and apathetic to the scene. The sun set as we climbed Folly Mountain, luckily barely a contour line compared to the Rockies, but enough to make us happy to descend down the other side. I had the Disney tunes on, and it felt like there was a calmness, and inevitability to the ride in the dark. With a big last push to Truro, we were within 45 miles of the airport, a distance I was happy with, given the storm. We were planning to get there as early as possible to minimise time battling the elements and try and get some rest and recovery. Not how I wanted the leg to end, and I was getting increasingly twitchy about ensuring we had the distance, but I was both grateful and desperate to be ready for the flight.

They weren't joking about the storm, and it was a significant effort to leave the warm, dry motel room to push through the final miles. The wind was in our faces as expected and the rain battered down relentlessly; thankfully Nicole was downgraded to a tropical storm by now, so we were relatively safe from extreme winds, but it was still not easy going. Waves of rain overcame us, and we could do little but get our heads down and try and believe it would be over soon. Finally, the airport came into sight, but frustratingly we had to ride three sides of the square to get to the entrance. We got in and couldn't register we had made it, there were still so many jobs to do, we took no time to celebrate and set about unpacking and preparing to dismantle the bike. True to his word Mark turned up with the brand new freehub and even a couple of beers which went down very well. Our next visitor was Dominic from Cycle Touring Life. Cycle Touring Life had been our very first sponsor and this had meant so much in terms of giving us a foot in the door and the confidence we needed to push our sponsorship further. They were suppliers of the frame bags and panniers for the bike with some nifty other bits and bobs like a bike specific multitool and then made an immense effort to help us get sorted after the accident in Malaysia... If this generosity wasn't enough, Dominic had come to take us out to dinner! We had hoped to stay with him after the ferry crossing but when this was cancelled, we couldn't route via him and I'd been sad to miss the opportunity to meet him. However, when he heard about our predicament, he was adamant he would come out to Halifax to see us! And he brought the essential bike packing boxes too. Forgoing the packing until tomorrow, we now had a short amount of time to rest and were delighted to be wined and dined by Dominic and his lovely wife Clare. Sitting and socialising in a restaurant that didn't do fast food felt like a complete novelty. It was just the antidote we needed to end the longest stint and we slept very soundly that night with the sense that everything was coming together.

A lie-in until 8am the next day was a complete luxury, but we were soon up and at 'em, packing the bicycle at the same time as switching the freehub. It seemed to take longer than ever to get everything in the two boxes for the last time, and when the airport shuttle almost refused to put the boxes on before the flight, we were becoming a bit frazzled. The check in process wasn't straightforward either and with a massive bill for taking the bikes as luggage we were not impressed when the security officer insisted that we unpack everything, because they wouldn't fit through the X-ray machine. Eventually we compromised and took a few large items out to allow her to see the rest and were given some tape to repair them again before negotiating security.

Back in Montreal in no time it was surreally busy, and we felt like we were in some strange nether world between flights. I had been trying to negotiate Stevie some more legroom, especially with the risk of his knee flaring up on the long-haul flight, but to no avail as it was an extra £1,000 to get him into business class. We resigned ourselves to doing the best we could in economy and eventually settled down on our last flight to the finish line.

Instead of a triumphant finish to the longest leg of our trip it was a cold and broken Hallelujah.

Vancouver
Day 20
11636
miles

Elmonton

The Rockies

The Prairies

Winnipeg

Canada

200mi

Sault St.
Marie

Ottawa
Montreal

Quebec

Halifax
Day 161
16295miles

121
122
123
124
125
126
127
128
129
130
131
132
133
134
135
136
137
138
139
140
141
142
143
144
145
146
147
148
149
150
151
152
153
154
155
156
157
158
159
160

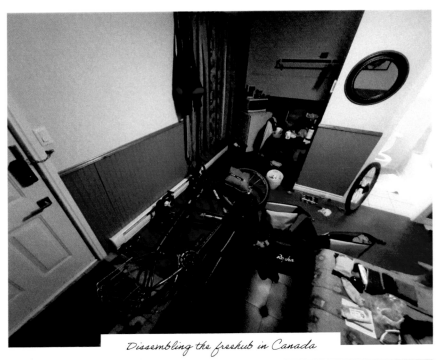

Dissembling the freehub in Canada

Tim the tin opener

Swollen knee in Canada

Booties on hands in minus 10 degree Canada

Endless praries

Full moon above Banff

waiting for the road to open Canada

Tough climbs Canada

As close as I got to a bear Canada

part 6: europe, return leg

Day 163–170, Lisbon, Portugal to Parentis-en-Born, France

WE STUMBLED off our final flight of the trip bleary eyed and not feeling well rested, and the immense relief at receiving the boxes of tandem safely for the final time was ruined when we had to have a debate with the customs officer as to whether the tandem was a used bike or not and whether we should be paying tax on it!

Stevie had the bike rebuilt in record time and it was a relief to roll out to some warmer weather into the streets and cycle lanes of Lisbon. Navigating through the city kept us on our toes, but once we got out into the countryside we started to fade fast, and jet lag kicked in as we stopped for emergency coffee at a petrol station. Trying to take a shortcut to Santarém we ended up on a steep dirt track and Stevie was less than impressed. It was not the end we needed for a long day; but the town was picturesque, and we found the hostel we had booked, down a sleepy street with instructions to let ourselves in. The shared kitchen was decorated with typical blue and white Portuguese tiles, and I found a feast of food in the nearby supermarket, delighted to have so much fresh produce. It was nice to be back in Europe, as it felt familiar and we were welcomed well on the tandem, with all the old lads sitting outside cafés giving us a nod and a wave.

The weather was variable the next day and we got a couple of soakings as we headed northeast and had the first significant climb for weeks; our tired legs groaning as we winched our way up. The jet lag was still getting to us, and we struggled with feeling dozy as we failed to find an option for a coffee in the countryside. Our descent was hampered by the rain, and we skirted Castelo Branco to try and avoid the traffic and pushed through to a small village on the other side, where I'd found a casa to stay in. Arriving later than planned the streets were dark and empty and we spent some time going up and down the cobbled back roads until we found our destination. The casa owner looked surprised to have two soggy tandem riders turn up so late and it seemed that this was more of a sleepy tourist destination than a pitstop for those on the road. He got us settled into a lovely stone walled room and we tentatively asked about options for food nearby: there were none at this time of night! Taking pity on us the casa owner said they had a small snack menu, and we could order from that despite the late hour, a relief to say the least.

The "light snacks" resulted in two large freshly filled baguettes and a platter of cured meats, cheeses, crisps, and more bread: a veritable feast and we even washed it down with a cheeky glass of port: when in Portugal...

Despite the clear skies the next morning, we were warned of rain to come by our dot-watchers and it made for a tough start on the road knowing it was only going to get worse. It felt like it was uphill all day, and this turned out to be the case and then to make matters worse I got thoroughly lost on some backstreets of a small town by missing the turn. A frustrating network of cobbles seemed to take us round in circles and we lost time and energy trying to rectify my mistake: it felt like the day was doomed. Finally, we climbed again in the drizzle up to the large blue EU sign reading España: we had reached Spain!

And then everything seemed to change as we had a downhill and sunshine as we entered country number 18. Our moods completely lifted; we practised our extremely limited Spanish (probably less than a dozen words) as we pushed on until dark to stop at a roadside motel. In complete contrast to the night before, this was very much a pitstop, full of local workers and drivers and it turned out our practice had been worth it as they spoke no English. The poor lad behind the counter looked terrified as we tried to communicate through Google translate, but we had soon negotiated a room and somewhere safe for the bicycle. Venturing back down to the bar cum restaurant cum café it was soon clear we were to be immersed in Spanish culture as the food offering was all tapas. Making an executive decision and using my best guess at what everything was I pointed at a range of dishes lined up and we soon had a table full of food; it was all brilliant and I was definitely getting used to European eating; we had had so many takeaways in Canada that this felt like a real treat.

It was just as well we fuelled up as the next day the rain was pouring down and the locals stared in amazement as we got on the bike in the downpour; we could hardly explain to them we weren't doing this for fun. It turns out the Spanish don't really do big breakfasts, so we were soon hungry by the time we got to Salamanca and with the rapidly expanding Spanish I was learning from Google Translate I managed to order us brunch. I hadn't expected Spain to be quite so Spanish and having to put so much effort into communication at this point of the trip wasn't something I had anticipated.

Fuelled up, we were good to push on to a massive milestone in our trip: our second antipodal point of Alejos. It truly seemed half a world away from Wellington in New Zealand and gave us the sense that all we needed to do now was get back to Berlin. The sunshine was holding up, and we were riding well through Valladolid to get to a hostel pre-booked in a small town on the other side. Arriving about 6pm my heart sank as there was no one there, no one in the restaurant attached and no one picking up the phone. Another accommodation disaster loomed...

Eventually a lady emerged looking like we'd just woken her up from a siesta and spieled a torrent of Spanish at me. I managed to get across that my understanding was limited, and we settled on communicating via Google translate, which seemed to be going well until she typed, "It is very disappointing you don't speak Spanish," onto my phone. Feeling a bit crestfallen I decided not to take it personally or try and explain that we couldn't have possibly learnt the language of every country we were visiting.

We settled into the room before venturing to the restaurant for what looked like it would be another wonderful meal. The place was relatively busy, they weren't serving food from their main menu until 9pm but did have a few tapas options. We picked a few of these to start with but they all seemed to consist of greasy chewy sausages and by the time we could order anything else we didn't feel like eating much, so had a bowl of chips and went to bed. The greasy food, which was so much worse than the last few nights', didn't settle well and I ended up losing my dinner in the early hours. Feeling drained and with little appetite after the poor meal the previous night, more rain made for a tough start. It was a complete emotional rollercoaster now, any high seemed to be followed by deep low due to our mental exhaustion and it was harder each day to maintain motivation. We knew we had to keep going until the finish line and couldn't afford to slip or take a break.

But when the rain cleared, the countryside was picturesque and a friendly café serving a carb feast of Spanish omelettes in huge baguettes helped us make progress through sleepy villages and quiet roads. Kites wheeled over ploughed fields and we drifted for a bit along the large plateau we'd climbed up to in the centre of Spain. It didn't last though as we watched the storms blowing across us. We were hit as we went through Burgas, piling into a McDonald's to layer up with clothes we had hoped not to need again after Canada, we got all the layers on and feasted on hamburgers while surrounded by hordes of teenagers. It was surreal to be sitting there shivering amongst the bright lights and noise, knowing we would have to venture out into the rain and dark again and descend into the cold night. We were dreading it and it felt like an insurmountable challenge to finish the day, tempted as we were by the bright lights of the hotels, of the city we were in. But we sucked it up and, trying not to shiver too much, got on the bike and pushed hard up the last climb of the day to warm up before descending. The last miles were nowhere near as bad as we had feared, and we raced trains on the adjacent railway and enjoyed a quiet road as the parallel motorway took most of the traffic. We had made great progress but arrived at the hotel late at 9pm, but this time the Spanish eating hour held in our favour, and we were able to get a delicious three course meal before collapsing into bed.

The morning light revealed a vaguely alpine-like setting and we grabbed croissants from the bar with the locals, determined to get an early start and finish. The first mission was to get up and over the climb to Vitoria-Gasteiz. The temperature noticeably dropped with the elevation, and we watched the thunderous dark clouds of storms roll by, followed by spectacular rainbows, hoping we would dodge another drenching. Winding around some large lakes it was slow going and we were losing the momentum from our head start, with the most significant climb of the day to go. It was frustrating not to be able to pick up the pace and see the daylight hours slip away. It felt like there was nothing we could do. The descent was then ruined by a poor road surface, roadworks and rain. Stevie was suffering badly, and we were having to push up the steeper climbs due to the excruciating pain from his knee. His hands were so cold and soaked he lost feeling and grip, making changing gears difficult and braking dangerous. Despite our intentions to keep pushing on we had to stop to warm up in a busy café and lost yet more time. It was now dark, and we felt like we had lost the day and still had so far to go.

More descending on busy roads in the dark was attritional and passing through towns of Saturday night revellers we felt disoriented and lost, amongst the noise and bright lights. The day was never ending, and the next challenge was plunging into a suddenly quiet and dark road that wound between river and mountain, too narrow for comfort, with bends and rolling hills making it hard to stay clear of the traffic. Every hill was exhausting, and we pushed and pushed to try and make our destination for the day, the rain soaking us yet again. It felt like a culmination of all the challenges of our trip. More town riding slowed us down at the last until finally, much later than planned we crossed over a large bridge and into France. We were shattered.

The last thing we needed was more accommodation problems, but that was what we got, with the hotel I had booked shut by the time we got there. I was so frustrated I could have sat down and cried; I was just absolutely fed up with the continual fight with logistics; surely, we deserved a decent night's rest after such a big effort! Finally managing to get hold of someone to let us in, we were on the top floor; Stevie was so knackered he didn't even notice I had had to revert to my newfound Spanish to communicate despite the fact we were over the border. The room was tiny and there wasn't enough space to dry our sodden clothes, but a quick Google gave me the hope I needed to venture out again as I'd found wood fired pizza. Jogging through puddles in the dark I ran up to the beckoning light of the pizzeria, so thankful that something might go our way tonight. I stood dripping at the bar in the rather nice establishment and to my delight two of the best pizzas I had had for months were soon served up. I dashed back to the hotel with my treasure, and they were quickly devoured before we passed out with a dripping kit hanging from every hook, lamp, and door frame, in the futile hope it might be slightly drier in the morning.

To begin with it wasn't and we awoke to grey skies and drizzle obscuring most of the bay, but we had a slow start having breakfast at the hotel and doing some maintenance on the bike. We felt a bit washed out after what felt like a dramatic end to the day before, so everything was taking twice as long. Our tardiness paid off though and the skies cleared to brilliant blue and suddenly we were at the seaside with seagulls wheeling and shrieking overhead. France had a welcome sense of familiarity; we had cycled in the country many times before and were more used to the routine than in Spain, where we seemed to have struggled with food service times. It was a Sunday, and feeling proud I still knew which weekday it was, we made it our aim to get stocked up before everything closed at lunch. We rode up the coast, shivering at the sight of surfers braving the swells, and through small villages and towns towards Biarritz.

The Sunday morning traffic was surprisingly hasty and we got a few scoldings for missing the cycle lanes that appeared intermittently, as if we should be able to predict their existence. Feeling a bit flustered by this we reached Biarritz feeling completely out of place amongst the exclusive hotels and châteaux. Trying to stay on the right side of the French drivers we opted for a coastal route with a cycle path and were then a bit put out to be shouted at and waved down... Grinding to a halt I was ready to defend whatever misdemeanour had been perceived in my very best French and then I realised that the shouts were of excitement and "SteLa!"

We had been off Wi-Fi for a good 48 hours and given the trials of the day before, I had completely forgotten that Charles from the Tandem Club, who had been following us avidly, had said he would arrange to meet us. Having failed to keep him updated at my end, it had slipped my mind, and I had assumed he had much better things to be doing than tracking down a couple of exhausted tandemists. I couldn't have been more wrong! As far as I could make out, he and his wife had extended a stay in the region, instead of returning home to near Strasbourg, to meet us and I felt terrible they had gone to such lengths when I had failed to reply to his last message. They were a pleasure to meet and had everything we could have wanted/needed but were determined not to hold us up. His wife had baked a delicious apple cake and we enjoyed some with a cup of tea, before stuffing our pockets full of the remains and fresh fruit. We wished we could have stayed longer and had a proper chat, but we were running pretty late into the day. Charles gave us some great tips for the roads ahead to help with our progress. We couldn't believe someone had put so much effort in to track us down and support us and it was a real boost to the day. Arriving in the sleepy town of Parentis-en-Born late into the evening I was delighted to find the pizza van still open, but then peeved that I had another night unable to connect to Wi-Fi: the distances and timing were critical now and I needed to ensure we didn't have any more delays or accommodation disasters in the remaining 10 days.

Day 170: Parentis en Born to the Brandenburg Gate, Berlin

10 days to go, 1,000 miles.

It all suddenly seemed doable... except we still needed to factor in "buffer" mileage too as we dared not risk coming short!

Making a big effort to be ready and packed, in time for the hotels advertised breakfast (which we had accepted via text message and was advertised on all the literature), we were more than a bit put out when the hotel reception was still shut up and there wasn't a 'pain au chocolat' in sight. Having to venture out into the dark and rain with nothing to get us going, the beckoning lights of the bakery were very welcome and we did our best to eat quickly and brave the elements again. We were set for a day of deluge, but it brightened a bit, as did my mood, when we found yet another pizza van on the outskirts of Bordeaux and stopped for a pavement picnic. The carbs fuelled us well and we pushed through the rest of the day, with the roads getting smaller and quieter, before veering off the main road to a little farmhouse run by an English couple. As we rode up to an unlit building and closed gate, I feared the worst again, but Logis du Poirier was a delight and Ian and Jo gave us a tremendous welcome despite us being rather unusual guests. The room was beautiful, the shower pure bliss and with an endless supply of tea and coffee we felt truly spoilt. With the gift of a demi-bottle of Bordeaux we celebrated getting to three figures of distance left and had one of those extremely rare moments of contentment amongst the increasing stress of nearing the race to the finish line.

The next morning, we struggled to get on the bike; as much due to the immense breakfast we had consumed, as to our tired legs and poor Stevie's saddle sores. I could have stayed there for a month but the incentive of being able to finally stop, in hopefully less than 10 days, was a motivator. We rolled out through the countryside as thunderstorms rolled overhead, miraculously we seemed to be dodging them amongst the swirling winds and ominous clouds looming above with occasional claps of thunder to show us they meant business. At one point I had an unusual sensation from the backseat and looking down realised we were running a flat: it had been over 13,000 miles since the last puncture so I suppose we were overdue, and we cannot praise the Schwalbe Marathon Mondial tyres enough! Stevie as ever did a quick job getting it fixed, but not quick enough to avoid a drenching. We'd seen hail stones accumulating in the gutters, which we were relieved to have avoided, but were still pretty miserable to get drenched and were well into dusk by the time we got to Chavigny for the night.

Trying to decide whether to check into our hostel or order food first, I plumped for buying a late-night kebab and hoped the hostel owner would hang on for us. Navigating around the complex of old town streets it took some finding and then we were in a tiny attic room beside the grand wall of the castle. There was no heating, and the stay was uncomfortable in what would have been an interesting quirky room under different circumstances. The hostel owner suggested we might like to enjoy coffee in the herb garden in the morning and we didn't have the heart to tell him we would have to leave before dawn.

The morning bells rang out around the town, and we gratefully descended on one of the first boulangeries to open, having not really had our fill of takeaway the night before. We thought we were good for most of the morning, but somehow found ourselves pulling over for more baked goods and coffee, not too far down the road. We'd had a soaking early on and morale was becoming a battle every time we got wet. As we approached Tours a cyclist from the other direction gave us a massive "Whoop!" and pleased, yet bemused by their enthusiasm, we rode on.

I had a sneaking suspicion though, so was less surprised than Stevie, when the cyclist looped back around to come alongside us: Anisa is a very experienced audaxer and ultra-distance cyclist and we knew her from other ridiculous exploits such as All Points North and a range of audaxes. I had spotted from her social media that she was on a ferry to France and, ages ago she had suggested she might meet us, but I had never expected her to actually track us down!

We had intentionally not encouraged anyone to ride with us as our pacing is often different from solos, and the distances we cover are great with few stops; it would have put unnecessary pressure on us to try and have a normal cyclist along for the ride. Anisa is very much an extraordinary cyclist though and I knew she would understand our needs and would be more than capable of looking after herself on the road. So, when we took our lunch stood next to the bike or dived into the bushes for a pee, she didn't bat an eyelid at our feral traits and had some goodies to share. She even lent us her rear light as ours was fading fast. She kept pace easily as we picked up the Loire Valley and with the wind behind us it made for a cracking evening, and I was delighted by the company. Parting ways in Mer, Anisa dashed off to get a train. We did a supermarket sweep before having the night ritual of pannier explosion in a very spacious and modern apartment in the town.

The next day our plans for a cheeky McDonald's takeaway were foiled by midday opening on the outskirts of Orleans, so we settled for getting our heads down, riding the outskirts of the city before some tedious, but necessary, main road bashing to make progress. Then, in complete contrast we headed to a more minor track and through Rambouillet, a nod to the famous Paris-Brest-Paris run from there every four years. Stevie needed more local anaesthetic gel for his saddle sores because he now had a good routine for numbing the pain before getting on the bike, he was reliant on the anaesthetic, and it looked certain he would spend well over a month of the entire trip reliant on this analgesia to be able to sit on the raw ulcers that had developed on his posterior.

Stocked up on a range of pharmaceutical goodies, we dodged school run traffic before embarking on the last climb of the day in the dusk. We were going steadily when Stevie suddenly let out a yell, I jumped a foot in my stoker seat. There was a crunching sound. I couldn't figure out what had happened at first and then turned back around to see his lovely Exustar sunglasses crushed on the road – he had dislodged them and then we had ridden over them. He was gutted they had made it so far to be crushed now. Safer on the backseat and with less sunlight to worry about now I donated him mine to see us through the rest of the ride.

The hills kept coming the next day and looking at the gradients I opted to take the long way around rather than risk a walk: we'd had enough trouble lifting the bicycle out of the steps of the picturesque gite that morning! At our first café stop we noticed the World Cup was on and we had been so immersed in our own little world we hadn't even realised until this point. Slowed down significantly by traffic through Amiens I was constantly assessing and updating our route to try and keep things as smooth as possible, but some areas were just unavoidable, so it was yet another late finish. We expected to roll in the dark every evening now, despite leaving at or before dawn, but it was a real struggle to keep the night riding to a minimum and the rest and recovery time off the bike was a constant battle to maintain as a priority.

Leaving another luxury gite the next morning we were cornered by the owner's elderly mother who was very sweet and tolerant of my awful French, but convinced we couldn't be riding 100 miles a day, even when we wrote the figure down! Feeling ever so slightly put out by the scepticism we were quickly into thick mist. We were entering the Somme region and it looked as I had envisaged from school; misty, dank, muddy fields interspersed tragically with endless rows of graves. A sobering reminder of the history of the area. Particularly poignant was a message on an Australian Cemetery of "We stand with Australia" and knowing exactly how far away Australia was having ridden it, it felt dreadful that those had lost their lives so far from home.

A sleepy Saturday morning in the small village had us wondering where we would get supplies, when of all things, we came across a pizza vending machine. Delightedly keying in our order, we were rewarded with two pizzas posted out to us a short time later; not the pinnacle of Italian cuisine, but a very welcoming finding that was a 24-hour supply of cheesy goodness.

The mist persisted throughout the day, and we made it into Belgium almost without realising as there was no "Welcome to Belgium" signage, just a subtle shift in culture and architecture. The pace felt faster, the signs were brighter and there was definitely a more hectic feel compared to the relaxed state of France. Everyone seemed in a rush, and we dodged the melee across a poor road surface covered in potholes and then onto equally poor backroads. Needing to stock up for dinner we had the weirdest supermarket experience of the trip, with a place that looked more like an Ikea warehouse, with a central refrigerated room for cooled items, tiny tasting glasses of prosecco and then a checkout where one person scanned your goods and another took payment, but they didn't accept visa cards! Completely phased by the whole experience we luckily had enough cash, but I had certainly had enough of culture shocks by this point and we still had five miles to go.

The Airbnb I had booked was off the main road, but the best option I could find. This would have been fine if we hadn't been launched straight into a cobbled section that would rival the gnarliest on Paris-Roubaix! We settled for a mix of dismounting and rolling when it got too severe, genuinely worried about damaging the bike, but things only got worse as the cobbles petered out to an unpaved road and this petered out to a track and the track led us to what looked like a public footpath, with the lights of what I was sure was our accommodation, visible across two fields. Stevie was livid and tired, but we had no choice but to backtrack and take the long way around; weighed down by the evening's shopping. The roads leading in were still cobbled but at least rideable, but with a final climb as a kick in the teeth, to a small farmhouse with an apartment. I set about rustling up a curry in the sleek kitchen as quickly as possible to try and appease my poor exhausted husband and we ate in silence before he collapsed in bed, and I tried to wind down in the bath and not dread the cobbles back to the main road the next day.

Things seemed somewhat brighter in the morning and we had rested and eaten relatively well despite another late night. We decided to skip the cobbled section and pottered down to the metalled road (and, yes, we didn't start Strava until that point!), mooching back to the route in the drizzle. Trying to navigate on and off bike paths and up and down little climbs sapped our energy and we soon pulled over for a snack; seemingly living up to all the cliches of Belgium, we ordered plates of waffles not realising we got a mini waffle with our coffee too. Feeling bolstered a bit by the warmth and calories, we continued to try and navigate the cycle network of Belgium where the cycle paths seemed to come and go and weave on and off the pavements. Crossing one junction a car slowed down, honked their horn and someone was gesticulating angrily at us and shouting. Concerned we pulled over, confused as to how we had caused so much upset. A man got out waving some sort of ID card and spouting a torrent of angry Flemish (or at least we assumed it was Flemish because we didn't understand a word!). Finally able to get this across to the very angry man (who we also assume was some sort of off duty police/ traffic officer) he exclaimed:

"Do you want to die?!" in a dramatic fashion. We suggested we didn't but were still confused as to whether this was a question or a threat!

He pointed out that we had run a red light, not for the main traffic, but for the cycle path at a side road. We hadn't even seen the light and were moving with the main traffic as we were accustomed, but he was not impressed by this excuse.

"Next time I hope the car hits you so you will learn!!" He proclaimed, "You have money? It cost €272 for this mistake!!"

It was all we could do to say we were extreme sorry and no, we were not carrying that amount of Euros. Either sensing it would be more hassle than it was worth to try and arrest us on a Sunday afternoon, or he was after making a quick backhand buck from unsuspecting foreigners, we will never know, but eventually he drove off leaving us feeling stunned. At the next set of lights, we spotted our mistake: the bicycle light was definitely there, but at the same height as the main traffic lights, so well above our eye level and still green with the turning traffic so not making us any safer (we felt). We were completely put out by such an extreme and unwelcoming reaction to two people innocently riding a tandem and had made an honest mistake in a foreign country. I had had enough of Belgium by now, similar to Spain it felt unfamiliar, and we were at the limit of our tolerance, so it was a relief to push onto Holland that evening. Having to stop to adjust the brakes due to the persistent damp, set us behind yet again and it was dark by the time we reached the border.

Holland lived up to its cycling friendly reputation though and although we couldn't appreciate any views in the dark, we did appreciate the wonderfully sensible, straight, and easy riding bike paths which had us flying through the country at decent pace. Our mission for the evening was to get out of the other side and into Germany: back in the country we started, and we pushed hard to make it that night. From experience, I was aware that food options would be limited in Germany on a Sunday night, and passing through Venlo I convinced Stevie to pick-up late-night kebabs as we had the key code to let us in to our pre-booked accommodation later. Again, a problem with our visa card, which had worked perfectly everywhere else in the world, had me jogging around the town trying to find a cash point. By the time I had returned we devoured half of our feast right there, resigned to another late finish and too little sleep.

It was another drag in the morning, every day it was seeming harder and took longer to get on the bicycle; especially because it was raining again. We should have felt excited, triumphant, and delighted to be in our last country and approaching the finish line, but we were just knackered. Broken and exhausted. The days on the bike were getting longer and longer and it felt like we were running out of steam, that the ordeal would never end, and the challenges everyday brought were just too much for us to take emotionally and physically. Our friends and family were getting excited but the last thing we wanted to hear was: "you're nearly there!" because we still had so far to go... and that point was about to be proved big time!

Back to a maze of cycle networks, where there was no tolerance for us being in the wrong place, combined with a treacherous combination of tree roots, wet leaves and Stevie's sodden gloves trying to work icy cold levers, did nothing for our moods. Towns and traffic lights slowed us down, the rain was incessant, and we first needed to stop for more local anaesthetic gel for Stevie (a joy to describe in my basic German) and then to adjust our rapidly wearing brakes again in the wet conditions. We felt shattered already and checked the distance: 13 miles. We had made next to no progress.

Stopping for bockwurst and coffee to try and help us spring into action, we tried to pick up the pace, be smoother, more efficient, get into the race; but the incessant rain wore us down and we stopped again, chilled and hungry at 45 miles. It was 3pm and we had 70 miles to go.

There was little leeway now. Our nightly stops were aligned to make our 180-day target in three days' time. Everything we had worked for the past six months on the bike and 18 months preceding hung in the balance of a few days' performance. This fact didn't make it any easier and it seemed we had finally reached breaking point, having pushed too hard for too long without enough rest and recovery. The abysmal weather and lack of daylight was just making it too tough, but we just couldn't relinquish our goal having literally risked life and limb to come this far.

Despite this sense of futility, we got back on, initially determined to do whatever it took to make our daily target. Skirting around a big lake as the light started to fade a grand hotel taunted us with brightly lit rooms and the promise of warmth and comfort.

We push on.

Further up the road the surface deteriorated and the brakes ground with debris from the road. Our pace slowed and Stevie got colder still, already soaked through. Despite three pairs of gloves his hands could no longer sense the gears or brakes and tremors from his body shook the whole frame.

We are in a pickle.

It is one thing to invest all the energy we have into beating a world record, it is another to risk our own health and the decision is heartbreakingly clear: we must retrace to safety.

We had ridden 55 miles that day.

Riding the endless mile back down the road, I wrestle panniers off the bike and stand in my own personal puddle in reception, trying not to let my teeth chatter as we check into what is a rather posh hotel. Fast forward a few hours and both showered and having spent some time tucked up in bed, we are in the restaurant eating dinner hours earlier than we have for days. The early finish has finally given us the chance for recovery we needed and although our 180 day dream now hangs in the balance, I am just so grateful we are safe, and Stevie has some of the recovery he deserves. I'm desperate for it to end, to be able to sleep, to stay in my own bed and have a fridge full of food and cupboards of clean clothes. But the question was whether we raced to the finish or preserved what little strength we had left to arrive safe, calm, and composed.

Day 178, Haltern am See, Germany

Continuing our indulgence, we raided the immense buffet breakfast the next morning determined to make a strong start on the road. The pockets of our cycle jerseys bulged with pastries and semmel rolls as we slunk out past the waiting staff. To make matters better it wasn't actually raining for once and having bundled Stevie into most of his clothing with a newspaper down his front to add extra warmth, I was pleased my paranoia proved to be overkill and he was able to get a few layers off later in the morning. We still weren't making great progress with more networks of cycle paths and junctions in towns slowing us down and I conceded to stop for a morale boosting McDonald's. On the way out of town someone was waving at us from the side of the road:

"Would you like a cup of tea?" Scott shouted, and we could hardly refuse such a British invitation. Scott was another avid dot watcher/tandem stalker and we found out later had made an epic 680 km round trip to meet us. And we had almost rode on past!

He not only had Yorkshire tea, but a car full of snacks, bicycle tooling and lube and some brilliant SteLa shaped chocolate letters that didn't see the end of the day. But most importantly he had a pair of waterproof gloves that he could lend Stevie to avert anymore frozen hand disasters. We were quite overwhelmed by such a wonderful gesture and regrettably were probably too dazed to express our sincere and heartfelt thanks properly. As always, we had to get going far too soon and approached what I had warned Stevie looked to be a fairly large town called Bielefeld...

Bielefeld, is in fact a major city; but so little known there is a whole conspiracy theory as to whether it actually exists, the basis of which is down to three questions:

Do you know anybody from Bielefeld?

Have you ever been to Bielefeld?

Do you know anybody who has ever been to Bielefeld?

We are still unclear what our answer would be, as we gradually became ensconced in bright lights and tall buildings that seemed to emerge out of nowhere. Dodging trams and riding through a Christmas market, it was entirely surreal and even otherworldly, having been avoiding the large confluences of civilisation for so long. I tried to justify that it had looked much smaller on the map, but Stevie was unconvinced. The rain set in just in time for it to get dark and we were running late again trying to get out of the other side of the city. A cycle lane on the wrong side of the road was pretty grotty and we were worried about some noise from the back wheel until:

"Slam!"

I was illuminated by headlights with a van bonnet inches from hitting me. A right turner from the other direction hadn't been looking at the bicycle path and with all the traffic coming through Stevie hadn't been able to factor in whether he had seen us. We had found we automatically had priority, far more so than in the UK, on these paths, but never took it for granted. There was no doubt that the driver was in the wrong and almost caused a pile up behind too, but all I could see was the bright lights and bonnet inches from disaster. It was a stark reminder of the danger of the road, and we quickly swerved and rode ourselves out of the way, I was sobbing and quivering with shock. Stevie remained calm and steadfast, but the thought settled on us both with solemnity: we have to get home safe.

Thankfully, the traffic quietened down on the way to Hamelin, but this highlighted that the noises we had heard from the back wheel were real and consistent, and Stevie already had a sneaking suspicion what was going on. The last thing we needed was an apartment on the third floor, and locking the bike up in the rain, the rear wheel had to be detached and carried up for inspection while I went on the hunt for supplies. Stevie inspected the wheel and established that it was indeed the bearings that were starting to grind, only able to get to one side the worst were inaccessible so he regreased them as best he could, then got washed, ate dinner and then it was 2am. It was as if time was slipping away, and one disaster was followed by another.

Our options were to sleep in and wait for a bike shop to open, push on and try every bike shop on route, or ride on and ignore the crunching sound for 200+ miles. It had come so far, maybe, just maybe we could make it? We both felt that waiting in Hamelin would jeopardise our 180-day target and after the previous night's near miss we didn't fancy being out in the dark any longer than we needed to, so we decided for option b. to push on and try bike shops. I had been on the case to Hope International again and by mid-morning, when we had established the first few bike shops didn't have what we needed, we had a message saying that their retailer in Hanover, "My BikeTime" had the bearings in stock but it would be a significant detour into the city. We had actually been riding ok on the damaged wheel thanks to Stevie's maintenance, so we had a gamble to make again, between adding the distance and stress and probably missing 180 days or risking everything to press on.

It felt like we had a chance though and we concurred to press on and keep everything crossed. A headwind didn't help but we made steady progress for the first 60 miles and gained a false sense of confidence. We had yet another fantastic visit from some tandem club dot-watchers, Andreas and his wife who had tracked us down by car to see if we needed anything or a bed for the night and we had the foolish confidence to say no.

And then the noises returned, and got worse, and worse. It sounded like we were riding on metal gravel (which I suppose we were as the bearings disintegrated in the hub) and I could feel the increasing friction through my seat post. It was, of course, raining and dark again by this point too and we still had 40 miles to our final nights stop and 160 miles to go to Berlin.

We stopped at a bus stop in the rain, and I knew we couldn't go any further. Stevie was talking of the risk of the wheel seizing up entirely, but all I could do was cry torrents of tears to match the downpour above.

We had failed.

Everything we had given, everything we had overcome, and now we had failed. Over 18,000 miles travelled and the crucial 160 miles to go and we couldn't ride the bicycle. The sense of despair was more overwhelming than anything I had ever experienced, and I just wanted to lie down and wait for everything to end.

And then I sensed a tiny glimmer, a minuscule hope, a remote possibility.

Squinting through tears at the bright light of my phone and trying to type through my sobs I checked the opening hours of the bike shop in Hanover: it was open until 7pm.

It was currently 5pm.

The nearest place to stay was two miles away and we would need to get there regardless, even though I felt like collapsing in the middle of the road. But there was a chance, a small chance that we could get the wheel to the bike shop in time as it was about 50 miles away. Springing into action we limped the bike to the guesthouse and were almost unsurprised when it was closed and no one answered the door or phone, but quickly made the decision to lock the bicycle in an open garage and take the wheel out and hope for the best. Then the first two taxi companies were either fully booked or unable to comprehend my awful German and it seemed we were scuppered, until the third came through and said they would be there in 10 minutes. We called "My BikeTime" and they immediately put the workshop on standby for the wheel, despite it rocking up within 30 minutes of their closing time. What should have been a 10-minute job turned into 40 minutes as the bearings were so badly seized after our prolonged use and abuse; but the mechanics and shop staff stayed late and miraculously got the problem fixed. Even the taxi driver waited and was ready to whisk the wheel back to the bike as soon as it was ready. It cost us 200 euros for the taxi alone, but the budget had gone out of the window now and it was a case of whatever it takes.

By 8pm that evening we had everything fixed and were back on the bike!

We had got back to the still deserted guesthouse, to find a note from Andreas who had spotted our tracker stopped moving early and come back to see if he could help. Finding the bicycle minus us and the wheel in the garage, he had left a kindly note, but I'm not sure who was more surprised, him or us, when we bumped into him riding back to the road! He offered accommodation yet again, but now we were set, we had fixed the wheel and we had a plan, and we were riding to Berlin for 180!

The night was then blissfully calm and quiet (not just because the rear wheel was silent), the traffic and rain had gone too and I was almost enjoying myself for what felt like the first time in weeks. We had a hotel with a key code and had the packs of emergency rations we had carried all the way around the world for dinner, so we had nothing to lose by riding into the night now (except sleep, but that could come later!) Our audax training kicked in and we made the most of the late evening finally rocking up at midnight to a deserted town.

I had dreamt about our grand arrival for so long; and Stevie will concur that there probably wasn't a day on the whole trip we didn't think about it. I imagined us triumphantly riding through the Brandenberg gate midafternoon, well rested and spruced up the night before, with a 40- to 50-mile processionary stage left. But this had all gone out of the window with the hypothermic episode and the 55-mile day a few before. The last day was now set to be a full one, with approximately 120 miles left to ride and it certainly wasn't over yet. Being the 180th day we tried to convince ourselves it would be fine if we ran over and didn't quite make the distance in time, agonising over whether we would push through into the night and risk arriving in the early hours of the morning or just accept with the events of the last few days, another night's sleep might be warranted...

We set the alarm for 4am.

Waking up had the strange sense of disorientation, when you know you should still be asleep, like getting up for an early flight. We packed up as quickly as we could and slunk out of the hotel where we'd had well under four hours rest. Riding into the dawn we struggled with drowsiness and stopped to fuel up on coffee and bockwurst. There was a headwind to Berlin, and we expected nothing less at this point, but it was cold too; bitterly cold. The down booties came out for Stevie's hands again, and bundled up in all our winter gear yet again, we certainly didn't look like people about to set a world record and didn't feel like it either. The countdown was on though and it felt surreal to have less than 100 miles to go: surely, we could ride that?! We had been averaging over 100 miles a day for the best part of six months! Surely one last effort would do it?!

Another garage for more coffee and fuel at 70 miles... about 50 left. Our quintessential training ride, known as the fixed fifty, came to mind but summer spins around quiet Derbyshire lanes were a long way away and we were still a long way off yet.

20 miles to go.

The roads got busier and I frantically tried to keep track of the routing as the weather and light deteriorated. I was determined to get the best route and navigated a mixture of bike paths, bridges and road crossings, trying to predict what I couldn't see up ahead. A bike path on the wrong side of the road saw drizzle turned into sleet, and Stevie dazzled by the headlights of the cars on the other side of a barrier. There was nothing I could do to help.

10 miles to go.

The traffic built up more and we were sharing the bike lanes with a mixture of all sorts of bicycles, but undoubtedly none as well travelled and desperate as us. I tried to stay vigilant, looking in all directions at busy junctions and crossings; just hoping and praying we would stay safe for the last few miles. The sleet was undoubtedly verging on snow now and blasting into our faces. I had messages coming through from dot watchers cheering us on from the comfort of their homes, and when a message from Jenny Graham cropped up, I was overwhelmed with excitement. She was watching our arrival, so similar, yet so different, from hers, years before. The challenging conditions made it hard to get truly excited though and the road dragged on endlessly. As ever I was over distance, and it felt like we would be stuck in between the traffic lights, getting colder and colder indefinitely. Other cyclists sped around us, but we had no option but to grind on, though losing speed each time we stopped. The lights changed ahead of us yet again and I looked up from my shelter from the blizzard behind Stevie's back.

And there it was!

The Brandenburg Gate unmistakably towering ahead, illuminated against the darkness. It was a couple of traffic lights away: we were so, so close.

The lights changed, and it reared up ahead of us and we finally veered away from the traffic and under the arches where we had started six months before. There were cheers and shouts and then we stopped.

My job wasn't done yet, as I needed to get the photos and video required by Guinness and stop Strava. But when those essential jobs were done, I looked around to see family and friends we had missed so dearly, and it felt indescribably surreal.

We had stopped. And we could stop at last. It was over.

And thanks to our mental fatigue and miscalculation over the past few days it was indeed day 180, but this meant our total ride time, and therefore our record to be verified by Guinness, would be 179 days 12 hours and 26 minutes.

We were so pleased and proud we pushed through: We did what we said we were going to do.

And we had sacrificed our grand finale too: I had had images of glorious daylight photographs of our success, but in a snowstorm in the pitch black, it was all we could do to get the couple of requisite photos needed before we got ourselves, and our frozen friends and family back to the hotel.

Brandenburg Gate
Berlin
Day 180
1875miles

Bielefeld 179
178
Germany
177
176
Holland
Belgium
175
174
173
France
172
171
170
169
Biarritz
168
100mi
167
Burgos
166
Spain
165
164
Lisbon 184
Day 162
163 Portugal
16295miles

The light snack dinner in Portugal

Charles from tandem club found us on the road in France

Storms in France

Getting the tandem in and out of the gite

Plenty of pizza in Europe

Cobbles in Belgium

Chauvigny France

Snow on panniers at finish

Finally seeing the Brandenberg gate

Arrivés

epilogue

OF COURSE, we had to ride to the hotel. We stowed the bike and removed the panniers for the last time, brushing off the snow that was encrusted on them. We were soon warm, dry and ready to face civilisation, wearing wonderfully clean, fresh clothes that weren't Lycra. My parents were there, as were Michael (Stevie's brother), Ela and Stefan. Sitting down to dinner, to our complete surprise Jen, Joe, Karina and Matt walked through the door, and this turned into a theme for the weekend when Nikki and Matt unexpectedly appeared after breakfast the next morning too. It felt so unreal to see everyone and try and catch up on six months of news.

Unfortunately, I tried to catch up on six months of cocktail drinking that night too, relieved not to have an alarm set the next day, but this rapidly backfired when a very professional Simon Hare, from BBC East Midlands, interviewed us live the next morning and I prayed I didn't look too green around the gills. As wonderful as it was to see everyone, one of the best bits was that we now had help rounding up bike boxes, which ended up taking us all over Berlin, and we could merrily pop them and ourselves in a taxi to the airport two days later.

We had two issues on the way back though: firstly, Stevie forgot when he had entered Europe last and the stamp from Lisbon was so faint, I had to go and retrieve him from a customs interrogation as to whether he had overstayed his welcome in Europe! And secondly after 10 flights and no damage, the baggage handlers dropped the bike leaving a dent in the top tube. We were gutted.

We were collected from the airport by Stevie's dad, and whisked over for one of his mum's legendary Sunday roasts before descending on our local haunt: the Hole in the Wall. We had told people we were coming, but we never expected the pub to be that packed! We were completely blown away; especially by those who had travelled a considerably distance like Jane and John, Peter Madley and Gerald Davidson and we were presented with printouts and spreadsheets of our stats. Pete from the Tandem Shop in Telford was there too and immediately offered an overhaul of our poor tired bicycle and to repair the damage: by the time we got her back four months later she was as good as new! Big Phil who helped set up the website stopped by and Deano from Huub had a bottle of fizz for us. Adele and Andy had brought Geoffrey, our faithful hound who looked no worse for wear having spent 6 months with "Aunty and Uncle". We couldn't have asked for a better homecoming. Many hours later we stumbled home, delighted to get in and shut the door on the world for a bit!

The next few weeks were tough. I was back at work doing night shifts just over two weeks later because my previous job had let me down on an offer to take me back on. The 186-mile commute, when still getting used to riding a solo bike again was not what I needed, but we needed the income, having borrowed money to see us through the last part of the trip. A low point came on my way along the river track in the dark, where I came skidding off on ice and was forced to walk about a mile feeling like the biggest fraud who couldn't get herself to work on a bike: never mind the world.

But I knew I needed a new focus and set about finding a different role alongside my Veterinary shifts by branching into project management; on the basis I seemed to have mostly been doing that around the world. Feeling like I needed a sporting challenge too, I toyed with ultra-cycling events for a while before settling on doing an Iron Distance triathlon and taught myself to swim freestyle to keep myself occupied. This all kept me busy enough to ward off the "post adventure blues" I had heard about. The same couldn't be said for Stevie.

His saddle sores were still healing up well into the new year and riding the bike wasn't an option for him for many months. Currently a house husband, he had no job to come back to and was a rather lost soul for quite a long time. I tried my best to help but he was struggling with the come down too and it took many months to readjust.

I had another fear too: the record still needed to be verified and having processed over nine hours of video footage, thousands of photos and a multitude of other forms of evidence I waited helplessly for the verdict on our record. When it finally came through in February, my relief was immense, but it turned out Stevie had already taken it as a given; a good illustration of how our roles differed throughout the trip.

Come July 2023, eight months after our return, we are both back on bicycles again, including an enjoyable jaunt to York Rally on our beloved refurbished tandem and enjoying the summer we missed last year. And I got around my Iron Distance Triathlon!

We still get asked, "What's next?" and will both answer, "nothing like this ever again!"

Not only was the expense, over £40,000, immense, but the physical and mental toil something we will never put ourselves, our families or each other through again. We are massively proud of our achievement, and we have nothing more to prove.

We did what we said we were going to do.

acknowledgments

Firstly, I would like to acknowledge those who have gone before and inspired this crazy idea in the first place: most notably Mark Beaumont, Jenny Graham and Tandem WoW, but so many others in the sphere of cycling and endurance. Many of these featured on our podcast: Stoked to be Here and have amazing stories of their own.

The support we received from our sponsors turned the idea into a reality and we are deeply grateful to the Tandem Shop/ Bicycles by Design (especially Pete), Huub (especially Deano), Cycle Touring Life and Woho (especially Dominic and Samuel for saving the ride with new panniers), Co-Motion Cycles, Exustar, Alpkit, Extra UK and Brooks saddles, Schwalbe, Ride with GPS, Epic Ride Weather, Follow my Challenge (especially Rob) and Village Biltong. A special mention goes to Derby Brewing Company and the Hole in the Wall and all the amazing staff and patrons who supported our leaving do and grand return; although the ""one for the road"" could have undermined the entire attempt!

Although not an official sponsor, Hope Technologies came through in our darkest times on the ride and were instrumental in us achieving our 180-day target. A special shout out to Biketime Hannover for saving the day.

Simon Hare and the crew at BBC East Midlands did a great job cheering us off and gave us a warm welcome back too.

And then there is an extensive list of those who made

everything possible on and off the road and we must beg forgiveness for forgetting anyone as there were just so many! Big Phil helped set up www.stelatandem.com and published the last set of blogs when my tech skills were failing, Mr E and Megan dispatched parcels around the world and cheered us from the start, as did Michael, Katie, Ela, Sherlock and Stefan; Mark for Hungarian hospitality, Ruso advised us where to find a laptop in Tbilisi, Meera and Deepak gave us a proper Audax India welcome in Bengaluru, Dinesh found us with the tyre in Chennai, Sumanta brought boxes in Kolkata, Julio and Tasi did the same in Singapore, Rob and Juliane hosted us in Perth, Nasi showed us such kindness after the crash in Malaysia, Dr Rich and Dr Laura from World Extreme Medicine and Dr Sarah were always on hand for advice, Tom and the MacGyver of Gibson got us digs for the night, KeyWee Rob organised the box and kit drop off by Chris in Auckland, Alex and Trish treated us to beers in the hot tub to celebrate halfway, Gwen and Ed were the best absent hosts in Dunedin and Liz and Shane laughed through the drama in Melbourne, Moray and Jose welcomed us to Canada, a string of wonderful hosts in Canada included Tim, Denise, Barefoot Sue, Andrea and Stephen, Mark Beaver collected the vital freehub in Halifax, Charles and his wife tracked us down in France, as did Scott with the brilliant gloves in Belgium, Anisa was a joy to ride with for a day and Andreas and Britta were on standby to save the day at the end.

And that's not to mention all the daily remote support too from the likes of Peter Madley, Gerald Davidson, Micheal Kennedy, Charles Kendall, Nigel Calladine, Alex Bojko, Graham Nix, Paula Johnson, Janet Powell, Hilary Collins, Andrew Parsons, Steve Webster, Jane and John, Andy Thomas, Colin and Dianne (and Matilda), Scott, KeyWee Rob, Mark Hedberg and so, so many more– – I read every comment!

Lizzy Banks was the only person up to this point who really

knew what was going on behind the scenes and cheered us on as if we were in the yellow jersey.

The home guard was kept by Adele, Andy, Janet and Dawn for looking after Geoffrey; and Doxy who sadly (but expectedly) passed away during our trip.

I feel we both owe a huge apology to our parents who must have been on tenterhooks for the whole six months. From my parents waiting in a blizzard at the Brandenburg Gate to Stevie's mum who commented on every single post on Instagram, Facebook and Twitter your support and faith in us was on a different level. The financial subsidies when we repeatedly rebooked flights were much appreciated too! I think it is safe to say, we would not be the people we are without you, so this is as much your achievement as ours.

And Stevie.

It seems strange to acknowledge and thank the other half of you, and saying "I couldn't have done it without you," is obviously a massive understatement. It takes something quite special to have such an intense co-existence for six months, and my pride in who we are as a team cannot be expressed in words. You are, and always will be, my hero.

Maybe one day you will hear his side of the story and what really happened...

Charities:
Sustrans: www.sustrans.org.uk
Mind: www.mind.org.uk
Vetlife: www.vetlife.org.uk

appendices

<u>Kit list at the start:</u>
1 Co-Motion coupled tandem
<u>On the Bike:</u>
2 racks: 1 Tubus titanium, 1 alloy, 2 Brooks B17 carved leather saddles (one standard, one short).

1 Woho frame bag, 1 Woho top tube bag, 2 x Almighty cups, 2 x Woho dry bags, 4 x Cycle Touring Life Erro panniers, 1 foam mat (cut in two, multiple uses), Bungies and straps, 1 x combi Hiplok, 2 x small Hiploks.

<u>Sleep system:</u>
1 x Alpkit Ordos tent, 2 x Alpkit Cloudbase mats, 1 long, 1 standard Pipedream sleeping bags, 2 x silk liners, 2 x Alpkit air pump dry bags

<u>Wash kit:</u>
Sudocrem Cream, toothbrushes x 2, toothpaste, hairbrush, beard brush, moisturiser, toothpicks, soap, shampoos, cotton buds, menstrual cup, P20 Sunblock, Smidge insect repellent, multi-vitamins, prebiotics, electrolytes, tissues, 2 x ear plugs/eye masks, 2 x facemasks, hand disinfectant.

<u>First aid kit</u>:

4 x wound dressings, sterile swabs, triangular bandage, superglue, skin suture, 4 x wound wipes, steri-strips, 2 x bandages, gloves, tape, tick hook, thermometer, bite cream, sleeping mat/tent repair.

Med's bag:

Needles/syringes, pulse oximeter, antihistamines, pain relief, anti-inflammatories, Imodium, rehydration sachets, anti-malarials, water purifier tablets, travel sickness meds, Ibuprofen gel.

SAM splint, Combat tourniquet, Nasopharyngeal tube, Space blanket.

Cook kit:

2 Tupperwares, food bags, 2 x sporks, 2 x mugs/cups, gas canister, Alpkit Kraku stove, water purifier, aluminium pot and kettle, pot handle, 1/3 of a sponge.

Emergency rations (dehydrated 2 main meals, 2 breakfasts).

Clothing:

2 x SteLa tandem caps, 1 x thick hat, 1x buff, 2 x flip flops, 2 x leggings/PJs, 1 x vest, 1 x swimwear, 1 x headscarf, 1 x casual shorts, 1 x boxers, 3 x socks, 1 x sealskin socks, 2 x Huub toe covers, 2 x Huub leg warmers, 2 x Huub bib shorts, 2 x Alpkit cycling shorts, 2 x sports bra, 2 x Huub base layers, 2 x Huub long sleeve Thunderbirds jerseys, 4 x Huub short sleeve Thunderbirds jerseys, 1 x Huub gillet, 1 x Huub cycling gloves, 1 x cycling gloves, 2 x thin gloves, 1 x thicker gloves, 2 x canvas clothes bags, 2 x Exustar windproofs, 2 x Altura Waterproofs, 2 x HiVis gilets, 2 x down jackets, 1 x pair down booties, 1 x sports towel

2 x Exustar SPD sandals, 2 x Exustar helmets, 2 x Exustar transition sunglasses.

Power:

1 x Solar panel, 1 x USB multiplug, 1 x power-bank, Charging leads, 4 x rechargeable AA batteries, 2 x AA batteries.

Tech:

2 x mobile phones, GoPro and GoPro stick/stand/phone mount, Spare GoPro battery, 2 x Memory cards, Garmin ETrex GPS, Coros GPS watch, 1 x spot tracker (courtesy of Follow My Challenge), 1 x kobo e-reader, headphones.

Miscellaneous:

2 x Pen/1 x sharpie, Laminated sheet A4, hairbands, braid cotton, diary and logbook, card reader, wallet plus dollars, 2 x debit cards, 1 x credit card, head torch, 2 x musette sack, paperwork (passport copies, insurance docs, visas, magic letters, control sheets), 2 x Passports, 2 x GHIC, shoe covers, 1 x exposure Light.

Maintenance Kit:

Cable ties (lots), spare Schwalbe Mondial tyre, 4 x Schwalbe aerothan inner tubes, Turbo morph mini floor pump, 20 x alcohol wipes and sandpaper patches, 2 x spare chains, flat duck tape, latex gloves, 2 x chain lube, 2 x long gear cable, electrical tape, mini penknife, disc pad spacing tool, Presta-Schrader valve adapter, 4 x bottom bracket bearings, Bird cassette hyper-cracker, ultralight custom chain whip, spoke key, 11 speed power chain link, 2 x spare pulley wheels, 1 x spare carbon crossover belt, belt lube, multitool, reduced brooks tension spanner, chainset peg spanner, chain extractor, chain wear indicator, 3 x tyre levers, small adjustable wrench, Alan keys 2,3,4,5,6,8mm, S&S coupling tightening wrench, 25 x glue-less patches, 6 x pairs spare brake pads, 1 bottle rack container.

People:

1 x captain, 1 x stoker.

Full route

Stats:

- Total distance: 18,194.9 miles (as recorded by the on-bike Garmin GPS)
- Total time: 179 days 12 hours and 25 minutes
- Average moving speed: 13.0mph
- Max speed: 53.9mph (descending in Turkey, day 16)
- Minimum average speed day: 8.89mph, day 34 India (monsoons and roadworks)
- Maximum distance in a day: 158.9 miles, day 130 Canada (tailwinds in the Prairies)
- Longest moving time: 10hrs 53mins, day 145 Canada
- Average moving time: 7hr 58mins
- Accommodation: 10 nights camping, 8 Airbnbs/homestays, 11 hosted (free), 2 on flights and 149 hotels/motels
- Punctures: 14 including the 7 in 24 hours in Turkey: we covered 13,814 miles without a puncture!
- 64.75 pizzas consumed (where 8 slices=1 pizza regardless of diameter), equivalent to a third per day.